The Politics of Aid Selectivity

With the ending of the political dichotomy in world politics around 1990, the good governance principle came to occupy an important position in judgements about political regimes in developing countries. Good governance became an important objective in the policies of many aid-giving Western countries and the main international financial institutions, such as the World Bank. Increasingly, however, good governance and market-oriented economic reform came to be subsumed under one heading, leading to what has been called a post-Washington Consensus.

This book describes in detail the policies of aid selectivity adopted by the World Bank, the Netherlands and the United States since the end of the 1990s. The main assumptions underlying the policies, as well as the key decisions related to the selection of developing countries, are analysed and critically evaluated. A comparison is made between policy making in these three cases and different approaches to selectivity in the United Kingdom. The book brings out the conflicts that may exist between foreign assistance agendas and the desire of governments in developing countries to set priorities for their national development policies.

The Politics of Aid Selectivity is the first extended analysis of selectivity policies of important bilateral and multilateral aid donors and combines a policy-analytical with a quantitative-empirical approach. The book is relevant to students of various sub-fields of development studies and policy analysis, among other areas, and also has international appeal to researchers and policy-makers working in the area of foreign assistance.

Wil Hout is an Associate Professor of World Development at the Institute of Social Studies in The Hague and currently serves as Dean of the Institute. He is the author of *Capitalism and the Third World*, co-editor (with Jean Grugel) of *Regionalism Across the North–South Divide* and co-editor of three Dutch-language volumes on issues of international relations and political science.

Routledge studies in development economics

1 **Economic Development in the Middle East**
   Rodney Wilson

2 **Monetary and Financial Policies in Developing Countries**
   Growth and stabilization
   Akhtar Hossain and Anis Chowdhury

3 **New Directions in Development Economics**
   Growth, environmental concerns and government in the 1990s
   Edited by Mats Lundahl and Benno J. Ndulu

4 **Financial Liberalization and Investment**
   Kanhaya L. Gupta and Robert Lensink

5 **Liberalization in the Developing World**
   Institutional and economic changes in Latin America, Africa and Asia
   Edited by Alex E. Fernández Jilberto and André Mommen

6 **Financial Development and Economic Growth**
   Theory and experiences from developing countries
   Edited by Niels Hermes and Robert Lensink

7 **The South African Economy**
   Macroeconomic prospects for the medium term
   Finn Tarp and Peter Brixen

8 **Public Sector Pay and Adjustment**
   Lessons from five countries
   Edited by Christopher Colclough

9 **Europe and Economic Reform in Africa**
   Structural adjustment and economic diplomacy
   Obed O. Mailafia

10 **Post-apartheid Southern Africa**
   Economic challenges and policies for the future
   Edited by Lennart Petersson

11 **Financial Integration and Development**
   Liberalization and reform in sub-Saharan Africa
   Ernest Aryeetey and Machiko Nissanke

12 Regionalization and Globalization in the Modern World Economy
Perspectives on the Third World and transitional economies
Edited by Alex E. Fernández Jilberto and André Mommen

13 The African Economy
Policy, institutions and the future
Steve Kayizzi-Mugerwa

14 Recovery from Armed Conflict in Developing Countries
Edited by Geoff Harris

15 Small Enterprises and Economic Development
The dynamics of micro and small enterprises
Carl Liedholm and Donald C. Mead

16 The World Bank
New agendas in a changing world
Michelle Miller-Adams

17 Development Policy in the Twenty-first Century
Beyond the post-Washington consensus
Edited by Ben Fine, Costas Lapavitsas and Jonathan Pincus

18 State-Owned Enterprises in the Middle East and North Africa
Privatization, performance and reform
Edited by Merih Celasun

19 Finance and Competitiveness in Developing Countries
Edited by José María Fanelli and Rohinton Medhora

20 Contemporary Issues in Development Economics
Edited by B.N. Ghosh

21 Mexico Beyond NAFTA
Edited by Martín Puchet Anyul and Lionello F. Punzo

22 Economies in Transition
A guide to China, Cuba, Mongolia, North Korea and Vietnam at the turn of the twenty-first century
Ian Jeffries

23 Population, Economic Growth and Agriculture in Less Developed Countries
Nadia Cuffaro

24 From Crisis to Growth in Africa?
Edited by Mats Lundal

25 The Macroeconomics of Monetary Union
An analysis of the CFA franc zone
David Fielding

26 Endogenous Development
Networking, innovation, institutions and cities
Antonio Vasquez-Barquero

27 Labour Relations in Development
Edited by Alex E. Fernández Jilberto and Marieke Riethof

28 The Crisis of Rural Poverty and Hunger
An essay on the complementarity between market and government-led land reform for its resolution
M. Riad El-Ghonemy

29 **Globalization, Marginalization and Development**
Edited by S. Mansoob Murshed

30 **Programme Aid and Development**
Beyond conditionality
Howard White and Geske Dijkstra

31 **Competitiveness Strategy in Developing Countries**
A manual for policy analysis
Edited by Ganeshan Wignaraja

32 **The African Manufacturing Firm**
An analysis based on firm surveys in sub-Saharan Africa
Dipak Mazumdar and Ata Mazaheri

33 **Trade Policy, Growth and Poverty in Asian Developing Countries**
Edited by Kishor Sharma

34 **International Competitiveness, Investment and Finance**
A case study of India
Edited by A. Ganesh Kumar, Kunal Sen and Rajendra R. Vaidya

35 **The Pattern of Aid Giving**
The impact of good governance on development assistance
Eric Neumayer

36 **New International Poverty Reduction Strategies**
Edited by Jean-Pierre Cling, Mireille Razafindrakoto and François Roubaud

37 **Targeting Development**
Critical perspectives on the Millennium Development Goals
Edited by Richard Black and Howard White

38 **Essays on Balance of Payments Constrained Growth**
Theory and evidence
Edited by J.S.L. McCombie and A.P. Thirlwall

39 **The Private Sector after Communism**
New entrepreneurial firms in transition economies
Jan Winiecki, Vladimir Benacek and Mihaly Laki

40 **Information Technology and Development**
A new paradigm for delivering the Internet to rural areas in developing countries
Jeffrey James

41 **The Economics of Palestine**
Economic policy and institutional reform for a viable Palestine state
Edited by David Cobham and Nu'man Kanafani

42 **Development Dilemmas**
The methods and political ethics of growth policy
Melvin Ayogu and Don Ross

43 **Rural Livelihoods and Poverty Reduction Policies**
Edited by Frank Ellis and H. Ade Freeman

44 **Beyond Market-Driven Development**
Drawing on the experience of Asia and Latin America
Edited by Makoto Noguchi and Costas Lapavitsas

45 **The Political Economy of Reform Failure**
Edited by Mats Lundahl and Michael L. Wyzan

46 **Overcoming Inequality in Latin America**
Issues and challenges for the twenty-first century
Edited by Ricardo Gottschalk and Patricia Justino

47 **Trade, Growth and Inequality in the Era of Globalization**
Edited by Kishor Sharma and Oliver Morrissey

48 **Microfinance**
Perils and prospects
Edited by Jude L. Fernando

49 **The IMF, World Bank and Policy Reform**
Edited by Alberto Paloni and Maurizio Zanardi

50 **Managing Development**
Globalization, economic restructuring and social policy
Edited by Junji Nakagawa

51 **Who Gains from Free Trade?**
Export-led growth, inequality and poverty in Latin America
Edited by Rob Vos, Enrique Ganuza, Samuel Morley, and Sherman Robinson

52 **Evolution of Markets and Institutions**
A study of an emerging economy
Murali Patibandla

53 **The New Famines**
Why famines exist in an era of globalization
Edited by Stephen Devereux

54 **Development Ethics at work**
Explorations – 1960–2002
Denis Goulet

55 **Law Reform in Developing and Transitional States**
Edited by Tim Lindsey

56 **The Asymmetries of Globalization**
Edited by Pan A. Yotopoulos and Donato Romano

57 **Ideas, Policies and Economic Development in the Americas**
Edited by Esteban Pérez-Caldentey and Matias Vernengo

58 **European Union Trade Politics and Development**
'Everything but arms' unravelled
Edited by Gerrit Faber and Jan Orbie

59 **Membership Based Organizations of the Poor**
Edited by Martha Chen, Renana Jhabvala, Ravi Kanbur and Carol Richards

60 **The Politics of Aid Selectivity**
Good governance criteria in World Bank, US and Dutch development assistance
Wil Hout

The Politics of Aid Selectivity
Good governance criteria in World Bank,
US and Dutch development assistance

Wil Hout

LONDON AND NEW YORK

First published 2007
by Routledge
2 Park Square, Milton Park, Abingdon, Oxfordshire OX14 4RN

Simultaneously published in the USA and Canada
by Routledge
711 Third Avenue, New York, NY 10017

First issued in paperback 2014

Routledge is an imprint of the Taylor and Francis Group, an informa business

© 2007 Wil Hout

Typeset in Times by Wearset Ltd, Boldon, Tyne and Wear

All rights reserved. No part of this book may be reprinted or reproduced or utilised in any form or by any electronic, mechanical, or other means, now known or hereafter invented, including photocopying and recording, or in any information storage or retrieval system, without permission in writing from the publishers.

British Library Cataloguing in Publication Data
A catalogue record for this book is available from the British Library

Library of Congress Cataloging in Publication Data
A catalog record for this book has been requested

ISBN 978-0-415-37860-4 (hbk)
ISBN 978-0-415-51164-3 (pbk)
ISBN 978-0-203-94578-0 (ebk)

For Sophie and Oscar

Contents

List of illustrations xiv
List of acronyms xvi
Preface and acknowledgements xviii

1 Introduction 1

1.1 The emergence of the 'good governance' agenda 1
1.2 The reinvention of development assistance 2
1.3 Aid selectivity 4
1.4 Outline of the book 5

2 The paradigm shift in development assistance 10

2.1 Introduction 10
2.2 Reorientations in economic theory 12
2.3 The rethinking of development policies 16
2.4 Good governance and aid effectiveness 19
2.5 Conclusions 21

3 The World Bank and performance-based allocation 24

3.1 Introduction 24
3.2 The World Bank and governance 25
3.3 Governance and performance-based allocation 28
3.4 Evaluation 40
3.5 Conclusions 48

xii *Contents*

4 The Netherlands and the selection of recipient countries 50

    4.1 Introduction 50
    4.2 First steps: the selection of preferential countries (1998–2002) 51
    4.3 A change of course: the reduction to 36 partner countries (2003–7) 58
    4.4 Evaluation 61
    4.5 Conclusions 68

5 The United States and the Millennium Challenge Account 70

    5.1 Introduction 70
    5.2 Foreign aid and governance: the US political and institutional framework 71
    5.3 The Millennium Challenge Account 74
    5.4 Evaluation 89
    5.5 Conclusions 95

6 Selectivity and good governance in the United Kingdom, Denmark and the European Union 97

    6.1 Introduction 97
    6.2 Assistance policies of the United Kingdom 98
    6.3 Assistance policies of Denmark 103
    6.4 Assistance policies of the European Union 106
    6.5 Conclusions 113

7 Quantitative-empirical analyses of World Bank, Dutch and US aid selectivity 115

    7.1 Introduction 115
    7.2 Research design and methodology 115
    7.3 World Bank 119
    7.4 The Netherlands 123
    7.5 The United States 127
    7.6 Conclusions 131

8 Conclusion 134

    8.1 The challenge of aid selectivity 134
    8.2 Governance quality and aid effectiveness 135
    8.3 Definitions of governance 136
    8.4 Causes of 'bad' governance 137

8.5 Methodology and quantification 138
8.6 Bias towards selection 140
8.7 Indeterminacy of governance quality 140
8.8 The importance of poverty reduction 141

Appendix A: Interviews 143

Appendix B: The Country Policy and Institutional Assessment (CPIA) 144

Appendix C: IDA borrowers, by per capita income, 1999 151

Appendix D: Selection criteria of the Millennium Challenge Account 153

Appendix E: Low-income and lower-middle-income countries in the analyses 157

Notes 159
Bibliography 167
Index 182

Illustrations

Figures

3.1	IDA's performance-based allocation mechanism under IDA14	41
5.1	Stages of the MCA compact development process	87

Tables

2.1	The paradigm shift in the international aid agenda	22
3.1	IDA allocations and commitments by performance quintile, 2000 lending strategy	34
4.1	Criteria for country selection	54
4.2	Allocation of delegated ODA funds, 2000	57
4.3	Official Development Assistance allocated to partner and exit countries, 2004	62–3
5.1	MCA's budget, 2004–7	79
5.2	Selection criteria of the Millennium Challenge Account	80
5.3	Eligible, threshold and compact countries, fiscal years 2004–6	82
5.4	Signed Millennium Challenge Compacts, 2004–6	86
5.5	Millennium Challenge Compacts, allocation by type of activity	88
6.1	Major recipients in the UK's country aid programme, 2005/6	99
6.2	Major recipients of Danish development assistance, 2004	105
6.3	Regional breakdown of commitments of external assistance managed by EuropeAid and DG Enlargement, 2001 and 2005	110
6.4	Major recipients of EU Official Development Assistance, 2005	111
6.5	Sectoral and regional breakdown of commitments of external assistance managed by EuropeAid, 2005	112
7.1	World Bank, eligibility stage	120
7.2	World Bank, level stage	122
7.3	The Netherlands, eligibility stage	124
7.4	The Netherlands, level stage	125

7.5	The US Millennium Challenge Account, eligibility stage	128
7.6	The US Millennium Challenge Account and USAID, level stage	130
B1	Categories and judgements on the CPIA, 1999–2004	147
B2	Categories and judgements on the CPIA, since 2005	150

Acronyms

ACP	group of African, Caribbean and Pacific countries (European Union)
ARPP	Annual Report on Portfolio Performance (World Bank)
CAS	Country Assistance Strategy (World Bank)
CDF	Comprehensive Development Framework (World Bank)
CEO	chief executive officer
CPIA	Country Policy and Institutional Assessment (World Bank)
CPR	Country Performance Rating (World Bank)
DAC	Development Assistance Committee of the Organisation for Economic Co-operation and Development
DFID	Department for International Development (United Kingdom)
DGIS	Directorate-General for International Cooperation (the Netherlands)
EDF	European Development Fund (European Union)
EPA	Economic Partnership Agreement (European Union)
EU	European Union
FY	fiscal year
G-7	group of seven major industrialised countries (United States, Japan, Germany, United Kingdom, France, Italy and Canada)
GAO	Government Accountability Office (United States)
GDP	gross domestic product
GMV	governance, human rights and peace-building (the Netherlands)
GNP	gross national product
HIPC	highly indebted poor countries
IBRD	International Bank for Reconstruction and Development (World Bank)
ICP	IDA Country Performance
IDA	International Development Association (World Bank)
LICUS	low income country under stress (World Bank)
LPF	Lijst Pim Fortuyn (the Netherlands)
MCA	Millennium Challenge Account (United States)

MCC	Millennium Challenge Corporation (United States)
MDGs	Millennium Development Goals
MEPI	Middle East Partnership Initiative (United States)
NGO	non-governmental organisation
ODA	official development assistance
OECD	Organisation for Economic Co-operation and Development
OED	Operations Evaluation Department (World Bank)
PBA	performance-based allocation (World Bank)
PCPI	Post-Conflict Progress Indicators (World Bank)
PEFPAR	President's Emergency Plan for AIDS Relief (United States)
PRBS	Poverty Reduction Budget Support (United Kingdom)
PREM network	Poverty Reduction and Economic Management network (World Bank)
PRS(P)	Poverty Reduction Strategy (Paper)
PSA	Public Service Agreement (United Kingdom)
SDR	Special Drawing Rights (International Monetary Fund)
SFRC	Senate Foreign Relations Committee (United States)
SWAp	sector-wide approach
UNDP	United Nations Development Programme
USAID	United States Agency for International Development

Preface and acknowledgements

This book is about the recent trend in development assistance policies to be more selective in the choice of countries that receive aid. The approach derives its theoretical legitimacy from claims made in the donor community where aid works, but only in contexts characterised by 'good' governance and policies. The focus on the quality of governance and policies in developing countries represents a policy reorientation of some major bilateral and multilateral aid donors, which is politically very significant. Aid selectivity has been introduced with the explicit aim to give new legitimacy to development assistance policies that had come under attack in the 1980s and 1990s.

This book aims to analyse the policies of aid selectivity adopted by three donors: the World Bank, the Netherlands and the United States. It is felt that an analysis of the policy theories held by these donors and of the ways in which selectivity policies have been implemented over the last decade is called for in order to shed light on the validity of the policy reorientation. This study is built around case studies of the donors' policies, based on a review of policy documents and interviews, as well as a quantitative-empirical analysis of policy choices related to the selection of aid recipients and the allocation of aid over the recipient countries.

Several paragraphs of Chapters 1, 3, 4, 5 and 8 have been based on my article 'Political Regimes and Development Assistance: The Political Economy of Aid Selectivity', which appeared in *Critical Asian Studies* 36(4): 591–613. For Chapter 4, I have drawn on my article 'The Netherlands and Aid Selectivity, 1998–2005: The Vicissitudes of a Policy Concept', which was published in the *Netherlands Yearbook on International Cooperation* (Assen: Van Gorcum, 2007). These parts are used with permission of the publishers.

I would like to thank all those people who have contributed in one way or another to the publication of this book. The Staff Group States, Societies and World Development at the Institute of Social Studies has provided a conducive environment for research and was a source of financial support for travel purposes. Dick Robison, Garry Rodan and Kevin Hewison have stimulated my initial thinking about aid selectivity and have made me reflect on the 'larger picture'. Nico van Niekerk at the Dutch Policy and Operations Evaluation Department has been a valuable 'sparring partner' for the analysis of Dutch aid selectivity. I have very much enjoyed working on the Dutch case for the Policy and Operations Evaluation Department with Dirk-Jan Koch (currently at the Dutch Ministry of Foreign Affairs), who shares part of the 'intellectual property' of Chapter 4 in this book. I gratefully acknowledge the collaboration of staff at the Dutch Ministry of Foreign Affairs, the World Bank and the Millennium Challenge Corporation, whom I have been able to interview about their work (see Appendix A). Two anonymous reviewers have made useful comments, which are reflected in the design of the book.

Oegstgeest, 2007

1 Introduction

1.1 The emergence of the 'good governance' agenda

The attention of most Western policy-makers to the nature of political regimes in the developing countries is of relatively recent origin. For many, the end of the Cold War was a watershed between negligence of and renewed attention for non-Western political systems. Part of the lack of concern during the Cold War was attributable to the seemingly rigid power relations that characterised the era, while part of it was a function of political manipulation.

On the one hand, many Western politicians turned a blind eye to the political repression and violation of basic political rights and civil liberties in the countries that belonged to the Soviet Union's sphere of influence. For instance, dissident movements such as Czechoslovak *Charta 77* and Polish *Solidarność* received little attention from Western politicians during the period of Soviet dominance of Central and Eastern Europe, as these politicians feared to disrupt the fragile political balance between the East and West.

On the other hand, the attitude of many Western politicians towards developing countries was coloured by the position of the latter countries in the bipolar Cold War world. Statements such as 'He may be a son-of-a-bitch, but he's *our* son-of-a-bitch' and 'The enemy of our enemy is our friend,' although both older than the Cold War, can be cited as credos in the foreign policies of both superpowers and their allies in the post-Second World War period. Concerns related to the maintenance of the two opposite Cold War alliances explain the long-term affiliation of the West to Mobutu's Zaire, and the superpowers' shift of allegiance between Menghistu's Ethiopia and Siad Barre's Somalia in 1977 without any concern for these countries' internal politics.

With the ending of the political dichotomy in world politics around 1990, attention for the nature of political regimes in developing countries has clearly gained momentum. Along with the emphasis on market-oriented policies, which had been the dominant trend in economic policies suggested to the developing countries after the Reagan–Thatcher 'revolution' of the early 1980s, the attention for the principles of governance of developing countries achieved prominence. 'Good governance', the term that has been *en vogue* since the publication of a World Bank report on Africa (World Bank 1989), became an important

2 Introduction

objective in the policies of many aid-giving Western countries and the main international financial institutions, such as the World Bank.

Looking at the post-Cold War period in retrospect, the attention for governance issues in developing countries seems to have been part of a more general trend, which produced a remarkable comeback of development issues and development assistance policies on the international agenda. The United Nations' Millennium Declaration, the Monterrey Consensus on the financing of development and the Millennium Development Goals (MDGs) are witness to the increasing salience of poverty reduction in international policy arenas. Key global players in the domain of development assistance, such as the United Nations and the European Union (EU), are increasing their contributions to the global funds for development. The likely failure to achieve several of the MDGs is perceived by many as a major sign of the continuing relevance of poverty as the main contemporary global social problem.

Critics of the international project that produced the MDGs have commented that the MDGs are little more than a technocratic fix for the issue of poverty that have served to cement a compromise among politicians from a variety of backgrounds and with highly distinct national constituencies. Some see the MDGs even as 'a simplistic vending machine model that largely ignore[s] institutional factors and governance' (Hulme and Chhotray 2006: 4). It is highly plausible that the depoliticised nature of the MDG agreements has contributed to their success in international policy circles. This is not, however, equivalent to saying that the adoption of the MDGs has resulted in the downplaying of governance concerns among the most important development assistance agencies. On the contrary, recent documents issued by several agencies witness a continuing concern with issues of governance in development assistance strategies. Examples of policy documents that stress governance include the United Kingdom's 2006 White Paper on poverty reduction and governance (Secretary of State for International Development 2006), the paper on governance and anti-corruption tabled at the World Bank and International Monetary Fund (IMF) Development Committee's meeting in Singapore of September 2006 (Development Committee 2006) and the European Commission's governance statement related to the 'European Consensus on Development (European Commission 2006b; see also Chapter 6).

1.2 The reinvention of development assistance

Recent concerns about development, poverty and governance have followed a period of widespread scepticism about development theory and policy. The late 1980s and early 1990s were an episode of doubt both about the intellectual foundations of development and the targets and instruments of development policy.

The theorising about development in the 1980s and 1990s showed many signs of a discipline that was trapped in an impasse (Booth 1985) or was in crisis (Leys 1996). The main pillars of post-Second World War development thinking had come under attack (Schuurman 2000: 8–13). First, the quick pace of economic growth in some developing countries in the East and South-East Asia challenged the schematic 'North–South' frame of analysis as well as the very notion of the Third World, which had underpinned much of development studies. Second, notions of progress, which had arguably been equally important as the idea of the Third World, turned increasingly vacuous as a result of increasing international inequality, the apparent failure of African countries to develop and the imminent ecological emergency. Third, the role of the state as a central tool of development policies was put more and more into question.

Apart from the crisis in theorising, the scepticism about development policy was fuelled by the apparent inability of aid to lift countries out of poverty (cf. Burnside and Dollar 1997: 1). Interpretations of the East Asian success stories of development in the 1980s and 1990s stressed the importance of domestic factors, although assessments of the relative contribution of the market and the state differed. What the interpretations seemed to agree upon, however, was that foreign aid had been only marginally important, if at all (Wade 1990; World Bank 1993). Accounts of the impact of development assistance on the poorest countries, focusing on the abuse of funds by corrupt regimes and the continuation of policies harmful to economic growth, contributed to the spread of cynicism about the usefulness of aid (cf. Bauer 1991: 45–9).

The general scepticism about development policy brought about a stagnation of the worldwide spending on development assistance during the first part of the 1990s and resulted in a real decrease of funds after 1996 (Organisation for Economic Co-operation and Development 2006b). Several initiatives, most importantly at the Organisation for Economic Co-operation and Development (OECD) and the World Bank, aimed to counter this trend by rearticulating the objectives and reasserting the effectiveness of development assistance.

The report *Shaping the 21st century* can be interpreted as an attempt of the donor community, brought together in the OECD's Development Assistance Committee (DAC), to reformulate the objectives of development aid in the light of declining aid levels (Development Assistance Committee 1996). Although the DAC (1996: 1) acknowledged that 'the efforts of countries and societies to help themselves have been the main ingredients in their success', the committee emphasised the continuing relevance of development assistance:

> [T]he record also shows that development assistance has been an essential complementary factor in many achievements: the green revolution, the fall in birth rates, improved basic infrastructure, a diminished prevalence of disease and dramatically reduced poverty. *Properly applied in propitious environments, aid works.* . . . We have learned that development assistance will only work where there is a shared commitment of all the partners. . . . We have seen, on the other hand, the countries in which civil conflict and bad governance have set back development for generations.
> (Development Assistance Committee 1996: 1, italics added)

4 Introduction

On the basis of its analysis of development needs, the DAC formulated three development targets – some with several sub-targets – that would subsequently be used in the context of the MDGs (Development Assistance Committee 1996: 9–10; see also Chapter 2).

The World Bank set out on a similar enterprise as the OECD in the mid-1990s. Two reports published towards the end of the decade (Burnside and Dollar 1997; World Bank 1998) produced an argument on aid effectiveness that tied in with the emerging discourse on governance. The *Assessing Aid* report phrased the objective of the reassessment as follows:

> *Assessing Aid* is a contribution to this ongoing learning process. It aims to contribute to a larger 'rethinking of aid' that the international community is engaged in – a rethinking in two senses. First, with the end of the cold war, there is a group that is 'rethinking aid' in the sense of questioning its very existence in a world of integrated capital markets. In response to this trend, *we show that there remains a role for financial transfers from rich countries to poor ones*. Second, developing and developed nations alike are reconceptualizing the role of assistance in light of a new development paradigm. *Effective aid supports institutional development and policy reforms that are at the heart of successful development.*
>
> (World Bank 1998: ix, italics added)

The message contained in the last sentence of the quote – that aid is effective if given to countries with good governance and policies – would become a central element of the approach to development assistance of various bilateral and multilateral donors.

1.3 Aid selectivity

This book focuses on the emphasis on good governance that has characterised and in some cases even dominated the foreign assistance agendas of some of the important bilateral and multilateral aid donors in the 1990s and the early twenty-first century. In particular, this study analyses the introduction of governance quality as a selection criterion for development assistance.

Development assistance policies have always been influenced by ideas that became fashionable in academic circles or the development community more broadly. Because of the highly complex nature of policy interventions in developing countries, almost all development agencies have traditionally tried to monitor the success and failure of their approaches to development problems. The attention for what works and what does not in development has frequently produced new approaches to policy making and implementation (cf. Nederveen Pieterse 2001).

In this book the argument is made that the concept of selectivity is one of the latest of policy fashions related to development. It is argued (in Section 1.3 and Chapter 2) that the notion of aid selectivity was the product of the reassessment of development assistance in the 1990s that followed upon the period of crisis in development theory and policy making. For a variety of reasons, many of which revolved around the political necessity to find ways out of the intellectual and policy impasse that development was in, an 'effectiveness discourse' was adopted in the development community. The language of effectiveness resonated well with broader concepts of government policy making deriving from the so-called 'new public management' approach. In development policy making, the emphasis was placed on effectiveness in the first place as a defensive tool to rescue development assistance strategies in an increasingly hostile world.

Aid selectivity thus needs to be seen as a highly political concept, adopted by policy makers to distinguish contemporary approaches to development from those that had come under attack in the late 1980s and early 1990s. Aid selectivity is a concept that aims to give new legitimacy to development assistance by focusing on well-defined targets, new delivery mechanisms and greater attention for the recipients of aid (see Section 2.5 for more details).

The analyses contained in this book focus on one specific part of the aid selectivity agenda: the selection of aid recipients on the basis of considerations on governance quality, which are being applied alongside traditional poverty-related criteria since the end of the 1990s. Country selectivity is the most visible, and arguably the most political, part of the aid selectivity agenda, as this element is the clearest response to the criticism that aid monies have often been used to support countries with insufficient capacity to produce results.

The next chapters are an attempt to analyse the ways in which country selectivity has been implemented in various contexts. The cases of the World Bank's performance-based allocation mechanism, the Dutch policy on the selection of aid recipients, and the United States' Millennium Challenge Account (MCA) have been chosen as these are the clearest examples of contemporary policies based on country selectivity. The analysis of these cases serves to establish how country selectivity has been applied by several important aid donors, what the strengths and weaknesses of the principle are and what future the concept might have in development assistance policies.

1.4 Outline of the book

This book is both about the making of policy and about the way in which policy ideas are being implemented. A substantial part of the book deals with the analysis of policies that claim to apply the argument of aid selectivity to development assistance. The analysis of three main cases of aid selectivity – the World Bank's performance-based allocation mechanism, the Dutch selection of preferential and partner countries, and the US MCA – aims to bring out the *policy theory* that is guiding important decisions with respect to foreign assistance. Policy analysis serves here to highlight the central assumptions underlying policy decisions, as well as the relationship (or the lack of it) between the assumptions held and final decision-making.

Introduction

In addition to studying the policy theories supporting aid selectivity, this book also attempts to analyse the implementation of selectivity policies in the case of the World Bank, the Netherlands and the United States. This part of the analysis, which tries to establish the impact of certain key variables on the selection of recipient countries and the allocation of aid over recipients, is performed with the use of quantitative-empirical techniques. The objective of this part of the analysis is to establish to what extent the choices reflected in country selection and allocation can be explained on the basis of the very criteria that were applied in the policy theory of the respective donor country or organisation.

Chapter 2 provides an analysis of the paradigm shift that occurred in the thinking about development assistance at the end of the 1990s. The discussion in this chapter builds on the interpretation of good governance and development assistance in sections 1.2 and 1.3. Chapter 2 argues that the emergence of the selectivity agenda has been the result of a successful 'framing' of development policy in terms of effectiveness and governance. The framing exercise can be interpreted as part of the move away from the Washington Consensus, which emphasised pro-market reforms in developing countries. The move to a new paradigm was underpinned by a reorientation in economic theory, a rethinking of assistance modalities and a reinterpretation of the preconditions of aid effectiveness. In economic theory, the increasing prominence of the new institutional economics and the emphasis of information for the functioning of markets has led to a rethinking of the role of the market in development. Importantly, the proper working of the market was increasingly seen to depend on certain institutions, such as a system of property rights, the rule of law and contract enforcement. In the mid-1990s, policy-makers started to question publicly the prevalent methods of aid delivery. The effectiveness of project-based assistance was increasingly questioned, and the emerging discourse revolving around the principles of 'ownership' and 'alignment' led to the introduction of the sector-wide approach and budget support. Finally, the concern with the effectiveness of aid was instrumental in the thinking about the quality of governance ('good governance') as an important co-determinant of successful development assistance policies. The rethinking of the use of development assistance produced changes in the objectives, modalities and conditions of aid. For a good number of donors, selectivity proved to be the keyword in all three dimensions: the central objectives of assistance policies were reduced to a set of quantifiable targets (the MDGs), aid delivery was focused more on specific sectors in developing countries (sector-wide approaches), preferably with limited donor intervention (budget support), and the number of targeted countries was reconsidered in the light of overall governance quality (country selectivity or ex post conditionality).

Chapter 3 contains an analysis of the performance-based allocation mechanism implemented by the World Bank's International Development Association (IDA) since 1998. The introduction of the IDA's approach to aid selectivity is analysed against the background of the changes in thinking about governance in World Bank circles, where changes were particularly evident under the presidency of James Wolfensohn. Issues of governance and governance quality were addressed by the World Bank primarily in the context of public sector management and the regulatory framework of a well-functioning market economy. The introduction of the Country Policy and Institutional Assessment (CPIA) as the Bank's primary tool to judge policies and governance in countries eligible for IDA support since IDA12 (1999–2002) is analysed as an attempt to develop a relatively apolitical measurement device. The so-called governance discount (later renamed 'governance factor'), which is based on a sub-section of the CPIA items, is discussed in the light of the World Bank's attempt to enhance the role of governance quality in its performance-based allocation policy. The chapter contains an analysis of the implementation of this policy, to the degree that this is possible given the relative lack of transparency of the decision making process at the World Bank. The chapter is concluded with an evaluation of policy-based allocation, focusing primarily on the policy theory, the methodology and the role of the World Bank as a multilateral institution.

Chapter 4 reports on the case study of Dutch development assistance policy, in which the selection of recipient countries on the basis of governance quality has played a central role since 1998. The chapter analyses two stages of aid selectivity. During the first stage (1998–2002), when social democrat Eveline Herfkens was Minister for Development Cooperation, a group of 22 developing countries (the so-called '19+3') was selected for structural bilateral assistance from the Netherlands on the basis of three criteria (socio-economic policies, the good governance record and the extent of poverty). Next to the programme to support the 22 'preferential' countries, three important thematic programmes – focusing on environmental issues, human rights, peace-building and good governance, and private sector development – were provided with substantial government funds. The second stage (2003–5), under christian democrat minister Agnes van Ardenne-Van der Hoeven, demonstrated a change of course. The new minister decided to merge the programme of structural bilateral aid with the environmental and the human rights, peace-building and good governance programmes into one bilateral programme aimed at the support of 36 'partner' countries. Chapter 4 concludes with an evaluation of the policy theory that was used during the two phases of aid selectivity, the methodology that was applied in the selection of the 22 preferential and 36 partner countries, and the implementation of the selection process.

Chapter 5 analyses the US MCA, which was launched by President Bush in 2002 and came into operation in 2004. The MCA is understood as an attempt of the Bush administration to reorient US development assistance policies, which until then had revolved mainly around the activities of the US Agency for International Development (USAID) and had been very much subject to strategic and foreign policy considerations. The chapter discusses the MCA's legal framework and, more specifically, the mandate of the Millennium Challenge Corporation, the government agency that was created to implement the MCA. The analysis highlights the three sets of criteria that were applied in the selection of recipient countries – governance quality, social policies (focused, in particular, on education and health) and economic policies – and discusses their application in the selection of so-called candidate, eligible and threshold countries. Further, the allocations to the nine current Compact countries are discussed. The chapter concludes by evaluating the MCA's policy theory, the choice of the selection criteria and the selection methodology, and the role of the Millennium Challenge Corporation.

Chapter 6 contains a discussion of three cases in which development assistance has become increasingly selective, but where such results have not been achieved through the adoption of mechanisms of country selectivity. The analysis of the United Kingdom's development assistance policy since 1997 focuses on the increasing emphasis on poverty as a criterion for aid, alongside the move to different aid modalities. The section on the United Kingdom's aid policy also discusses the desire to implement ideas of 'mutual accountability' between the donors and recipients of aid, as well as the relationship to progress on achieving the MDGs and new ideas on monitoring governance quality. The analysis of Denmark's policy on development assistance zeroes in on the country's decision, made around 1990, to restrict aid to a limited number of countries and a small number of sectors, for which sector-wide programmes were formulated. The discussion of Denmark's aid policy brings out the country's overriding concern with poverty in developing countries. The analysis of the development policy of the EU is concentrated on its attempt to provide assistance to a wide array of developing countries. The dispersion of EU development funds is explained with reference to the increasingly diverse nature of its membership, which calls for assistance programmes to the former colonies of the EU countries (the so-called ACP countries), countries in Latin America, as well as the countries in the direct 'neighbourhood' of the EU, such as those on the Balkans, in the area of the former Soviet Union and on the Mediterranean rim and in the near Middle East. The section on the EU discusses recent attempts to limit aid to a series of sectors in which the organisation feels it possesses certain comparative advantages.

Chapter 7 contains a quantitative-empirical analysis of the impact of selectivity principles on the development assistance policies implemented by the World Bank, the Netherlands and the United States. All three cases are analysed in identical ways in order to highlight important similarities and differences among assistance policies based on country selectivity. In the first part of the analyses, the selection of aid recipients by the three donors is related to a set of variables reflecting recipient needs (poverty, human development), donor interests (trade relations) and several governance indicators. The aim of the logistic regression analyses of the so-called 'eligibility stage' is to establish how well the choice of recipients can be explained by reference to variables that are central to the policy theory on aid selectivity. The second part of the analyses of the three cases focuses on the allocation of development assistance monies across recipient countries. Multiple regression analyses are performed with absolute aid levels as dependent variable in order to establish the explanatory power of the variables mentioned above in the so-called 'level stage' of country selectivity.

Chapter 8 reflects on the implications of the study of the three cases of aid selectivity for wider debates about development assistance and the role of governance criteria. This chapter focuses on aspects of the policy theory that informs selectivity policies, the methodology used to select recipient countries, and the implementation of aid selectivity.

2 The paradigm shift in development assistance

2.1 Introduction

In a recent book, Bøås and McNeill have argued that trends in development policy, to a large extent, are the consequence of the successful 'framing' of policy analyses and policy recommendations. As they put it, '[a]n effective "frame" is one which makes favoured ideas seem like common sense, and unfavoured ideas appear unthinkable' (Bøås and McNeill 2004: 220–1). Ideas related to governance quality and selectivity have been the result of framing exercises in the development discourse that took place during the 1990s. This chapter discusses the paradigm shift in development assistance policies that resulted from the reframing of the development discourse that dominated previously.

In earlier days – and most definitely in the first several decades after the end of the Second World War – the thinking about development assistance was fairly uncomplicated (cf. Thorbecke 2000: 19–28). There was widespread agreement among theorists and policy-makers that the lack of development in large parts of the world was caused by the existence of certain 'gaps'. The gaps that were emphasised varied according to the theoretical and disciplinary background of analysts and policy-makers concerned. According to some, development was lagging behind because of a lack of capital and infrastructure. Others stressed the lack of education and training on the part of people inhabiting the recently independent countries. Yet others pointed at the lack of institutional sophistication and management skills characterising the public sector in many developing countries. The differences of opinion on the causes of the lack of development did not, however, preclude agreement on the main remedy to help with filling the gaps: the provision of development assistance.

The consensus about the merits of development assistance that dominated the 1950s and 1960s was challenged in the following period. Issues such as the dependency-enhancing impact of aid, the limited influence of grassroots organisations on the implementation of assistance programmes, the detrimental environmental impact of development projects and the imposition of certain policies on developing country governments have resulted in the breakdown of the earlier agreement on the virtues of development aid.

The scepticism about the usefulness of development assistance increased even further with the rise of the so-called Washington Consensus. The Washington Consensus was grounded intellectually in neo-classical economics and was characterised by a belief in the salutary impact of market processes. It was sceptical about government intervention into the economy and emphasised that markets work best if left to themselves (Fine 2001: 132–5). The Washington Consensus was shorthand for the preferences of Washington-based policy-makers in the World Bank, International Monetary Fund (IMF) and US government, and was aimed originally at Latin America after the debt crisis of the 1980s. Later, the policy precepts were applied in various other contexts, as well. John Williamson, who coined the term 'Washington Consensus', referred in particular to ten policy measures (Williamson 2000: 252–3):

- Fiscal discipline
- A redirection of public expenditure priorities towards fields offering both high economic returns and the potential to improve income distribution, such as primary health care, primary education and infrastructure
- Tax reform (to lower marginal rates and broaden the tax base)
- Interest rate liberalization
- A competitive exchange rate
- Trade liberalization
- Liberalization of inflows of foreign direct investment
- Privatization
- Deregulation (to abolish barriers to entry and exit)
- Secure property rights.

The late 1990s witnessed a paradigm shift in development assistance, away from the Washington Consensus, which was felt to be one-sided and overly economistic. Policy-makers and theorists seem to have rallied behind a limited set of ideas that, together, represent a new form of consensus about development aid. The new consensus about development assistance was nurtured by the Comprehensive Development Framework introduced by World Bank President James Wolfensohn (see further in Chapter 3) and cemented into policy terms, first in the United Nations' Millennium Declaration (September 2000) and later in the so-called Monterrey Consensus, the agreement reached at the Financing for Development summit meeting of March 2002.

The heads of state and government who assembled in Monterrey agreed on the following objectives of development policies:

> Our goal is to eradicate poverty, achieve sustained economic growth and promote sustainable development as we advance to a fully inclusive and equitable global economic system. ... Achieving the internationally agreed development goals, including those contained in the Millennium Declaration, demands a new partnership between developed and developing countries. We commit ourselves to sound policies, good governance at all levels

and the rule of law. We also commit ourselves to mobilizing domestic resources, attracting international flows, promoting international trade as an engine for development, increasing international financial and technical cooperation for development, sustainable debt financing and external debt relief, and enhancing the coherence and consistency of the international monetary, financial and trading system.

(Monterrey Consensus 2002: points 1 and 4)

The Monterrey Consensus built on a set of concepts and theoretical ideas that had evolved over the 1990s and that challenged the previous orthodoxy of the Washington Consensus.

The paradigm shift in development assistance came about as a result of at least three influences. In the first place, a reorientation in economic theory, away from the pure neo-classical emphasis on general equilibrium models and the role of the market, led to increased attention for institutions and information deficits. In the second place, the rethinking in development circles of favoured means of development policies such as projects and technical assistance resulted in an emphasis on programmes, sector-wide approaches and demand orientation ('ownership'), which were thought of in function of poverty reduction. Finally, the concern with the impact of development assistance culminated in a research project on the conditions of effective aid implementation and led to the emphasis of 'good' policies and governance structures as determinants of aid effectiveness. These three influences are discussed in Sections 2.2–2.4. Section 2.5 contains some concluding remarks.

2.2 Reorientations in economic theory

The relevance of the dominant neo-classical economic analysis for development has been questioned since, roughly, the end of the 1980s. Building on the work of Ronald Coase, Douglass North (1990: 15) emphasised that the neo-classical equilibrium model assumes a frictionless world where economic transactions can be made without costs. In the context of the general equilibrium model, the analysis of individual behaviour is based on the assumptions that individuals have perfect information about the transactions they wish to make and that the market is absolutely transparent. All information about transactions is assumed to be reducible to one figure: the market price.

Several research programmes in economics – summarised as 'non-neoclassical' perspectives by Hoff and Stiglitz (2001: 397) – have been instrumental to the reorientation of development policies away from their almost exclusive concern with the functioning of markets. The new institutional economics, associated most directly with Douglass North, emphasised the role of institutions and forms of governance in development. Information-theoretic economics, linked principally to the work of Joseph Stiglitz, stressed the role of governments in solving problems arising from various kinds of market failures.

According to the new institutional economics, transactions lead to costs that follow from the procurement and processing of information. These costs cannot be deduced directly from the price of goods and services. This view leads to an interest in institutions: 'when it is costly to transact, institutions matter' (North 1990: 12). It is argued that institutions reduce transaction costs by internalising transactions (Nabli and Nugent 1989: 1336–7). Certain transactions take place within organisations, rather than in the market, because certain costs (such as surveillance and quality control) can be avoided in that way.

Property rights are seen as instruments for the internalisation of external effects. It is argued that property rights help to increase economic efficiency and lead to economic progress, because the certainty and trust needed for making transactions is enhanced. Since the delimitation and enforcement of property rights is considered to be relatively costly, it is assumed that property rights are generally established when certain resources are becoming scarce, for instance as a result of population growth or technological change (cf. Clague 1997: 19–20).

Mancur Olson (1997) and others have pointed at the role institutions play in solving problems of collective action. The production of public or collective goods is argued to be problematic in those cases where individuals who are benefiting from the public good do not feel compelled to contribute to the costs of the good (Clague 1997: 21). Particularly in circumstances where individuals can hide as free riders within a large group, 'underproduction' of the public good is a likely outcome. Institutions are seen as instruments that can monitor individuals' behaviour and convince or force them to take their share of the costs involved.

In their analysis of the contribution of the new institutional economics to development theory, Lin and Nugent (1995: 2342–53) emphasised the role of households in the development process vis-à-vis tribes and clans. They argued that, in the early phases of the development process, the replacement of collective mechanisms – for instance, for the regulation of property – by 'self-supervision' through households leads to a reduction of transaction costs. The increased importance of technology in production, and of capital, leads to a substantial reduction of the efficiency of the household level. The development of markets and institutions for credit and payments is taken to be a necessary condition to achieve higher degrees of specialisation and a more complex division of labour. This change is assumed to produce a change in contractual forms: rent and share contracts will give way to fixed wage contracts, which will gradually become the dominant form. Gradually, the state takes the place of traditional institutions and steadily assumes responsibilities in regulation, tax collection and the production of collective goods. Expansion of the geographic scope of exchange is expected to lead to the expansion of market externalities (such as technology and information, which both have important characteristics of public goods). The state is in a better position than other institutions to internalise such externalities and provide public goods by virtue of its monopoly on the use of force and the collection of taxes.

According to Douglass North (1987: 422–5), there is a connection between the development of specific institutions and economic progress. Economies based on personal exchange, with a dominance of small-scale production and local trade, tend to advance very slowly, as specialisation and division of labour play a marginal role. Economies dominated by impersonal exchange without third party enforcement, reflected in trading at traditional bazaars and production through serfdom and slavery, tend to have high transaction costs and limited trade benefits. Only a third form of economic organisation, impersonal exchange with third party enforcement, would be conducive to sustained economic growth. In such a context, significant benefits will result from economic specialisation, and economic agents can enter into long-term transactions – such as investment – without needing to worry about the security of their possessions.

Institutions, North (1995: 20) argued, are not neutral actors: 'Institutions are not necessarily or even usually created to be socially efficient; rather they, or at least the formal rules, are created to serve the interests of those with the bargaining power to create new rules.' According to North, the creation of institutions should not be seen as inevitable, even where such institutions would contribute to general social welfare. Institutions are highly *path dependent*, which implies that existing institutional frameworks are resistant to change, because of the entrenched interests of certain social and economic groups. This means that countries that have a history of less efficient institutions cannot hope for sudden improvements in their institutional make-up.

North claimed that 'adaptive efficiency' is a more relevant objective for developing economies than 'allocative efficiency'. Institutions need to adjust to changing circumstances and need to contribute to efficient economic processes under new conditions:

> Allocative efficiency is a static concept with a given set of institutions; the key to continuing good economic performance is a flexible institutional matrix that will adjust in the context of evolving technological and demographic changes as well as shocks to the system.
>
> (North 1995: 26)

In addition to the foregoing, North argued that political institutions can only be stable when they are supported by social organisations that have an interest in their continued existence. Western history, in his view, has showed the importance of the rule of law and the safeguarding of civil liberties and political rights: 'While economic growth can occur in the short run with autocratic regimes, long-run economic growth entails the development of the rule of law and the protection of civil and political freedoms' (North 1995: 25).

In contrast to the new institutional economists, Joseph Stiglitz was more explicit about the arguments for government intervention into the market economy. Stiglitz argued that markets often do not produce the benefits predicted by neo-classical economics because of various forms of 'market failure'. Market failure, in his view, is often related to the unequal access to information of different economic actors. Such market failure, in particular resulting from imperfect and costly information, would be more prevalent in less-developed countries than in the industrialised world. Moreover, in the former countries 'nonmarket institutions that ameliorate its consequences are, at least in many instances, less successful in doing so' (Stiglitz 1989: 197). Differences in the level of development between industrialised and developing countries can be attributed 'to differences in economic organization, to how individuals (factors of production) interact, and to the institutions which mediate those interactions' (Stiglitz 1989: 197).

As a consequence of the fact that market processes fail to reach a general or partial equilibrium – Stiglitz argued – economic actors are faced with the existence of multiple equilibria and will often be ignorant about the way to move from an inferior to a superior equilibrium. This results in the prevalence of coordination problems: 'even though each individual may know that there is another equilibrium at which all would be better off, individuals are unable to coordinate the complementary changes in their actions necessary to attain that outcome' (Hoff and Stiglitz 2001: 390).

According to Hoff and Stiglitz (2001: 416–26), there are several important theoretical arguments for government intervention in economic processes. First, intervention may be necessary to solve coordination problems that cannot be addressed successfully by independent economic actors. Affirmative action, aiming to secure labour market participation of underrepresented groups, is an example of such action. Second, governments may decide to provide economic actors with information, with the objective of changing their behaviour. Information about pollution, for example, may impact on the use of certain production techniques. Third, interventions may change the dynamics of the political process. Such interventions, such as the privatisation of a state monopoly, would be considered 'deep' interventions (Hoff and Stiglitz 2001: 419) as they change the rules of the political game. Finally, and most importantly, governments may intervene with an eye to changing the distribution of wealth. Such interventions would have a direct impact on the behaviour of economic actors but would also have a lasting effect, as the distribution of wealth in succeeding generations will be affected.

Stiglitz's contributions to economic theory were directly related to his role in policy making at the World Bank. In 1997 and 1998, Stiglitz, in his position as chief economist of the World Bank, called for the incorporation of some of his ideas into the Bank's precepts – this came to be known as the 'post-Washington Consensus'. Stiglitz summarised his position by arguing that

> the policies advanced by the Washington Consensus are not complete, and they are sometimes misguided. Making markets work requires more than just low inflation; it requires sound financial regulation, competition policy, and policies to facilitate the transfer of technology and to encourage transparency, to cite some fundamental issues neglected by the Washington Consensus.
>
> (Stiglitz 1998b: 1)

16 *Paradigm shift in development assistance*

In Stiglitz's view, the Washington Consensus erroneously adopted an anti-government stance: 'focusing on the fundamentals is not a recipe for minimalist government. The state has an important role to play in appropriate regulation, social protection, and welfare' (Stiglitz 1998b: 25). Governments would have an important role to play, in particular, in the correction of the aforementioned market failures.

The innovations in economic theory that have been discussed in this section have nuanced the neo-classical, equilibrium-oriented understanding of markets, but markets have nevertheless remained central elements in the explanation of development and growth. The essential continuity between the period of the Washington Consensus and the currently dominant post–Washington Consensus has been captured well by Craig and Porter (2006: 93) who characterised the two phases as stages in the development of neo-liberalism, from a 'conservative' to a more positive 'inclusive' variant. As was shown above, the argument of the 'non-neoclassical' economists still hinges on the development of an efficient allocative mechanism and a productive division of labour. Market processes are assumed to generate wealth, and as such there is no alternative development mechanism to the market. Scholars assume, however, that markets will not develop spontaneously and that institutional mechanisms are necessary for the good functioning of markets. Good and efficient markets, according to them, can develop and function only in the context of institutions that allow the market to work. A system of property rights, the rule of law and contract enforcement are all seen as market-related institutional prerequisites for development. The state, as an enforcement mechanism of contracts and rights, is clearly instrumental to all this.

2.3 The rethinking of development policies

The awareness, in the mid-1990s, that poverty had persisted despite decades of development assistance programmes and major improvements in the lives of large parts of the population around the world, spurred a rethinking of the objectives and means of development aid (e.g. Development Assistance Committee 1996: 6–7; United Nations Development Programme 2000: 16–29). In various fora, the international donor community started to reflect on the perspectives for development cooperation. The Organisation for Economic Co-operation and Development (OECD), and its Development Assistance Committee (DAC) in particular, proved instrumental in the refocusing of development thinking.

A landmark document in the process of rethinking development policies was the DAC's report *Shaping the 21st Century* (Development Assistance Committee 1996). This report introduced a set of international development targets that were to become the basis for the Millennium Development Goals. The targets formulated by the DAC, on the basis of the outcome of several international conferences, were the following (Development Assistance Committee 1996: 9–11):

- To reduce the proportion of people living in extreme poverty by one-half in 2015;

- To make substantial progress in the improvement of primary education (to achieve universal primary education by 2015), gender equality (to eliminate gender disparity in primary and secondary education by 2005), basic health care (to reduce infant and child mortality by two-thirds by 2015 and reduce maternal mortality by three-fourths during this period) and family planning (to create access to reproductive health services for all individuals of appropriate ages, including safe and reliable family planning methods, by 2015);
- To implement national strategies for sustainable development by 2005 to ensure that the loss of environmental resources is effectively reversed at both global and national levels by 2015.

The achievement of the international development targets would, in the view of the industrialised countries that make up the OECD, not be the sole responsibility of the donors. The attachment of policy conditionalities to aid programmes was no longer felt to be sufficiently effective (Killick et al. 1998: 161–7; Collier 2000: 300–3). It was argued that past experience had demonstrated that developing countries have insufficient incentives to adopt policies in exchange for aid – which led to the much quoted statement, 'Aid does not buy policy reform' – and that new means had to be found to ensure implementation of sound policies.

The key to solving this problem was found in 'ownership'. This principle implies that development programmes need to be based on 'agreement and commitment from developing country partners, through their own national goals and locally owned strategies' (Development Assistance Committee 1996: 9). Ownership would also imply, in the view of the DAC, that development goals do not only reflect the preferences of developing country governments, but are the outcome of civil society involvement:

> As a basic principle, locally owned country development strategies and targets should emerge from an open and collaborative dialogue by local authorities with civil society and with external partners, about their shared objectives and their respective contributions to the common enterprise. Each donor's programme and activities should then operate within the framework of that locally owned strategy in ways that respect and encourage strong local commitment, participation, capacity development and ownership.
> (Development Assistance Committee 1996: 14)

The ownership of national development strategies would enable donor countries to adopt an approach that would later, in donor parlance, be referred to as *alignment*. This term would be used to signal that developing country governments are in control and that donors 'base their overall support on partner countries' national development strategies, institutions and procedures' (High-Level Forum on Aid Effectiveness 2005: 3).

Other principles for development assistance formulated by the DAC in 1996 were coherence and greater coordination (later also labelled *harmonisation*). *Coherence* implies that instruments adopted in different policy areas should work together (Development Assistance Committee 1996: 14). Thus, development cooperation efforts should not be undermined by limiting access to foreign markets for products originating from developing countries, maintaining subsidies for agricultural and other producers who compete unfairly with producers in the South, or imposing technical, sanitary and other requirements for imports that producers in the developing world are not able to meet (cf. Development Assistance Committee 2001: 95–101). *Coordination* or *harmonisation* means that donors adopt 'common arrangements at country level for planning, funding (e.g. joint financial arrangements), disbursement, monitoring, evaluating and reporting to government on donor activities and aid flows' (High-Level Forum on Aid Effectiveness 2005: 6). The adoption of this principle should lead to a sharp reduction of transaction costs for developing country governments.

Building on the principles referred to in this section, new forms of aid delivery have been introduced that were assumed to enhance the effectiveness of development assistance. Two forms, the sector-wide approach and budget support, deserve more elaborate discussion here, given their increasing popularity in the international donor community. It was argued that both forms offer better opportunities for alignment with recipient countries' objectives and lead to donor harmonisation more easily.

The sector-wide approach was introduced as a means to concentrate development efforts in particular sectors in developing countries. The choice of sectors would need to be made by developing country governments in a participatory process of the kind that was referred to above and could involve social sectors (such as health or education) or other sectors that were deemed important for the country concerned (such as rural development, water or sanitation). The development of these sectors would be supported by donors in an integrated way:

> Agencies make their contributions towards a single sector policy and expenditure programme, under government leadership, striving to use as far as possible common management and reporting procedures to disburse and account for all funds. ... Sector programmes imply a different approach to aid management from what development agencies are used to and organised for. It requires development agencies to fully take into account locally owned sector strategies. And it calls for greater modesty and an acceptance of what may be a slow process of change, relying on partnership-building rather than on the implementation of a blueprint. Extending this form of support greatly depends on the country context and is premised on a number of prerequisites, including the ability of the partner country to fulfil the responsibilities of adequate financial governance.
>
> (Development Assistance Committee 2001: 77)

Linked to the introduction of the sector-wide approach was the preference that many donor countries have shown for forms of programme aid, such as balance of payments support, debt relief or general budget support. Programme aid results in the provision of financial resources to recipient governments, either for earmarked purposes (such as help with solving balance of payments problems or paying off outstanding debt) or to support government expenditure generally. The provision of programme aid is usually made dependent on the assessment of a recipient country's macro-economic stability, which is predicated on an agreement of the country concerned with the IMF (Dijkstra 2006: 3).

The logic behind the choice for a sector-wide approach and budget support, which transpires in the quote from the *DAC Guidelines on Poverty Reduction* (Development Assistance Committee 2001) above, was that donors assumed that such aid modalities could be used only in countries with sufficiently good governance mechanisms. As many decisions regarding the use of aid funds would need to be made locally, they were to be monitored by donor governments only from a distance, thus requiring proper budgetary and accounting procedures on the part of the recipient governments.

2.4 Good governance and aid effectiveness

Hermes and Lensink (2001: 3) have pointed out that in the first half of the 1990s there was 'no consensus on the nature of the relationship between aid and growth'. The usefulness of policy conditionalities as instruments in aid allocation was, moreover, criticised fiercely (Hermes and Lensink 2001: 7–8; Thorbecke 2000: 45). Concerns with aid effectiveness and policy conditionalities resulted in the setting up of various research programmes, the aim of which was to determine the conditions under which aid would be effective.

In particular, the research done by the World Bank, in a group around David Dollar, resulted in the 'powerful narrative' (Court and Maxwell 2006: 17) that aid works only in countries with good governance and good policies. The World Bank's research on aid effectiveness derived its influence, according to one commentator, primarily from five characteristics: '(a) the analysis was timely, (b) the policy implications were compelling, (c) the authors had credibility, (d) the story line was presented simply and clearly, and (e) the authors deliberately set out to achieve impact' (Masood Ahmed cited in Court and Maxwell 2006: 17–18).

Several World Bank working papers (Burnside and Dollar 1997, 2004; Collier and Dollar 1999) and the report *Assessing Aid* (World Bank 1998) arrived at the conclusion that aid has a positive impact on growth in developing countries that have good policies and governance. The message according to the World Bank was as follows:

> The development strategy emerging from this view is two-pronged – put in place growth-enhancing, market-oriented policies (stable macro-economic environment, effective law and order, trade liberalization, and so on) and ensure the provision of important public services that cannot be well and equitably supplied by private markets (infrastructure services and education, for instance). Developing countries with sound policies and high-quality public institutions have grown much faster than those without – 2.7 percent

compared with –0.5 percent per capita. Put simply, failures in policymaking, institution building, and the provision of public services have been more severe constraints on development than capital markets. ... The key recommendation from these findings is not that finance should go only to well-managed countries. Rather, we recommend that aid be allocated on the basis of poverty and economic management. Among countries with similar poverty levels but different policy regimes, more finance should go to the countries with better management.

(World Bank 1998: 11, 15–16)

The first two studies on the effectiveness of aid (Burnside and Dollar 1997; World Bank 1998) both used an index that was supposed to reflect the quality of governance and policies. Burnside and Dollar (1997: 19–20) constructed a 'policy index' using data on countries' budget surplus, rate of inflation and trade openness. They performed regression analyses on 56 countries for which data were available on six four-year periods between 1970 and 1993. Burnside and Dollar found that the level of aid had contributed positively to economic growth, when controlling for the policy index. Countries with good policies were showed to have a positive impact of aid on growth. In countries with poor policies, aid did not, however, influence economic growth in a positive direction.

The *Assessing Aid* report used an 'index of economic management', which was calculated as the weighted sum of the inflation rate, the budget surplus, trade openness and institutional quality (World Bank 1998: 121–3). The latter was a composite of indicators related to bureaucracy, corruption, the rule of law, the risk of expropriation, nationalisation and breach of contract. The *Assessing Aid* report arrived at similar findings as Burnside and Dollar's earlier study: during the 1970–93 period, aid was found to have a positive effect on economic growth in countries with good economic management.

In a subsequent analysis, Collier and Dollar (1999: 6–8) estimated the impact of aid on economic growth using the 1997 CPIA (Country Policy and Institutional Assessment) rating (see Chapter 3 for more detail on this), and applying their analysis to 86 countries in the period between 1990 and 1996. Despite the differences in the methodology, Collier and Dollar's study confirmed the findings of the two initial reports on aid effectiveness.

Responding to the findings of the three World Bank reports discussed so far, many researchers criticised certain aspects of the analyses and questioned the validity of the results and conclusions. Critics have addressed methodological and empirical problems related to, among other things, the use of cross-country regressions and the construction of the policy index (Lensink and White 1999: 3–6), issues of model specification and the distorting impact of influential observations and outliers (Hansen and Tarp 2000: 122, 2001: 561; Dalgaard and Hansen 2001: 27–33; Roodman 2004: 30–41), the inclusion of additional data (Easterly *et al.* 2003: 3–4), the impact of external shocks on the aid-growth relationship (Guillaumont and Chauvet 2001: 79), and the impact of factors such as political stability, democracy and post-conflict reconstruction (McGillivray

2003: 3–4). In addition to their criticism, Hansen and Tarp (2000: 116–18, 2001: 559) reported findings that suggest that aid would lead to increased growth in developing countries, irrespective of the quality of governance and policies.

In an attempt to respond to their critics, Burnside and Dollar (2004: 12–13) re-analysed their original data, using the governance indicators compiled by a team from the World Bank Institute (Kaufmann *et al.* 1999) to establish the impact of governance and policies. Burnside and Dollar (2004) performed a cross-sectional analysis of aid given to 124 countries during the 1990s. Their findings confirm the results of the three earlier World Bank studies. Changes in the operationalisation of the governance and policy indicators and variations in the number of countries and years included did not seem to affect the central conclusion: Burnside and Dollar argued that their findings indicated that good policies produce higher levels of economic growth, both directly and indirectly through the interaction with aid. Taking issue with the arguments of their critics, Burnside and Dollar (2004: 19) claimed that 'there is far more evidence that aid spurs growth conditional on institutions, than for the competing hypothesis that aid has the same positive effect in all institutional environments'.

2.5 Conclusions

The previous sections have illustrated that the international aid agenda has undergone considerable change over the past decade. Important modifications concerned the policy preferences of multilateral and bilateral aid donors, and the modalities of aid given to developing countries. Without doubt, the main driver of the changes in the aid agenda has been the concern with the impact of development assistance.

The issue of aid effectiveness came onto the international political agenda in the mid-1990s as a result of empirical observations on the persistence of poverty and the lack of economic development in large parts of the developing world, and analytical concerns related to the incentives for reform by developing country governments. Table 2.1 presents a schematic interpretation of the logic behind the recent paradigm shift in the international aid agenda.

At least three important dimensions can be distinguished with respect to the concerns about aid effectiveness, related to the objectives, modalities and conditions of development assistance. First, the focus on macro-economic fundamentals in the Washington Consensus and on market-oriented structural adjustment policies meant that there had been relatively little attention for poverty reduction as an objective of development assistance during the 1980s and the first half of the 1990s. Poverty assumed its prominence in the development debate only gradually during the latter half of the 1990s. Second, the prevalence of donor-driven aid agendas had implied an emphasis on forms of assistance (such as project aid and technical assistance) that failed to recognise the recipients' preferences. It became increasingly clear that this characteristic of aid implied that the aid relationship had only limited impact on realities in the developing countries. Third, policy makers had gradually come to recognise that

Table 2.1 The paradigm shift in the international aid agenda

Findings	Problem definition	Causes	Remedies	Operationalisation
Insufficient growth and insufficient poverty reduction in many developing countries	Aid insufficiently effective in terms of aid objectives	Too little attention for poverty, too much focus on macro-economic conditions	Focus on aspects of poverty	Millennium Development Goals: quantifiable targets for poverty reduction
Insufficient incentive for policy reform on the part of developing country governments	Aid insufficiently effective in terms of aid modalities	Aid modalities too much driven by donor preferences	Focus on ownership, alignment of aid with recipients' policies would lead to prevalence of recipients' preferences	New aid modalities: sector-wide approaches, budget support, PRSPs
	Aid insufficiently effective in terms of aid conditions	Policy ('ex ante') conditionalities had proved to be ineffective	Emphasis on policies and governance ('ex post conditionality')	Selectivity on the basis of policy and governance criteria

policy conditionalities, which were among the favoured instruments of development agencies to induce change in recipient countries, were only partly effective because of principal–agent problems affecting donor–recipient interaction (cf. Killick et al. 1998: 161–7).

The recent paradigm shift in the international aid agenda is reflected in changes related to the objectives and modalities of assistance and in the conditions that are attached to the provision of aid. Selectivity is the key principle in all elements of the new aid paradigm: the objectives are limited to a certain set of quantifiable targets; aid modalities and targeted sectors are selected in response to recipient countries' preferences; and recipient countries are chosen on the basis of criteria related to policies and governance. The latter element is often referred to as 'ex post conditionality' to signal that it is a criterion that judges past performance; as such, it is distinct from 'ex ante' conditionality, which relates to the promise to implement certain policies in a following period.

The attention for poverty reduction as an objective of development assistance has been operationalised in the Millennium Development Goals, which are a set of quantifiable targets for action on health and education issues. The focus on the preferences of recipient countries has led to a discourse of recipient 'ownership' of assistance programmes and has produced an emphasis on new aid modalities, such as sector-wide approaches and budget support. These new aid forms are believed to facilitate the 'alignment' of aid programmes with the policies adopted by recipient governments. The PRSP (Poverty Reduction Strategy Paper) approach initiated by the international financial institutions is advocated as an instrument to engage civil society in poverty reduction policies, and a means to enhance therewith the legitimacy of such policies. The introduction of a different type of conditionalities, which would be based on an assessment of implemented policies and governance arrangements in aid-receiving countries instead of promises concerning future policy reform, was believed to enhance donors' credibility in formulating and applying criteria. It is argued that this approach enables donor countries to select recipients on the basis of certain eligibility criteria.

3 The World Bank and performance-based allocation

3.1 Introduction

The World Bank, the world's most important multilateral development institution and a major player in the financing of development policies, has been at the forefront of discussions about issues of governance and development since the 1980s. During the 1990s and at the beginning of the twenty-first century, the Bank has consistently focused on the issue of governance and has set the global agenda on governance quality in the context of development policies and strategies. The Bank's influence on the development agenda, which may stem less from the originality than the propagation of views, was captured appropriately by Gavin and Rodrik (quoted in Gilbert and Vines 2000: 19): 'Once the Bank gets hold of an idea, its financial clout ensures that the idea will gain wide currency.'[1]

The World Bank's concern with governance issues sprang from its realisation that structural adjustment had not worked (Miller-Adams 1999: 106–8). In the introduction to a report on sub-Saharan Africa, in what is perhaps the first statement on the impact of governance on the development process, World Bank President Barber Conable wrote:

> A root cause of weak economic performance in the past has been the failure of public institutions. Private sector and market mechanisms are important, but they must go hand-in-hand with good governance – a public service that is efficient, a judicial system that is reliable, and an administration that is accountable to its public. And a better balance is needed between the government and the governed.
>
> (World Bank 1989: xii)

Towards the end of the 1990s, the World Bank's concern with governance was integrated with the assessment framework that it had applied for lending countries, the Country Policy and Institutional Assessment (CPIA). This integration resulted in the setting up of the governance-oriented performance-based allocation system that has been operational since 1998.

This chapter analyses the thinking in the World Bank about governance and the application of the governance criterion in its lending policies.[2] Section 3.2

traces the evolution of the Bank's attention for governance. Section 3.3 discusses the application of governance-related criteria in the allocation process of the International Development Association (IDA), the division within the World Bank that is responsible for concessionary lending to developing countries. In Section 3.4, the World Bank's approach to performance-based allocation is evaluated, while Section 3.5 concludes this chapter.

3.2 The World Bank and governance

One of the first fruits of systematic analysis of governance and development by the World Bank is a discussion paper of 1991, originally published for internal purposes only. In this paper, staff members ascribed the World Bank's recent attention for governance issues to the fact that 'the relatively good growth performance of developing countries between 1965 and 1980 helped conceal the deep-seated problems of governance'; since the early 1980s, however, 'the emergence of a climate of relative scarcity began to expose governance issues in many countries' (World Bank 1991: 1).[3]

From the outset, the World Bank has acknowledged its own limitations in implementing policies on governance. One major limit to World Bank activities was felt to derive from the Bank's mandate:

> [T]he Bank cannot be influenced by the political character of a member; it cannot interfere in the partisan politics of the member; it must not act on behalf of donor countries in influencing the member's political orientation or behavior; it cannot be influenced in its decisions by political factors that do not have a preponderant economic effect; and its staff should not build their judgments on the possible reaction of a particular Bank member or members.
> (World Bank 1991: 3)

The World Bank's original concern with governance was chiefly its implication for proper development management (World Bank 1991: 17–18). For this reason, the Bank's interpretation had a primarily technocratic overtone (Leftwich 1994). The Bank defined governance as 'the manner in which power is exercised in the management of a country's economic and social resources for development', yet limited its concern to 'the rules and institutions which create a predictable and transparent framework for the conduct of public and private business and to accountability for economic and financial performance' (World Bank 1991: 1).

The four main issues that the World Bank considered to be relevant for its work were (i) capacity and efficiency of public sector management, (ii) accountability, (iii) predictability and the legal framework for development (iv) and information and transparency. The definition of governance and the concern with public and private business has led the Bank to focus on measures to increase governance quality mainly in relation to the functioning of markets.

The *quality of public sector management* was considered important because of the role of government in the adoption and implementation of rules to make markets work effectively and in the correction of market failures (World Bank 1991: 3). The Bank's role in public sector management was seen primarily in terms of public expenditure management, civil service reform, and parastatal reform and privatisation (World Bank 1991: 8).

Accountability was defined chiefly in terms of ensuring financial accountability and accountability for economic performance. An important objective in this respect was to avoid 'capture' of public resources by narrow special interests and the use of public resources for private gain (World Bank 1991: 5, 27–38).

Predictability and the legal framework for development related to the adoption and implementation of rules. The World Bank stressed that a focus on the rule of law is necessary as one of the preconditions for economic development. The rule of law would imply that there is a set of rules that is known in advance; rules are actually in force; there are mechanisms to ensure rule application; rule adjudication takes place through an independent judiciary; and there are procedures for the amendment of rules when they are no longer appropriate. In the context of the legal framework, some of the symptoms of poor governance were considered to be arbitrariness in the application of rules and the existence of excessive rules and regulations hindering the functioning of markets and leading to rent-seeking practices (World Bank 1991: 6, 38–48).

Information and transparency were considered to be important aspects of governance because of their potential impact on development management. In particular, narrowly based or non-transparent decision-making was seen as a problem for development. The availability of information and transparency of decision-making was judged to be critical for the proper and efficient functioning of a competitive market economy and to be a safeguard against corruption, wastage and the abuse of authority (World Bank 1991: 11–13, 48–53).

During the presidency of James Wolfensohn, the World Bank's thinking about governance received a boost. The earlier focus of the World Bank on policy prescriptions of the Washington Consensus (see Chapter 2) was amended with the adoption of the Comprehensive Development Framework.[4]

Under the new framework, the Bank's emphasis moved away from its almost exclusive focus on macro-economic fundamentals to a more comprehensive treatment of social and political contexts. Wolfensohn put it in a speech to the World Bank Board of Governors about the implications of the Asian financial crisis on the Bank's work in 1998:

> Too often we have been too narrow in our conception of the economic transformations that are required – while focusing on macroeconomic numbers, or on major reforms like privatization, we have ignored the basic institutional infrastructure, without which a market economy simply cannot function.... Too often we have focused too much on the economics, without a sufficient understanding of the social, the political, the environmental, and the cultural aspects of society.
>
> (Wolfensohn 1998: 11–12)

The components of the new development framework that was outlined by Wolfensohn included 'the essentials of good governance' (transparency, participation, free information, anti-corruption policies and a well-qualified civil service), the regulatory framework for a working market economy, social policies focused on health and education, the build-up of infrastructure, and policies for environmental sustainability (Wolfensohn 1998: 13–14).

The World Bank President's views were supported intellectually and theoretically by Chief Economist Joseph Stiglitz, whose appointment in 1997 signalled a break with the Washington Consensus and a move towards the 'post-Washington Consensus' (Pender 2001: 403; see Chapter 2 for further detail about the theoretical frameworks involved). In Stiglitz's view, the emphasis of the Washington Consensus on the liberalisation of trade, macroeconomic stability and privatisation did not provide appropriate guidance for development policies. Stiglitz (1998b: 15–18) argued that market-oriented policies would need to be complemented by a 'redesigning' of the regulatory framework of the market economy. In particular, the creation of a legal framework in combination with regulation would provide markets with the information they would need to function effectively. The role of the government would be essential in this context, as it 'should serve as a complement to markets, undertaking actions that make markets work better and correcting market failure' (Stiglitz 1998b: 26). In Stiglitz's view (1998a: 26–7), the role of the World Bank would be to assist developing countries to create the institutional legal and regulatory framework that is required to attract foreign capital.

The changing orientation towards development policy is reflected in successive issues of the World Bank's flagship publication, the *World Development Report* (cf. Cammack 2002). The *World Development Report 1999/2000*, bearing the title 'Entering the 21st Century', stressed 'the need for a holistic approach', which was reflected in the Comprehensive Development Framework (World Bank 2000: 20). The World Bank argued that successful development policies would require a stable macro-economic environment, would be 'owned' by the country concerned and be formulated in partnership with civil society, the private sector and donor agencies. Such policies should take into account structural, human, physical and sectoral priorities:

> *Structural* elements include honest, competent governments committed to the fight against corruption; strong property and personal rights laws supported by an efficient and honest legal and judicial system; a well-supervised financial system that promotes transparency; and a strong social safety net.
>
> *Human* development includes universal primary education and strong secondary and tertiary systems, and a health system that focuses on family planning and child care.
>
> *Physical* concerns center around the efficient provision of water and sewerage; expanded access to reliable electric power; access to road, rail, and air transportation and to telecommunications; preservation of the physical

environment; and a commitment to preserving cultural and historical sites and artifacts that buttress indigenous cultures and values.

Sectoral elements include an integrated rural development strategy, a strong urban management approach, and an enabling environment for the private sector.

(World Bank 2000: 21)

Notwithstanding the World Bank's adherence to the post-Washington Consensus, its approach to development and governance has retained its focus on the role of markets. The *World Development Report 2002*, entitled 'Building Institutions for Markets', started from the assumption that 'income from participating in the market is the key to boosting economic growth for nations and to reducing poverty for individuals' (World Bank 2002: 3). The main task of governments is defined as the regulation of markets (cf. Jayasuriya and Rosser 2001: 388–91; Fine 2003: 4; Öniş and Şenses 2005: 275): when building institutions governments 'first need to assess what is inhibiting market development or leading to certain market outcomes'. The main concern of policy-makers should be to assess what kind of information is lacking to let markets function properly, whether the definition and enforcement of property rights is clear, and whether there is too little or too much competition. Importantly, institutions should be designed 'so that the incentives of market actors are aligned to achieve the desired outcome' (World Bank 2002: 10). The ensuing definition of 'good governance' is also based heavily on the functions of the governance regime for the effectiveness of markets:

Good governance includes the creation, protection, and enforcement of property rights, without which the scope for market transactions is limited. It includes the provision of a regulatory regime that works with the market to promote competition. And it includes the provision of sound macroeconomic policies that create a stable environment for market activity. Good governance also means the absence of corruption, which can subvert the goals of policy and undermine the legitimacy of the public institutions that support markets.

(World Bank 2002: 99)

3.3 Governance and performance-based allocation

Since 1977, the IDA has been implementing performance-assessment criteria to its lending portfolio. In the first instance, performance was assessed by quantitative indicators primarily reflecting economic achievement (such as gross national product (GNP) growth and saving rates), coupled with qualitative judgments on administration and economic management (Hicks *et al.* 1982: 24; Kapur *et al.* 1997: 1152). As of 1989, according to a memorandum written in October of that year, country performance would be assessed as 'high', 'moderate' or 'low' by 'knowledgeable' Bank staff members, on three criteria: short-run economic management (mainly of demand), long-run economic management (primarily supply-side restructuring) and countries' poverty-alleviation record as reflected in social service delivery and reforms removing labour market distortions. This assessment would lead to quite differing allocations for the three performance categories – the ratio of per capita allocations was set at 3.2:2:1 – for all except the most populous (China and India) and smallest countries (Kapur et al. 1997: 1153).

The Country Policy and Institutional Assessment – called Country Performance Rating (CPR) prior to 1998 (World Bank Operations Evaluation Department[5] 2001c: 1) – has been key to the IDA's performance-based allocation mechanism. Over the years, the performance assessment mechanism has changed considerably, in terms both of content and of methodological and operational sophistication. This section discusses the evolution of performance-based allocation. First, the CPR mechanism is described. This is followed by an analysis of the CPIA, which has been the main instrument of performance monitoring since 1998. Next, the introduction of an explicit governance criterion (the governance discount and the ensuing governance factor) is discussed, including the way in which the governance criterion is used in the determination of the allocation of IDA resources. Finally, the recent amendments concerning IDA14 are analysed.[6]

3.3.1 Country performance rating before 1998

The CPR mechanism that was applied prior to 1998 consisted of three categories: a country's short-term economic management, long-term economic management and poverty alleviation policies. Countries were rated on a scale ranging from 1 to 5 on each of the three items, which were weighed equally. Short-term economic management included monetary, fiscal, exchange rate and pricing policies. The assessment of long-term economic management focused on structural policies, most notably external and domestic trade regimes, private sector development, tax and financial sector policies, governance ('accountability, openness and predictability of government actions'), natural resource management, the quality and allocation of public expenditures, agricultural policies and programmes, human resource management (including gender aspects), public sector management and infrastructure. The evaluation of poverty alleviation policies included measures promoting the delivery of social services and the reduction of biases against the agricultural terms of trade and the demand for labour (World Bank Operations Evaluation Department 2001c: 4–5).

In its review of the application of the CPR, the Operations Evaluation Department (OED) emphasised that the ratings were originally performed without guidance to staff on how to rate policies on the 1–5 scale. Moreover, no weights were assigned to individual components of the three items and no written justifications for the ratings were required. It is assumed that governance had a weight of no more than 3 per cent in the overall CPR (World Bank Operations Evaluation Department 2001c: 5–6).

During the negotiations on IDA10 (1993–6), the CPR methodology was changed to include several new components to the item on short-term economic management (external account management and debt management) and to update the definitions of governance and natural resource management that were part of the item on long-term economic management. The governance component was amended to include community participation in programmes and projects and the diversion of resources from development to non-development (military) purposes. In addition to the changes in the CPR items, IDA portfolio performance was added to the CPR with a weight of 20 per cent (World Bank Operations Evaluation Department 2001c: 6–7).

In the preparations for IDA11 (1996–9), the weight of IDA portfolio performance was reduced, first to 10 per cent and later to 7 per cent of the overall CPR. An important innovation in this period related to the formulation of clearer criteria for scoring countries' policy performance. To this end, descriptions were made of the types of policies that would correspond with particular scores. Scores ranged between 2 for low performance and 4 for high performance; scores of 1 and 5 were to be assigned to countries that were persistently low or high performers (World Bank Operations Evaluation Department 2001c: 7).

Apart from the introduction of criteria for policy types, the weights of the different items in the CPR were specified during IDA11. Macro-economic stability, which replaced short-term economic management, received a weight of 25 per cent. The item on structural reforms, which combined long-term economic management and poverty reduction, was given a weight of 65 per cent. The remaining 10 per cent was allocated to IDA portfolio performance. As a result of this exercise, governance was no longer an explicit component on the structural reforms item. Instead, it was decided that 'performance assessments put a great deal of weight on *governance, commitment*, and *credibility*' (1995 CPR instructions cited by World Bank Operations Evaluation Department 2001c: 8). In 1996 and 1997, some governance-related components (civil administration and legal and regulatory framework) were added to the policy assessment instruments, at the same time reducing the weight of IDA portfolio performance to 7 per cent (World Bank Operations Evaluation Department 2001c: 8–10).

3.3.2 Introduction and implementation of the CPIA

During the negotiations on IDA12 (1999–2002), a major overhaul of the CPR system was undertaken. This resulted in the replacement of the CPR by the CPIA and the removal of the portfolio performance indicator from the CPIA into the allocation process. Importantly, the representatives of the donor countries (usually referred to as IDA deputies, cf. International Development Association 2001c: 1) stressed the need for changes to the CPIA methodology, in particular in respect of its equity, transparency and simplicity. The issue of equity related to the comparability of performance assessments across countries and regions and led to benchmarking and a greater role of sector specialists in the rating system. The problem of transparency was raised because of concerns about the secrecy of the assessment process, and this was addressed by disclosing the quintile rating of countries' performance as of 2000. The question of simplicity concerned the number and unequal weight of items and indicators used in the CPR; this issue was taken up by limiting the CPIA to 20 indicators of equal weight (World Bank Operations Evaluation Department 2001c: 10).[7] During IDA12 and IDA13 (2002–5), the CPIA was adapted repeatedly to accommodate comments originating from both World Bank management and the IDA deputies. These changes involved, among others, the indicators on policies and institutions for environmental sustainability, gender (which earlier related more generally to equality of economic opportunity) and social protection and labour (earlier focusing on safety nets) (World Bank Operations Evaluation Department 2001c: 13). The overall structure of the CPIA, however, did not change fundamentally until the revision that was undertaken in the negotiations leading up to IDA14 (2005–8).

The assessment of country performance on the basis of the CPIA has become a process involving three steps (World Bank Operations Evaluation Department 2001c: 13–14; interview, 2 June 2005):

- *Country-team work*: The rating process is initiated by country teams (consisting of between two and six staff members for smaller countries to between six and ten staff for larger countries), composed of the country desk officers and the local country officers, headed by the country director. The country-team work leads to the production of initial ratings for all countries involved.
- *The review process*: The review process involves, first, a benchmarking exercise of a set of countries (increasing from 5 in 1998, 11 in 1999 and 2000, to 17 in 2004) that are analysed in-depth and whose scores serve as the reference point for the rating of other countries. The ratings of the benchmark countries in particular regions are reviewed and revised by the chief economists responsible for those regions, as well as by the networks of specialists (e.g. on gender, governance and private sector development), leading to the eventual 'freezing' of the benchmark ratings. The scores of the country teams are subsequently compared with the ratings of the benchmark countries and, where this is considered necessary, the country ratings are revised.
- *Decision-making*: The central CPIA manager submits the country ratings to the Board of Directors that endorses the ratings.

3.3.3 The governance criterion and IDA allocation

The increased general attention for governance issues within the World Bank during the 1990s, analysed in Section 3.2, was reflected in greater emphasis in both performance rating and allocation of IDA loans and grants beginning in 1998. The revision of the performance assessment methodology, expressed in the adoption of the CPIA, included the insertion of six governance-related indicators, together making up 30 per cent of the CPIA:

32 World Bank and performance-based allocation

- policies and institutions for environmental sustainability (indicator 10, see Appendix B)
- property rights and rule-based governance (indicator 16)
- quality of budgetary and financial management (indicator 17)
- efficiency of revenue mobilisation (indicator 18)
- quality of public administration (indicator 19)
- transparency, accountability and corruption in the public sector (indicator 20)

The first of these indicators was subsumed under the item on structural policies, whereas the other five together constituted the item on public sector management and institutions.

Despite the fact that a country's overall CPIA rating was influenced significantly by the scores on the six governance-related indicators, it was felt that the governance record of borrowing countries had too little impact on the final allocation. The World Bank argued, in particular, that the 30 per cent weight of the governance-related indicators resulted in insufficient reduction of the allocation to countries with very poor governance profiles. For this reason, starting in 1998, the World Bank introduced the so-called *governance discount* into the allocation procedure, the application of which resulted in a reduction of countries' performance rating by 30 per cent and an eventual reduction of IDA allocation by 50 per cent. The governance discount was applied for countries that received an unsatisfactory rating (scores 1 or 2) on three or more of the six governance-related indicators in the CPIA, or received unsatisfactory ratings on at least two of these indicators and procurement practices in at least 30 per cent of IDA-supported projects were rated unsatisfactory (World Bank Operations Evaluation Department 2001a: 15).

Evaluation of the application of the governance discount demonstrated, according to the OED, that the methodology 'did not capture some countries with famously poor governance' and that it 'seems, in practice though not intent, simply to further reduce IDA allocations to the lowest ranking performers in the CPIA exercise overall' (World Bank Operations Evaluation Department 2001c: 31), while 'a small improvement can bring a country above the threshold' (World Bank Operations Evaluation Department 2001a: 16). For these reasons, the OED argued that incentives for countries to reform their governance structure were too weak: 'It is clear that the allocation process needs further study to achieve greater equity and a more substantial cut in lending for governance non-reformers even though their other ratings may be average' (World Bank Operations Evaluation Department 2001a: 51).

This criticism of the governance discount led to the introduction of the *governance factor* during the negotiations on IDA13. The governance factor would be calculated as (average governance rating/3.5)$^{1.5}$, where the average governance rating is the average score on the six governance indicators. The average governance rating would be divided by 3.5, as this is the mid-point of the six-point scale, and the spread of the governance factor would be increased by applying an exponential of 1.5. The new measure would result in a 'reduced allocation to the bottom quintile, while substantially increasing the allocation to the top quintile and moderately increasing that of the upper quintile' (International Development Association 2001b: 5). The application of this measure implied that countries with an overall governance rating below the mid-point of the scale would experience a decrease of their performance rating, while those above the mid-point would see their performance rating increase. Moreover, the application of the exponential resulted in a larger effect of the governance factor for countries with scores that are further removed from the mid-point.

The allocation formula that was used during IDA12 and IDA13 was based on countries' relative poverty level (calculated in terms of their per capita GNP) and performance rating (based on CPIA and portfolio performance), taking into account the additional governance criterion (first, the governance discount and later the governance factor). All 78 IDA eligible countries (i.e. countries with a per capita GNP lower than the 'operational cut-off', which was set at $885 in 1999 and is currently $895) would get a minimum allocation of three million Special Drawing Rights (SDR).[8]

The allocation formula of IDA12 rewarded relatively good performers by allocating proportionally more funds to countries with higher scores on the performance rating (World Bank Operations Evaluation Department 2001c: 28–9):

- countries with a performance rating of 3.0 or less would be allocated funds on the basis of the following equation: (GNP per capita)$^{-0.125}$ × (performance rating)$^{1.75}$, and
- countries with a performance rating higher than 3.0 would be allocated funds on the basis of the following equation: (GNP per capita)$^{-0.125}$ × (performance rating)$^{2.0}$.

The IDA country performance (ICP) ratings were calculated as a weighted average of the CPIA score (80 per cent) and the IDA Portfolio Performance Factor (20 per cent), which was an assessment of the proportion of projects at risk in countries' borrowing portfolios.[9] The split in the allocation formula implied that countries that improved their performance rating by 10 per cent would receive an 18 per cent higher allocation if their performance rating is 3 or less and a 21 per cent higher allocation if their performance score is higher than 3.

The allocation formula was changed in IDA13, when the break in the formula was removed and population size was added as a criterion:

$$\text{Country allocation} = f[(\text{performance rating})^{2.0}, (\text{population})^{1.0}, (\text{GNP per capita})^{-0.125}]$$

This formula eliminated the discontinuity in the impact of performance on allocation that resulted from crossing the 3.0-divide. The break in the formula was taken out to avoid that an improvement in the performance rating by 3 per cent (from 2.9 to 3.0) would continue to lead to an increase of allocation of more than 40 per cent (International Development Association 2001b: 7). Population size was added as a criterion to enhance the manner in which the problems related to population pressure are addressed: countries with a larger population were to receive a proportionally greater share of the funds available (International Development Association 2003c: 3).

Operations Evaluation Department calculations on the IDA allocations regarding the lending strategy for 2000 have showed the impact of the performance-based lending methodology. The data in the fourth column of Table 3.1 indicate that the average annual allocation per capita for the 2002–4 period of countries in the top quintile was about 4.14 times that of countries with the lowest performance scores, and about 1.55 times that of countries with lower performance ratings.[10] Data in the fifth column show that the average allocation of the top quintile was 34 per cent above the overall average, whereas it was 67 per cent below the average for countries in the bottom quintile and 14 per cent below the average for countries in the fourth quintile.

The operationalisation of the lending strategy, which took place as usual through the formulation of Country Assistance Strategies[11] (CASs) for the borrowing countries and ensuing lending commitments for a three-year period, differed substantially from the normative allocations that are reflected in Table 3.1. Analyses by the OED showed that the ratio between the commitments to the top and lowest quintiles was 3.48 (which was nearly 16 per cent lower than the ratio in allocations), while the difference between the other quintiles was no longer very clear. As a result of this and 'because many in the top quintile are relatively small, the bulk of IDA lending, in absolute terms, goes to the middle-rated performers' (Gwin 2002: 50).[12]

Under IDA13, an additional lending target for Africa was introduced. The IDA deputies, with the French in a leading role, recommended 'that Africa's share should reach 50 per cent of IDA13 commitments as long as the performance of individual countries warrants it' (International Development Association

Table 3.1 IDA Allocations and commitments by performance quintile, 2000 lending strategy (fiscal years 2002–4, population weighted)

Performance quintile	Number of countries	Average performance rating	Average annual allocation per capita (in SDR)	Indexed annual allocation relative to total	Indexed annual commitment relative to total
Top	13	4.06	8.7	1.34	2.09
Upper	12	3.78	7.8	1.20	0.84
Middle	12	3.58	6.8	1.05	0.84
Lower	13	3.27	5.6	0.86	0.63
Lowest	12	1.91	2.1	0.33	0.60
Total	62	3.43	6.5	1.00	1.00

Source: OED 2001c: 53, 55.

2002a: 27, interview; 3 June 2005). The fact that the target on Africa has been met was due, to a large extent, to the allocation to post-conflict countries (see p. 36). It would have been doubtful whether Africa would have received 50 per cent of IDA13 lending if the post-conflict funds had not primarily been allocated to countries in this continent (interview, 3 June 2005).

So-called *gap* and *blend* countries took in a separate position in the IDA allocation process. Gap countries are countries that have a per capita income above the operational cut-off but are not creditworthy for IBRD (International Bank for Reconstruction and Development) lending, and as a result are eligible for IDA loans. In addition to gap countries, a number of small island states with income levels above the cut-off level that are not creditworthy for the IBRD are eligible for IDA assistance. Blend countries are countries that are eligible for both IDA and IBRD loans. These include Nigeria, India, Pakistan, Indonesia, Zimbabwe, Macedonia and several smaller developing countries; in 2000, the share of the four major countries (India, Indonesia, Nigeria and Pakistan)[13] was 20 per cent of total IDA lending commitments, while all other blend countries received approximately 7 per cent (International Development Association 2001d: 4–5; World Bank Operations Evaluation Department 2001c: 33).

In addition to its IDA allocation policies, the World Bank has developed instruments that aimed at building governance capacity and stimulating institutional development in countries with poor governance quality. The Poverty Reduction and Economic Management (PREM) Network, created in 1997 to fill the gap left by the elimination of the public sector management group several years before, started to focus on issues of economic policy, gender, poverty reduction and the public sector (World Bank Operations Evaluation Department 2001c: 19). Commencing with IDA12, CASs have, in the words of the OED, paid 'particularly thorough' attention to issues of corruption and accountability, capacity building, institutional development and public sector management (World Bank Operations Evaluation Department 2001b: 20).

In 2000, the PREM Network published a report on the reform of public institutions and the strengthening of governance that emphasised eight 'strategic governance objectives' for inclusion in CASs (World Bank Poverty Reduction and Economic Management Network 2000: 60–2):

- the improvement of public expenditure analysis and management to increase the efficiency of the use of public resources;
- the improvement of revenue policy and administration to increase public resources and reduce market distortions;
- the improvement of the public service to achieve more efficient use of public resources and more effective government action;
- the decentralisation of decision-making and service delivery to enhance the accountability, efficiency and effectiveness of government;
- the improvement of access to dispute resolution to increase growth, security and accountability;

36 World Bank and performance-based allocation

- the creation of institutions (such as parliamentary oversight bodies, public audit and data collection organisations) to improve accountability;
- the privatisation and restructuring of public enterprises to improve service delivery and enhance the efficiency of resource use;
- sectoral institution building (e.g. in the social sectors, agriculture and infrastructure) to improve service delivery.

Post-conflict countries started to attract much attention during IDA12. In order to deal with post-conflict reconstruction, a methodology of performance-based allocations to post-conflict countries was proposed for IDA13. This methodology consisted of three major components: eligibility criteria and criteria for the initial allocation, indicators of post-conflict performance and allocation criteria for the period beyond the first year.

In its proposal for post-conflict allocations, IDA indicated that eligible countries would be expected to have experienced highly devastating conflicts in terms of human casualties, displacement of people and/or physical infrastructure.[14] The initial allocation to post-conflict countries – expected to range between $10 and $20 per capita – would depend on an assessment of the prospects of peace, the needs of the country, the commitment of its government to sustainable development and moral hazard considerations relating to potential negative consequences of IDA funding for peace prospects and the possibility that IDA resources could lead to resumption of the conflict (International Development Association 2001a: 3–6). The Republic of Congo, Eritrea, Guinea Bissau and Sierra Leone were the first countries that received support under the post-conflict facility; in later years, Afghanistan, Angola, Burundi, the Democratic Republic of Congo and Timor-Leste were added to the recipients list (International Development Association 2002b: 8; interview, 3 June 2005).

Post-conflict performance would be assessed with a set of 12 Post-Conflict Progress Indicators (PCPI), which are adapted from the CPIA. The PCPI contained four items: security and reconciliation; economic recovery; social inclusion and social sector development; and public sector management and institutions. The scores of these items would be given in a range of 2–5 in order to facilitate comparison with the CPIA methodology.[15] Once the initial allocation is spent within the first post-conflict year, funds would be allocated for subsequent years on the basis of the performance indicators. For countries with good or very good performance, allocations could be increasing up to $30 per capita, while poor performers might fall back to levels of $5–10 per capita (International Development Association 2001a: 7–9).

The World Bank set up a task force in November 2001 to address the problems of 'chronically weak-performing countries' – some of which, such as Sierra Leone, would have come out of a conflict situation only recently – and to suggest approaches to help them 'get onto a path leading to sustained growth, development, and poverty reduction' (Task Force on the Work of the World Bank Group in Low Income Countries Under Stress[16] 2002: ii–iii). The key to the problem of low-income countries under stress (LICUS), according to the

Task Force, was that they have had 'poor policies and institutions' for a prolonged period and that 'they fail to meet the most basic governance requirements for development.... Circumventing (and ultimately removing) the governance obstacles to development is therefore a key element in the development support strategies toward LICUS' (Task Force on LICUS 2002: 5, 8). The approach to LICUS, that was proposed by the Task Force emphasised that the World Bank's activities should focus less on transferring financial resources and more on the transfer of knowledge, capacity building and the delivery of basic social services (education, health and infrastructure) to the poor, the latter often in collaboration with non-governmental organisations (Task Force on LICUS 2002: 31–8).

Under the influence of the adoption of the Millennium Development Goals (MDGs) as a result of the UN Millennium Summit (September 2000) and the 'Monterrey Consensus' on Financing for Development (March 2002), the IDA deputies emphasised that the MDGs should 'provide a basic point of reference for measuring country outcomes ... with countries themselves monitoring and reporting on progress' (International Development Association 2002a: 8).[17] In their view, PRSPs (Poverty Reduction Strategy Papers) and CASs should include targets for poverty reduction. During IDA13, the major implication of the adoption of the MDGs was to be found in the reformulation of some items of the CPIA (International Development Association 2002a: 42–3).

3.3.4 Changes under IDA14 (2005–8)

The preparations of the fourteenth replenishment of IDA resulted in a number of modifications to the system of performance-based allocation described in previous sections, without changing vital components of the system. The most important changes resulted from decisions to modify the CPIA, disclose IDA performance ratings, pay more attention to the debt situation of borrowing countries, and take into account the progress made by IDA eligible countries in achieving the targets specified in the MDGs (International Development Association 2005a: 18–35).

The adjustments to the CPIA methodology were initiated with the installation of a Panel of Experts, led by John Williamson, to review the content of the CPIA and the process involved in arriving at country scores. The panel's recommendations concerned simplification of the CPIA to reduce overlap between items, rethinking of the governance factor, adjustment of the rating scale, enhancement of accountability and borrowing country involvement, and disclosure of the ratings (World Bank 2004b: 3–14).

Following the suggestions of the Panel, the World Bank made significant modifications to the CPIA in 2004. Although the Bank did not incorporate all changes proposed by the Panel of Experts, the CPIA methodology that was applied for the first time in 2005 was different from that which had been used during IDA12 and IDA13. The major change undoubtedly was the reduction of the number of CPIA components to 16, while keeping the weights of the four items identical at 25 per cent of the total. The major adjustments were made to the first and second items (economic management and structural policies), reducing the number of components from five to three. Smaller changes were made to the item on policies for social inclusion/equity, while the fourth item (public sector management and institutions) remained unchanged (World Bank Operations Policy and County Services 2004b: 14–15). The revised CPIA is outlined in Appendix B.

In addition to following the Expert Panel's advice on the CPIA methodology, the World Bank decided to define the upper and lower ratings (1 and 6) and to introduce mid-points between the ratings 1 and 2 and between 5 and 6, where these had not been allowed previously. Also, the Board of Executive Directors decided that the numerical CPIA, instead of the quintile scores, would be disclosed as of 2005 and that the IDA CPRs would be publicly available from the same time onward (World Bank Operations Policy and County Services 2004b: 10).

The Expert Panel's recommendation to enhance the involvement of borrowing countries, by providing them with an opportunity to comment on performance assessments by World Bank staff, was qualified by the World Bank: 'Management is committed to prevent any dilution of accountability for the ratings. That accountability lies squarely with Bank staff. ... [I]t will make clear that country discussions should be seen as consultations not negotiations' (World Bank Operations Policy and County Services 2004b: 7). In addition, the World Bank indicated that 'client involvement' was seen as part of a 'continuous policy dialogue' aimed at identifying the areas where countries perform relatively poorly and where the Bank could assist in improving performance (World Bank Operations Policy and County Services 2004b: 21).

However, the World Bank decided not to act on the Expert Panel's comments regarding the application of the governance factor.[18] The Expert Panel had argued that the 'procedure is highly nontransparent: the very large weight given to the governance factor is not obvious from the complex formula' and that 'the implicit impact of governance on IDA allocation seemed ... excessive in light of the results of the available empirical literature' (World Bank 2004b: 8). The Bank indicated that research would be needed on the impact of changes to the governance factor before any decision could be made on this element of the allocation process. Such decision-making was deferred to the mid-term review of IDA14 at the end of 2006 (World Bank Operations Policy and County Services 2004b: 21; International Development Association 2005a: 46, note 61). It is unlikely that the governance factor will undergo dramatic change because there is considerable support among the larger donor countries, most notably the United States, to penalise the worst performers (interview, 3 June 2005).

The issue of results measurement in the light of the agreed MDGs and the link to IDA programmes and projects was again placed on the agenda of IDA14 at the first meeting of the IDA deputies (cf. p. 36); their meeting 'emphasized the central importance of development effectiveness and the results agenda' (International Development Association 2004a; cf. International Development

Association 2004e: 9). The proposals made by the World Bank management in June 2004 eventually found their way into decision-making. The proposals implied that 14 outcome indicators related to economic and human development would be monitored in the IDA eligible countries and that reports would be prepared for each future IDA replenishment round (International Development Association 2004c: 12; 2005a: 28–31, 52). It was decided that the results monitoring system would not play a role in IDA allocation, as the latter is determined largely by the existing performance-based mechanism (International Development Association 2004c: 1).

Discussions on IDA14 by the IDA deputies, which began in February 2004, started to take into account the implications deriving from the debt situation in borrowing countries. The IDA deputies

> discussed debt sustainability as an important dimension of IDA's country programs within a performance-based framework. It was agreed that there was a need for more country-specific analysis, and that the Bank should work closely together with other partners to explore how best to incorporate debt vulnerability considerations into the work of IDA.
> (International Development Association 2004a)

During the IDA14 replenishment negotiations, the problem of countries' debt positions was discussed mainly in relation to the limits that high levels of debt impose on the implementation of development policies. For this reason, countries with high, unsustainable debt levels became eligible for grants instead of loans.

Debt sustainability under IDA14 was operationalised as the risk of debt distress (interview, 3 June 2005). The risk of such distress would henceforth be determined on the basis of three debt variables (the ratio of debt to gross domestic product, the ratio of debt to exports and the ratio of debt service to exports) and countries' CPIA score. It was assumed that countries with better policies and stronger institutions would be able to sustain higher debt ratios, and thresholds were determined accordingly (see International Development Association 2004b: 4). A so-called 'traffic-light system' was developed to determine the eligibility of countries for grants (International Development Association 2004b: 4–5; 2005b: 10–11; Van Bolhuis 2005: 15–16):

- *Red light*: countries with a high risk of debt distress (i.e. with debt values well above the threshold) would receive all allocations as grants.
- *Yellow light*: countries with medium risk (i.e. with debt values close to the threshold) would receive 50 per cent of the allocation as grants.
- *Green light*: countries with low risk (i.e. with debt values well below the threshold) would be allocated only credit.

In order to reduce the moral hazard problem that is connected with the allocation of grants instead of loans to countries facing debt distress, grant allocations were cut by 20 per cent. This volume cut would be redistributed to IDA eligible countries in an 'incentives-related portion' (11 percentage points) and a 'charges-related portion' (9 percentage points). The former portion would be reallocated to all eligible, IDA-only countries and would be performance based. The latter portion would be earmarked to compensate for the costs involved in giving the grants and lent to blend countries with a gross national income below the operational cut-off (presently India, Indonesia, Pakistan and Azerbaijan), in proportion to their original allocation (International Development Association 2004b: 7–17; 2005a: 25–8; interview, 3 June 2005).[19]

The performance-based allocation mechanism that has been in operation since the inception of IDA14 in July 2005 can be summarised as in Figure 3.1 (adapted from Van Bolhuis 2005: 2, 22). Figure 3.1 illustrates that the IDA CPR is derived by combining scores from the CPIA and ARPP (Annual Report on Portfolio Performance), taking into account the governance factor. Together with data on population size and gross national income per capita, the IDA CPR leads to IDA country allocations. The latter are influenced by separate decisions regarding blend and post-conflict countries, as well as the outcome of the mechanism on grant allocations, which is related to judgements about countries' debt position. The country allocations finally feed into the formulation of CASs, which determine the actual IDA commitments.

3.4 Evaluation

This section contains a critical evaluation of the World Bank's mechanism of performance-based allocation. In particular, the discussion focuses on the policy theory adhered to by the World Bank and the IDA, the methodological problems connected to the performance-based allocation mechanism and the relationship of the allocative decisions to the overall role of the World Bank as a multilateral development institution.

3.4.1 Policy theory

Much of the discussion about the policy theory applied by the World Bank and the IDA to its lending to poor countries revolves about the persistence of neo-liberal assumptions in the allocative mechanism. Despite the calls for change – notably Stiglitz's emphasis on a 'post-Washington Consensus' and the acceptance and implementation of the Comprehensive Development Framework by the Bank (see p. 26ff. above) – the models applied by the World Bank and IDA still contain many remnants of the Washington Consensus (cf. Cammack 2002, 2004; see further Chapter 2).

With respect to the performance-based allocation mechanism, the neo-liberal remnants are most readily visible in the composition of the CPIA and the governance factor (cf. Alexander 2004: 2). The CPIA, in its pre-2004 as well as its post-2004 form, has contained an emphasis on economic management and structural policies, with components related to monetary, fiscal, debt, trade, financial

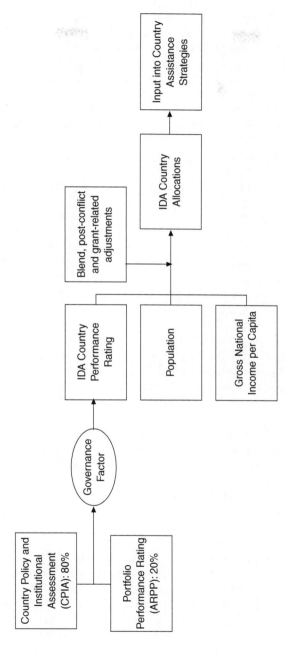

Figure 3.1 IDA's performance-based allocation mechanism under IDA14.

sector and business policies making up 50 per cent of the overall score (components 1–6 in Appendix B, part 2). Furthermore, several components of the item on social inclusion and equity have primarily been cast in terms of labour market participation of social groups, in particular women and the poor (components 7 and 10 in Appendix B, part 2). Finally, the CPIA's fourth item focuses on public sector management and institutions and is also the main input into the governance factor. This item is not so much remarkable for what it includes – although the component on property rights and rule-based governance (component 12 in Appendix B, part 2) definitely tilts the judgement into a more market-oriented direction – but for what it excludes. Generally accepted elements of governance, such as participation, accountability (or 'democracy'), the rule of law and the respect for human rights, which are included in such measurements as the World Bank's *Governance Matters* dataset and Freedom House's *Freedom in the World* index (cf. Gastil 1990; Kaufmann *et al.* 1999), are absent from the CPIA and the governance factor.

The content of the CPIA and the governance factor needs to be understood against the background of the World Bank's continuing adherence to the precepts of neo-liberal economic policies, which are carried on into the post-Washington Consensus. As it was put succinctly by Fine in his characterisation of the current understanding of market–state relations at the World Bank, the welfare- and governance-related elements of the CPIA can be understood as part of the Bank's continuing focus on the improvement of market-based allocation:

> Welfarism is needed in order to correct for market imperfections in the provision of health, education, and social and economic infrastructure more generally. Modernisation, at least in its non-economic aspects, can be disaggregated into a number of components broadly comprising the creation of good governance, on the one hand, and the beneficial aspects of civil society, on the other hand. In other words, modernisation within the post-Washington Consensus is the increasingly effective non-market means for handling market imperfections.... The pre-Washington consensus view of the state as a benign force for development has been lost in the transition to the post-Washington Consensus which has adopted from the Washington consensus an understanding of the state as being subject to capture by rent-seeking agents.
>
> (Fine 2001: 142–3)

In addition to the persistence of distinctly neo-liberal assumptions in the World Bank's approach to performance-based allocation, three other features of the Bank's policy theory are worth mentioning. In particular, these elements are (i) the depoliticisation of development, governance and aid; (ii) the technocratic, blueprint-oriented approach of developing countries' performance; and (iii) the lack of attention for certain 'deeper' causes of poor governance.

The World Bank's perspective on the need for and the implementation of performance-based allocation reflects a profoundly depoliticising approach to issues of development, governance and aid. In explaining the a-political or antipolitical character of the World Bank's policy theory, some scholars have referred to section 10 of Article IV of the Articles of Agreement, which specifies that

> [t]he Bank and its officers shall not interfere in the political affairs of any member; nor shall they be influenced in their decisions by the political character of the member or members concerned. Only economic considerations shall be relevant to their decisions, and these considerations shall be weighed impartially.[20]

At the same time, as others have made clear, this formula can explain the Bank's depoliticising nature only in part. The underlying source of depoliticisation appears to be the Bank's theoretical understanding of development and the role of aid and governance.

Ever since the embrace of the Washington Consensus, the most fundamental assumption of the World Bank's policy theory has been that markets are the ultimate source of wealth and development. The post-Washington Consensus, building on insights from information-theoretic and new institutional economics, has emphasised the role of institutions in correcting market imperfections and, in doing so, restricts the role of the state and politics to that of a regulator (see further Chapter 2 above). Fundamentally, political institutions are distrusted because of the inherent danger of rent-seeking behaviour (see the quote from Fine, 2001: 142–3 above). As Article IV, section 10, of the Bank's Articles of Agreement makes clear, the World Bank has been founded on the belief that it is possible to separate 'economic considerations' from politics – in other words, that it is feasible to formulate economic policies without consideration of power and interests. Many commentators with a background in international political economy (e.g. Harriss 2001: 117; Fine 2003: 16; Santiso 2003: 7–10) have correctly criticised the anti-political bias of the World Bank's policy theory and have emphasised that the ensuing notions of governance and aid have become unduly technocratic, leaving out elements of participation, democracy and human rights (as is the case with the understanding of governance), and empowerment and distribution (as in the concept of aid).

Connected to the mistrust of politics, and the de-emphasising of power and interests, is the Bank's technocratic, blueprint-oriented approach of developing countries' performance. George Abonyi (2004: 106–7) has noted that the approach to policy-based lending favoured by the World Bank and other international financial institutions has traditionally been 'rule driven', aiming at the implementation of 'a menu of international best practice' in borrowing countries. By taking this approach, the emphasis has been on 'doing the right things' rather than 'doing things right'. Thus, Abonyi (2004: 116–20) argues, the lending institutions have failed to recognise the political-economic dynamics resulting from differences of interests among social actors, and have had insufficient attention for the implementation and sustainability of reforms.

A consequence of the World Bank's technocratic organisational culture, which is reinforced by the dominance of economic, financial and other technical experts among the staff (Miller-Adams 1999: 6, 26), is that problems are cast in predominantly technical terms. Governance, understood primarily as public sector management, is a case in point (Leftwich 1994: 365–6; Miller-Adams 1999: 102). An added problem is that the specificities of local situations tend to be interpreted with rules that are assumed to be generally applicable. Local dynamics, as a result, fail to be recognised and get snowed under by a '"one-size-fits-all" set of "good" policies and "good" institutions' (Alexander 2004: 5). In the context of the performance-based allocation mechanism, this is most evident in the CPIA logic, which uses a uniform model of what is assumed to work in development processes, irrespective of the context to which it is applied (Kanbur 2005: 9; see further p. 45ff).

The final point to make on the policy theory behind the performance-based allocation mechanism concerns the lack of attention for certain 'deeper' causes of poor governance in developing countries. The current World Bank's mechanism treats governance quality as a variable that is virtually unrelated to the development process: the quality of governance is one of the elements composing the IDA CPR, and the latter rating is fed into the allocation formula together with GNP per capita and population (see Figure 3.1 and the formula on p. 33). The mechanism does not take into account possible covariations of the level of development and governance quality, although countries with low levels of development may well have poorer governance records than others, if only because they have fewer financial and human resources than richer countries (Kapur and Webb 2000: 13; Santiso 2001: 13; Abonyi 2004: 121).

In addition to this, external factors are effectively absent from the policy theory on performance-based allocation, although such factors may contribute to the absence of good governance. For instance, the ability of rulers to transfer capital abroad and hide it in foreign bank accounts, protected by banking secrets, may facilitate corruption and money-laundering practices (Kapur and Webb 2000: 13). More fundamentally, as argued by Moore (2001: 401), there are structural international causes for poor governance. The state of many developing countries, relying on 'unearned income' from the export of raw materials and the receipt of aid, has never felt the pressure to develop mechanisms of accountability to its citizens, as it was never reliant on their contribution to the state's revenue.

3.4.2 Methodology

The application of performance-based selectivity has invited much discussion about the methodological merits of the approach taken by the World Bank and IDA. A first set of methodological comments targets issues of measurement related to the CPIA and the performance-based allocation mechanism. The second set of criticisms is directed at the general use of governance indicators for the explanation of development and aid effectiveness.

A first and foremost measurement issue regarding the CPIA and the overall performance-based allocation mechanism relates to the empirical basis of the formulas. One issue that was touched upon above concerns the choice and weight of the indicators that constitute the CPIA and the governance factor. There is no empirically or theoretically grounded argument as to why, for instance, the CPIA is made up of four identically weighted items, or why the four items are composed of fewer or more unequally weighted components (Kanbur 2005; Lensink and White 1999: 11–13).

The composition of the governance factor and its weight in the overall allocation process has, similarly, not been justified. The criticism on the 'excessive' influence of governance on allocation that was voiced by the Expert Panel on the CPIA (see p. 38) received support from researchers in the World Bank's Africa division, who found that minor differences in ratings translate into major allocative consequences (Gelb *et al.* 2004: 18–19). These and similar criticisms, however, did not get a substantive response from World Bank management; the discussion on this issue was deferred to a later date.

Finally, it is unclear why the variable that is supposed to measure poverty (GNP per capita) has been assigned a weight of one-eighth of the performance rating in the calculation of the country allocation (see the formula on p. 33). The decision to raise GNP per capita to the power of -0.125 implies that countries will get only slightly lower allocations per capita when they get richer,[21] and this implies that relative poverty is not a decisive factor in the distribution of IDA funds. Alternative outcome variables – such as those related to the MDGs (cf. Kanbur 2005: 15) – have not yet been considered.

A second cluster of methodological issues relates to the use of governance indicators for the explanation of development and aid effectiveness. The publication of Burnside and Dollar's (1997; see Chapter 2) findings on the positive relationship among governance quality, aid and economic growth, and the subsequent publication of *Assessing Aid* with the same message (World Bank 1998), spurred a wealth of studies that questioned the World Bank's conclusions on these matters. First, a re-analysis of the relationship between the CPIA rating and economic growth by a group of economists led by former World Bank senior economist William Easterly showed that Burnside and Dollar's findings could not be replicated (reported in Alexander 2004: 7). In analyses that expanded Burnside and Dollar's dataset, Easterly *et al.* (2003) and Roodman (2004) found results that did not support the earlier World Bank conclusions on governance quality. Hansen and Tarp (2000, 2001) and Dalgaard and Hansen (2001) found that the size of aid may well have a positive impact on economic growth, irrespective of the policy and institutional environment. Finally, McGillivray's (2003) analysis demonstrated that policies seem to matter for aid effectiveness, but that this outcome is dependent on the external conditions that developing countries are facing. A recent re-analysis by Burnside and Dollar (2004), taking into account much of the quoted criticism, reports findings that are in line with their original conclusions. It proves difficult to draw firm substantive conclusions on the basis of previous quantitative work, but it seems fair to conclude that the 'strong' claim for governance-based selectivity has not been substantiated beyond reasonable doubt (cf. Lensink and White 1999: 5).

In addition to the doubts that were raised concerning the World Bank's claim of a solid relationship among governance, aid and growth, several authors have commented upon the methodological inconsistencies in the Bank's approach. Hopkins *et al.* (2000: 291–2) have pointed out that performance-based selectivity may lead to a methodological paradox: 'if good policy is positively correlated with economic success ..., a decision to direct aid away from countries where governments have poor policies entails a lower priority for poverty, at least over the short to medium term.' Likewise, Kapur and Webb (2000: 13) have indicated that poor, badly governed countries run the risk of ending up in a vicious circle of poverty and poor governance as a result of the implementation of performance-based selectivity. Santiso (2003: 19–22) has argued that policies aimed at implementing selectivity may be subject to circular reasoning, which results from the fact that governance is, at the same time, a condition for and an objective of development assistance.

3.4.3 Performance-based allocation and the World Bank's role as a multilateral institution

The implementation of the performance-based allocation mechanism is witness to the fact that the World Bank and the IDA are trying to maintain a precarious balance between their role as multilateral development institutions that are 'owned' by all members and their responsiveness to the major shareholders (cf. Woods 2000). The first factor leads to the requirement that all member states that qualify (because their GNP per capita is below the IDA's operational cut-off and they have insufficient access to capital markets) need to share in the resources that have been assigned to the IDA. In addition, this leads to certain accountability and transparency requirements. The second factor results in pressure from the Bank's major shareholders, which have great influence on decision-making due to the weighted-voting system and are also the main funders of the IDA in the successive replenishment rounds, to devise allocation rules that conform to their preferences and interests.

The role of the World Bank and the IDA as multilateral development institutions has come under attack, in particular, from groups and individuals because the outcome of the allocative mechanism is highly skewed in favour of countries with high ratings on the CPIA and the governance factor – criteria that are criticised precisely because of their neo-liberal bias. As Alexander (2004: 1) has put the criticism, the allocation logic 'helps make it possible to reward those that have already conformed to donor and creditor policy preferences'.

On top of the substantive argument related to possible biases, many commentators have pointed out that the Bank's practices lead to non-transparent and non-accountable decision-making (e.g. Kapur and Webb 2000: 17; Kanbur 2005: 8). With respect to the performance-based allocation mechanism, the lack of transparency and accountability has been evident primarily in the secrecy concerning CPRs and in the lack of scrutiny of the ratings by independent outsiders. In addition, the decision-making in the Board of Directors on the actual commitments made by the World Bank, which were shown to deviate from the allocations based on the Bank's own models (see Table 3.1 and the ensuing discussion), is highly confidential and not subject to public scrutiny. This lack of transparency opens up the possibility for representatives of the major shareholders to influence the Bank's spending in order to serve their own political interests. French pressure to increase Bank loans and grants to African countries, under the pretext of support to post-conflict countries, seems to be a case in point.

While the first point of contention has been removed by the decision of the Board of Governors to disclose country ratings starting in 2005, the second problem continues. The input into the country performance scores will remain the preserve of World Bank staff; as indicated previously (p. 38), the Bank's responsibility has been reaffirmed in recent decision-making. Moreover, the discretion of the Board of Directors to determine actual spending and thus to deviate from allocations on political grounds will fully remain in force.

Ravi Kanbur (2002: 22) has made the powerful argument that 'the Bank as a whole cannot possibly be viewed as an independent arbiter of social science research. It is owned by the rich countries, and it has operational policies that need to be defended.' Kanbur's (2002: 22) call for the 'farming out' of research to universities and 'transparently independent institutions' has not been taken into consideration by the management of the World Bank.

Steps towards greater transparency and accountability of World Bank practices would not solve the second problem that was mentioned above and that relates to the influence of the Bank's major shareholders and funders. Many authors have showed how the Bank's largest members have an undue influence on decision-making as a result of the system of weighted voting. A good example of this, mentioned by former vice-president of the Bank, Jozef Ritzen (2005: 100) was the decision of the G-7, the group of seven major industrialised countries, to support Russia with a $22.6-billion bailout package. These funds included approximately $6 billion from the World Bank, without prior consultation of the Board of Directors.

The manifestation of influence is, so to speak, only the tip of the iceberg. Interviews by Woods (2000: 134) report more subtle ways of influence by, in particular, but not limited to, the United States. A covert way of influencing is 'non-decision-making' (Bachrach and Baratz 1962), expressed, for instance, in the withdrawal of a proposal for particular loans or policies because of a lack of support from major shareholders. Such forms of influence, though real, would not be readily visible to any outside observer. In addition to this, indirect influence is exerted through the reproduction of the *esprit de corps* or organisational culture resulting from the recruitment of the Bank's multinational staff, almost exclusively, from a limited set of disciplines at a limited number of elite training institutions in a limited number of industrialised countries (Miller-Adams 1999: 27–30).

The dominance of one particular policy perspective on governance, development and aid, advocated by a limited set of member states, has effectively induced borrowing countries to shape their policies according to the mould that is preferred in World Bank circles. The rhetoric of developing country ownership of policies has not prevented the creation of a situation where borrowing countries potentially face a 'global–local double bind' (Gore 2004). The centrality of poverty reduction strategies to the World Bank's Comprehensive Development Framework and the CASs (see note 4) implies that countries need to have a PRSP assessed and approved by the Bank and the International Monetary Fund before they get access to IDA funds. As the institutions 'remain committed to Washington Consensus policies – macroeconomic stability, liberalization and privatization – as the core of what constitutes the sound policies that ideally should be at the heart of all PRSPs' (Gore 2004: 280; cf. Hatcher 2003: 643–4), developing countries are hesitant to include unorthodox policy measures that might endanger acceptance of the PRSP, even though these would respond better to calls for a 'nationally owned' development approach (Ellerman 2005). The noble principles laid down in the Bank's Comprehensive Development Framework may easily be undermined by other policy prescriptions, which run counter to the objectives of empowerment and ownership and thus reduce the framework to little more than a 'disciplinary' tool (Cammack 2004: 190).

3.5 Conclusions

This chapter has documented the implementation of selectivity by the World Bank, and more specifically the IDA, in its policy of lending to the poor countries of the world. The analysis demonstrated that the principle of performance-based allocation has taken shape since 1977. At first, during the 1980s and the better part of the 1990s, performance-based allocation was applied through the CPR mechanism, which included information on both short- and long-term economic and poverty alleviation policies of borrowing countries.

A more elaborate, and governance-related, mechanism of performance-based allocation has been applied since 1998, with the development of the CPIA and the introduction of specific governance criteria (first the 'governance discount' and later the 'governance factor'), alongside the 'portfolio performance' of borrowing countries. Despite the changes affecting the specifics of the mechanism, performance-based allocation has been established as a system that rewards countries performing well on the criteria of policy and governance defined by the World Bank. In particular, the (normative) allocation formula works to the benefit of countries that receive a score above the mid-point of the CPIA and the governance factor. Although actual lending commitments by the World Bank's soft-loan window IDA were shown not to keep pace exactly with the outcomes of the allocation mechanism, it was clear that actual loans and grants still benefit mostly those countries at the upper end of the distribution (see Table 3.1).

Recent innovations of the performance-based allocation mechanism have been implemented without affecting the logic introduced in 1998. The major inputs into IDA's allocative formula continue to be the evaluation of the quality of policies and governance institutions (while countries' wealth and population are secondary criteria). Elements such as the allocation to post-conflict countries and chronically weak-performing countries (the so-called LICUS), the allocation to heavily indebted countries, and the allocation of grants next to loans, were blended with the allocative logic that has existed since 1998.

The evaluation of the World Bank's performance-based allocation mechanism brought to light several weaknesses related to the policy theory in which the mechanism is rooted, the methodology applied and the connection between decisions on allocation and the role of the World Bank. The discussion of the policy theory indicated that the approach of the IDA to lending countries' performance remains dominated heavily by neo-liberal precepts and a technocratic outlook on governance issues (from which dimensions such as participation, democracy, rule of law and human rights are almost completely absent).

The conclusion on the methodology of the performance-based allocation mechanism was that the empirical basis for many of the measures applied by the World Bank and IDA seems to be weak. In particular, the composition of the CPIA and the governance factor that are used in the CPRs are insufficiently grounded in empirical knowledge. Moreover, criticism by various researchers of the World Bank's claims about the impact of governance quality on economic growth and aid effectiveness leads to serious doubts about the applicability of the methodological framework for the purpose of policy making on aid allocation.

Finally, the allocation mechanism implemented by the IDA was shown to be largely non-transparent and non-accountable. Decision-making on allocation is based on ratings that cannot be scrutinised by outsiders. The domination of the World Bank by its shareholders and fund-providers has given them disproportionate influence on decision-making. The dominance of one policy perspective on governance, aid and development has produced a straightjacket for the borrowing countries, which need to comply with the policy prescriptions set by the World Bank in order to qualify for aid.

4 The Netherlands and the selection of recipient countries[1]

4.1 Introduction

The late 1990s saw the introduction of several important changes in the orientation of Dutch development assistance. General discussions in the international policy community about the effectiveness of aid – fuelled, in particular, by the persistence of poverty in large parts of the world – gave rise to renewed attention among politicians and policy makers for the modalities of assistance (cf. Minister for Development Cooperation 1995: 39–40). The Dutch orientation to development assistance was changed considerably with the adoption of the so-called sectoral approach (modelled on the Sector-Wide Approach or SWAp applied by other donors during the 1990s and advocated through the Development Assistance Committee of the Organisation for Economic Co-operation and Development (OECD); see Section 2.3). The main objective of the sectoral approach was to support development within a social or economic sector by 'making contributions towards a single sector policy and expenditure programme, under leadership of the recipient government, with the use of common management and reporting procedures to disburse and account for all funds' (Policy and Operations Evaluation Department 2006: 16).[2]

Following the emerging policy consensus about the importance of the quality of governance for development in general, and for development assistance policies more specifically, the Netherlands opted for the introduction of the selectivity principle into its aid policy in 1998. The implementation of selectivity in Dutch aid policy took place in two stages. Under Social Democrat Minister[3] Eveline Herfkens, a first step was set with the selection of a group of countries for a 'structural bilateral aid relationship' (the so-called 19+3 or preferential countries). Alongside this selection, three 'issue-specific' programmes were set up: one for aid related to environmental policy, a second for aid in the context of governance, human rights and peace-building (the Dutch acronym being the GMV programme) and a third targeted at the development of the private sector in developing countries.

The second phase of selectivity was initiated in 2003 by Christian Democrat Minister Agnes van Ardenne-van der Hoeven. This phase involved the collapse of the list of preferential countries with the countries that had been selected for the environmental and the GMV programmes and the subsequent reduction of the number of aid recipients from 49 to 36 partner countries.

Section 4.2 focuses on policy formation in the 1998–2002 period, when Eveline Herfkens was at the helm of the ministry. In this section, the major considerations that gave rise to the policy of selectivity are analysed and some major aspects of the implementation of this new policy are described. Section 4.3 zeroes in on the term of office of Agnes van Ardenne, who changed course and collapsed the separate bilateral programmes into one partnership programme. Section 4.4 presents an evaluation of the major elements of the two recent phases in Dutch bilateral development assistance policies. Section 4.5 concludes the chapter.

4.2 First steps: the selection of preferential countries (1998–2002)

Eveline Herfkens, former Social Democrat Member of Parliament (1981–90) and former executive director of the World Bank (1990–6), became Minister for Development Cooperation in 1998 in the second government led by Social Democrat leader Wim Kok. Herfkens succeeded development cooperation veteran Jan Pronk, who had concluded his third term as Minister for Development Cooperation in the first Kok government.

As soon as Herfkens took over from Pronk, she appeared to be intent to change the orientation of Dutch development policy quite drastically – something that was sometimes referred to as the de-Pronking of Dutch development assistance. Herfkens seemed to feel that good intentions had come to stand in the way of effective policy making – a feeling that may have been linked to her Washington experience – and that a radical reorientation would be necessary in order to restore the credibility of Dutch aid policies (*NRC Handelsblad*, 9 September 1998, p. 3; 10 September 1998, p. 2).

The coalition agreement of the Social Democrat and right-wing liberal parties that laid the foundations of the second Kok government contained only brief references to development assistance. The coalition agreement stipulated as a condition for future development assistance relations that aid recipient countries would need to have a record of 'good policies, including economic policies, and good governance, to be ascertained by international standards' (Regeerakkoord 1998: 93). The concentration of aid 'on countries that *meet all criteria mentioned*' (Regeerakkoord 1998: 93, italics added) was adopted as the leading principle.

In a letter to Parliament of 5 November 1998, Minister Herfkens announced her resolve to restructure Dutch development aid policy. In the first instance, restructuring would involve 'structural bilateral assistance, in other words, the share of the budget that is delegated to the embassies (approximately 1.3 billion guilders annually)' (Minister for Development Cooperation 1998: 2). The background to this shift in policy, according to the minister, was that various reports on development assistance had proved that

aid effectiveness is very much reliant on the presence of good policies and good governance in the recipient country. In this respect, the quality of government policies across a number of areas is relevant: macro-economic and monetary stability, policies related to economic structure and economic reform, and socio-economic policies, but also transparency and integrity of government, separation of powers, political liberties and respect for human rights.
(Minister for Development Cooperation 1998: 2)

The minister argued that a concentration on fewer countries and sectors would enhance Dutch aid's contribution to poverty reduction and would increase its overall effectiveness.

Herfkens' 5 November letter indicated that the reappraisal of countries and sectors would, first of all, involve the 78 countries that had received more than one million guilders in Dutch aid in 1997. The letter spoke quite candidly about the envisaged selection process: 'The Netherlands will maintain its structural bilateral development relationship with the group of countries that meet the criteria of the aforementioned selection' (Minister for Development Cooperation 1998: 3). Countries that would not meet the criteria might qualify for continued aid, but in those cases assistance would only involve the 'use of specific aid instruments' and would be no more than 'a limited or occasional aid relationship' (Minister for Development Cooperation 1998: 3).

According to the 5 November letter, the criteria for the initiation or continuation of a structural relationship would be (Minister for Development Cooperation 1998: 3–4)

- the recipient country's socio-economic policy
- the recipient country's record of good governance
- the extent of poverty and the recipient country's need for aid.

In a communication to Parliament in 2001 in relation to a report of the Scientific Council for Government Policy, Herfkens disclosed the methodology used to select countries. According to her, the level of poverty was the first criterion in the selection. Subsequently, 'for the countries thus remaining, we set up our own selection process based on two criteria, namely, the quality of policy and the quality of governance.' Finally,

also other considerations played a role in the selection process, such as the Dutch capacity to implement aid (including the question of whether there is a Dutch embassy in the candidate country – without bilateral presence no bilateral aid relationship is possible) and donor density (received ODA per capita).
(Minister for Development Cooperation 2001: 6–7)

The 5 November letter was clear about the rating of countries on the first and third criteria. In order to rate socio-economic policy, 'the judgement of relevant multilateral organisations' would be followed; when this would prove to be insufficiently clear, ministry staff would rely on 'their own appreciation'. The rating of countries with respect to poverty and needs would rely on countries' IDA eligibility, but the amount of aid received and the degree of international aid coordination were taken as additional inputs (Minister for Development Cooperation 1998: 4). Later, 'the possible value added of a Dutch bilateral aid relationship and the feasibility of a multi-donor sector-wide approach under the leadership of the recipient country' (Minister for Development Cooperation 1999a: 3–4) were mentioned as additional points of attention.

It is to be concluded only from later communications of the minister to Parliament that the rating of recipient countries on the second criterion had been completed with the help of a set of 'benchmarks', including

> the integrity of the government apparatus, the avoidance of corruption, transparency in the management of public means, surveillance of government spending, the degree of public participation, separation of powers, legal security, democratisation and respect for human rights. In addition, the relative size of defence spending was included in this rating.
> (Minister for Development Cooperation 1999a: 4)

In a later response to questions from Parliament, the minister indicated that the rating of policy and governance quality should mainly be seen in 'relative terms'. According to the minister, an important consideration was the following:

> The first round of selection [of the countries that were eligible for IDA concessional loans] involved, in principle, relatively poorer countries and this means we were dealing with countries that suffer more than others from corruption, weak institutions and underdeveloped civil society because of their relative poverty. As further rounds of selection did not involve measurement with absolute standards, but focused on relative policy and governance quality, *I would argue that I have done justice to this correlation, as the relative rating involves a comparison with other countries in similar circumstances* (similar income bracket, similar region or otherwise).
> (Minister for Development Cooperation 1999b: 2, italics added)[4]

In addition to this, several other 'additional considerations' have been mentioned – which, interestingly, differ from the 'other considerations' brought forward in the minister's response to a report of the Scientific Council on Government Policy (see p. 52). The additional considerations mentioned were

> an assessment of the quality of the current development assistance programme, the activities of a country in supporting the rule of law in its region (such as the participation in peace initiatives), or ... existing socio-cultural or economic relations with the Netherlands.
> (Minister for Development Cooperation 1998: 4)

54 The Netherlands and recipient countries

A 2002 internal memorandum of the Deputy Director-General for International Cooperation – the second-highest civil servant in command of development assistance in the Ministry of Foreign Affairs (see note 3 of this chapter) – contained the most exhaustive and systematic discussion of the criteria used in the selection of preferential countries. These criteria are summed up in Table 4.1.[5]

Minister Herfkens updated Parliament about the operationalisation of her country policy in a letter of 26 February 1999. One of the issues that was raised

Table 4.1 Criteria for country selection

---

1 IDA performance rating (top, upper, middle, lower, lowest quintile)

2 Financial-economic and social policies of the recipient country
   a Financial-economic policies and structures
   b Social policies
   c Commitment of the recipient country to gender issues
   d Commitment to the environment
   e Commitment to the 20–20 targets

3 Situation of governance
   a Integrity and effectiveness of the government apparatus
   b Transparency of management of public means
   c Absence of corruption
   d Adequacy of surveillance of public finances
   e Functioning of Audit Office
   f Parliamentary control of government spending
   g Participation
   h Separation of powers, independence of judiciary
   i Extent of access to legal procedures
   j Fairness of parliamentary elections
   k Respect for human rights
   l Balance between spending on social issues and defence spending

4 Extent of poverty and need for development assistance
   a Gross national product in US dollars
   b Internal social and geographical distribution of poverty
   c Aid efforts of other donors
   d Degree of coordination of aid
   e Degree of access of the recipient country to the capital market/financing gap

5 Additional considerations
   a Assessment of the quality of the existing development assistance programme
   b Activities of the country in support of the regional legal order
   c Socio-cultural relations with the Netherlands
   d Economic and trade relations with the Netherlands
   e Expected future expansion of economic relations with the Netherlands:
   f Presence of government-to-government relations between other Dutch Ministries and the recipient country
   g Attention in Parliament for the country (number of Parliamentary questions and visits)
   h Geostrategic importance of the recipient country
   i Other considerations

Source: Deputy Director-General for International Cooperation (2002).

in that letter concerned the background of country selection. The structural bilateral relationship would result, in the minister's perspective, in a broad ranging and intensive relationship between the Netherlands and the preferential countries: 'Given the limited administrative capacity and budget available, such a relationship can only be established with a smaller number of countries than we are presently dealing with' (Minister for Development Cooperation 1999a: 2). On the basis of the criteria mentioned above, the minister claimed, an assessment was made of the situation of all potential aid recipients, which was 'anything but mechanical' and included quantitative and qualitative data provided by the Dutch embassies and multilateral institutions, in particular, the World Bank (Minister for Development Cooperation 1999a: 4). Eventually, the minister presented a list to Parliament containing 19 countries with which the Netherlands would start a structural bilateral aid relationship and three countries that, for political reasons, would receive aid for a limited period of time.[6]

In May 1999, the minister indicated that the ministry had considered favourably 'approximately thirty countries' in terms of their 'results and prospects as to policies and governance quality' (Minister for Development Cooperation 1999b: 4). The selection of preferential countries from this set was said to have been influenced by the estimated value added of a structural bilateral relationship with the Netherlands, as compared to relationships with other bilateral and multilateral donors (Minister for Development Cooperation 1999b: 5).

Continuity, measured by the 'size and quality of the Dutch development assistance programme', was also mentioned as an important element of decision-making:

> The establishment of an extensive Dutch bilateral programme in a country without a pre-existing programme and without Dutch diplomatic representation would be unnecessarily expensive. ... On the other hand, the abrupt exit from a country with substantial Dutch bilateral activity would result in undesirable capital destruction.
> (Minister for Development Cooperation 1999b: 5)

The 19 countries that were eventually chosen as preferential partners were Bangladesh, Bolivia, Burkina Faso, Eritrea, Ethiopia, Ghana, India, Macedonia, Mali, Mozambique, Nicaragua, Pakistan, Sri Lanka, Tanzania, Uganda, Vietnam, Yemen, Zambia and Zimbabwe. High-ranking civil servants have indicated that the final selection, given the diversity of criteria that were applied, had more features of 'weighing on the hand' rather than of precise measurement (interview, 10 December 2003). As it proved impossible to arrive at the desired number of approximately 20 preferential countries on the basis of quantitative indicators alone, qualitative considerations have played an important role in the final selection.[7]

For political reasons, three countries were added to the 19 preferential ones: South Africa, Egypt and the Palestinian Territories. The Netherlands wished to maintain a special relationship with these three countries: South Africa was selected to support the political transition after the end of the Apartheid era,

Egypt was included because the country found itself 'on the verge of a new phase of development', and the Palestinian Authority was felt to be an important partner given the ongoing Middle East peace process (Minister for Development Cooperation 1999a: 5).

Eritrea and Ethiopia would subsequently be removed from the list of preferential countries for the duration of the war they were fighting. Later, Parliament forced the Minister to take Pakistan and Zimbabwe off the list (in 1999) and to include Benin and Rwanda (in 2001). The list of temporary partners was changed with the addition of Indonesia in 2000 and the removal of the Palestinian Authority in 2001.[8]

As indicated before, the selection of 19+3 preferential countries coincided with the establishment of three 'thematic' programmes. Eleven countries were selected for the environmental programme, which aimed at fighting environmental degradation. A second programme related to human rights, peace-building and good governance activities in 15 countries; the aim was to set up activities together with partner governments. The third programme, aimed at the development of the private sector, would involve the (19+3) preferential countries, as well as an additional 17 countries (Minister for Development Cooperation 1999a: 6).

Five transitional countries in Eastern Europe and the former Soviet Union, which had received positive evaluations on the quality of their policies and governance, had belonged to the thirty countries that were considered for preferential status. The minister had ultimately decided that assistance to these countries would be channelled through the World Bank, as the Netherlands did not have an embassy in these countries (the exception was Bosnia-Herzegovina) and it was felt that the Netherlands, being the representative of four of these countries in the World Bank's Board of Executive Directors, 'would be able to exert direct influence on World Bank policy in these countries' (Minister for Development Cooperation 1999a: 8). The remaining six candidates that had not been included in the list of preferential countries were: Cape Verde, the Gambia, Ivory Coast, Mongolia, Rwanda and Senegal. In the case of Cape Verde and Ivory Coast, it was felt that the contribution of Dutch development assistance would be limited in the light of the presence of other donors. For the other countries, 'situation specific' circumstances were mentioned as the reason for Dutch non-involvement (Standing Committee on Foreign Affairs 1999: 107).

In a letter to Parliament of 10 November 1999, Minister Herfkens disclosed the allocation of the ODA budgets that would be made available to the embassies in 2000. The distribution of the ODA funds (approximately €700 million) over different categories of countries is given in Table 4.2.[9]

In an attempt to strengthen the methodology for the selection and screening of aid recipients, the Ministry of Foreign Affairs instituted the Task Force on the Allocation of Structural Bilateral Assistance in 2000. The task force reported on its findings in September 2000; its report is commonly referred to as the Timmerman Report (Timmerman et al. 2000). The methodology that was proposed by the task force has been applied in calculations of the multi-annual budgets,

Table 4.2 Allocation of delegated ODA funds, 2000

Preferential countries (17)	€376 million
Temporary partners (3)	€59 million
Environmental programme (7)	€53 million
Human rights, peace-building and good governance programme (13)	€92 million
Environmental and human rights, peace-building and good governance programme (5)	€50 million
Countries with a sustainable development treaty (3)	€21 million
Remaining ('exit') countries (24)	€47 million

Source: Minister for Development Cooperation 1999c: 9–10.

Note
The number of countries per category is indicated between brackets

primarily as a frame of reference for the decision-making on allocations. The outcome of the Timmerman model has played a role in cases where the discrepancy between the model allocations and the historical allocations had become too big; in those cases the model's results provided a legitimation of re-allocation decisions (interview, 3 December 2003).

The Timmerman model took a so-called *zero-base* approach. This implies that the model calculates what an optimal allocation of aid monies would be to achieve the greatest poverty reduction impact, without taking into account historical aid patterns. In practice, the model has been applied for decision-making on the distribution of the multi-annual growth (or decrease) of the structural bilateral aid budget; the disparity between the historical and the zero-base allocation provided one of the arguments to expand (or reduce) the budget allocated to certain countries (interview, 3 December 2003). The model outcome was not used as the overriding factor in budget allocations, as it was felt that (qualitative) considerations related to countries' absorptive capacity should play an important role alongside quantifiable indicators (interview, 10 December 2003).

The Timmerman model results in the calculation of a weighted average of several indicators, producing one score per country per year (Timmerman *et al.* 2000: 7):

- the need for aid (50 per cent), calculated on the basis of a country's gross national product, overall allocations of official development assistance, and official foreign debt, all expressed in per capita terms;
- the quality of governance and policies (50 per cent), calculated on the basis of World Bank data (the Country Policy and Institutional Assessment [CPIA] and the Portfolio Performance Rating) and the ministry's own assessment of a country's human rights situation.[10]

Policy considerations related to the importance of aid to Africa and to the least-developed countries have resulted in corrections of the country scores for these two groups. Least-developed and African countries are given a 50 per cent bonus on top of their country score. In addition, model outcomes are corrected for population (the square root of population size is used) and a threshold allocation of €10 million is applied to avoid dilution of the assistance effort (Haver Droeze 2003: 3; Keppels 2003: 5).

Since 1999, Dutch embassies have been required to submit 'country screenings' (these were called 'trend assessments' in 2003 and 'track records' in 2004–5). In this exercise, Dutch embassy staff in 44 recipient countries reported on the performance of these countries in relation to the criteria that were used in the country selection process of 1998 (see Table 4.1). The country screenings contained short qualitative descriptions of the situation in the country for most of the criteria in table 4.1, as well as quantitative ratings for the first four categories (IDA performance rating; financial-economic and social policies of the recipient country; situation of governance; extent of poverty and need for development assistance) on a scale ranging from 0 to 50. The average score on the country screenings was 33.4 (Hout and Koch 2006: Appendix A).

4.3 A change of course: the reduction to 36 partner countries (2003–7)

A few days after the presentation of the second Balkenende government[11] to Parliament, Minister for Development Cooperation Agnes van Ardenne-Van der Hoeven sent a letter to Parliament which contained her plans for development cooperation in the 2003–7 period. This letter, dated 17 June 2003, announced a change of course with respect to the country selectivity policy initiated by her predecessor, Eveline Herfkens. Van Ardenne indicated her resolve

> to concentrate further the Dutch expertise and financial means that are available for bilateral development cooperation, both in terms of the countries and the sectors involved, and to cluster aid within a smaller number of regions. In addition, I am contemplating a merger of the current list of 19 + 3 countries with the environmental policy and GMV (good governance, human rights and peace-building) lists, so as to arrive at one list of 'partner countries'. ... The reconsideration will be based, in the first place, on the central criteria of poverty and the perspective of improving policies and governance (better governance). ... I am contemplating the addition of complementarity and concentration to these criteria. Concentration is the process of combining knowledge and means in a limited number of countries with the aim of achieving the critical mass necessary to boost effectiveness. Critical mass is also achieved through complementarity: it is the value added that is realised by working together with other donors, be it governments, multilateral or civil society organisations.
>
> (Minister for Development Cooperation 2003a: 4)

The principles contained in the 17 June letter have subsequently been recast in policy terms; the end result of this process was the white paper *Mutual Inter-*

ests, Mutual Responsibilities: Dutch Development Cooperation En Route to 2015, which was sent to Parliament in October 2003. This white paper documents the minister's resolve to achieve thematic, sectoral and partner concentration (Minister for Development Cooperation 2003b: 3). Thematic concentration referred to the adoption of four 'priority themes': education, reproductive health, HIV/AIDS, and environment and water (Minister for Development Cooperation 2003b: 14–18). Sectoral concentration implied that the number of sectors of the development relationship would be restricted 'to two, or three at the highest' (Minister for Development Cooperation 2003b: 20). Partner concentration meant, in line with the statement of the 17 June letter, that the three existing lists for bilateral development cooperation would be merged into one list of partner countries (Minister for Development Cooperation 2003b: 18).[12]

In order to select developing countries for partner status, 'trend assessments' (see p. 58) were used to review the quality of the relationship between the Netherlands and the 49 countries that appeared on one of the three lists in the 1998–2003 period. In setting up the review, the ministry had explicitly decided against 'a "zero-base" analysis ... of all developing countries', because 'the success of a development cooperation relationship would be based, to a significant degree, on reliability and continuity. For this reason, only those countries with which the Netherlands has maintained a bilateral development relationship have been included' (Minister for Development Cooperation 2003c: 3).

The result of the review exercise was the establishment of 'one list of 36 partner countries, including Afghanistan, where the Netherlands is engaged in a significant and multi-annual development effort' (Minister for Development Cooperation 2003b: 20). The selection criteria, as summed up in the white paper *Mutual Interests, Mutual Responsibilities*, were the following (Minister for Development Cooperation 2003b: 19–20):

- poverty, operationalised as the eligibility of countries for concessionary loans through the International Development Association ('IDA eligibility');[13]
- the quality of policies and governance in recipient countries, operationalised as 'IDA performance' (calculated on the basis of countries' CPIA rating, their Portfolio Performance Rating and their governance score; see further Chapter 3);
- recipient countries' need for aid, calculated as the value added of a euro in aid, taking into account the involvement of other donors, the size of the total aid programme and the absorptive capacity of recipients;
- the value added of Dutch aid, which is partly a function of the complementarity of the Dutch aid effort and the concentration of aid (see the quotation from the 17 June letter on p. 58);[14]
- foreign policy considerations, such as the assumed contribution to regional stability (as in the case of aid to South Africa, the Palestinian Authority, Yemen and Egypt), the observance of treaty obligations (as applicable to the former Dutch colony of Suriname) and the maintenance of good relations

with poorer members of the Dutch constituency in the World Bank, the International Monetary Fund and the European Bank for Reconstruction and Development.

Application of these criteria has led to the termination ('phasing out' or 'exit') of the bilateral relationship with 13 developing countries, because these countries were argued to be relatively rich (Brazil, China, Ecuador, El Salvador, Namibia, Peru and the Philippines), to have relatively poor policies and/or governance (Cambodia, Guinea Bissau and Zimbabwe), or to have only a rather small Dutch programme (Bhutan, Brazil, Cambodia, El Salvador, Guinea Bissau, Honduras, Namibia, Nepal and Zimbabwe). Three additional countries (Angola, Sudan and Yugoslavia) are counted among the exit countries, on the basis of earlier decisions to terminate the aid relationship. India is a special case, because of its own decision in 2003 to stop requesting foreign aid. The final selection of partner countries is presented in Table 4.3, together with the exit countries and the allocation of official development assistance in 2004, which constitutes the bulk of Dutch bilateral aid.

The figures in Table 4.3 illustrate the variety of instruments that together constitute official development assistance to the 36 partner countries and the 17 exit countries. The figures in the second column indicate that the majority of funds (42.8 per cent) have been spent on sectoral support for programmes and projects related to education, health, water and rural development. In addition, major shares have been allocated to macro-economic support (18.3 per cent), governance, human rights and peace-building (14.7 per cent) and environmental programmes (12.3 per cent). Substantively smaller amounts have been devoted to post-conflict reconstruction in Afghanistan and Sudan (6.2 per cent) and private sector development (2.9 per cent). In addition to the latter category, the development assistance programme included a separate budget line for cooperation with the private sector (amounting to €111 million in 2004).

Minister Van Ardenne indicated that she had 'a clear preference of disbursing assistance funds through the government budget of the recipient country', as this would be 'a good way of implementing the government's resolve to stress the recipient country's responsibility as well as the coordination and harmonisation of donors' efforts'. The allocation of budget support would depend on three conditions: aid recipient should have a poverty reduction strategy (PRS) process in place; there should be an 'effective' policy dialogue on the quality of governance, including the political dimension, and poverty reduction; and progress should be monitored on the basis of indicators of institutional and policy reform (Minister for Development Cooperation 2003b: 21). In 2004, approximately €59 million of sectoral support (Table 4.3, second column) was given as sectoral budget support. In addition to this, €101 million of macro-economic assistance (Table 4.3, fifth column) was allocated to partner countries as general budget support (Policy and Operations Evaluation Department 2006: 59).

In order to facilitate the use of the budget support instrument, the track record has been used, as of 2004, as a tool for determining the modalities of aid. The general idea is that aid should be, as much as possible, in line with the policies and budgetary processes of the aid-receiving country. Using the parlance of the donor coordination exercises this is referred to as the 'alignment' of aid allocations. The track record has been applied to determine to what extent alignment, which is an important objective of the sectoral approach (see Section 4.1), is acceptable. The optimal form of alignment is general budget support, which implies a complete transfer of decision-making on the use of aid to the developing country and which is considered acceptable only in countries that score sufficiently well on the clusters of the track record. Countries that are rated insufficient on one or several aspects, are generally not eligible for budget support and may receive earmarked sectoral support or – in the most extreme case – project support (Department for the United Nations and International Financial Institutions 2004: 5–6).

The four clusters of the track record for 2004 and after have been labelled as poverty reduction, economic order, good governance and policy dialogue. The Dutch embassies are asked to score countries on two criteria per cluster, using a 4-point scale (good, sufficient, insufficient, bad).[15] In completing certain elements of the track record, embassy staff are requested to use external information, such as the CPIA and the governance indicators collected by a World Bank team led by Daniel Kaufmann (Department for the United Nations and International Financial Institutions 2004: 7–11).

4.4 Evaluation

In this section, the Dutch approach to aid selectivity will be assessed. The ensuing discussion addresses three issues in more detail: the policy theory used by the two consecutive ministers for development cooperation in the 1998–2007 period, the methodology applied in the selection process and the implementation of the selection.

4.4.1 Policy theory

As was demonstrated in this chapter, Dutch development assistance policy since 1998 has been permeated by discussions about the criterion of good governance and good policies. According to Minister Herfkens, the quality of governance and policies, together with the extent of poverty and the need for aid, would be the prime qualifying criterion for starting up or continuing a structural bilateral aid relationship (Minister for Development Cooperation 1998: 3–4). Under her successor, Minister Van Ardenne, the quality of governance and policies – reformulated as the perspective of improving policies and governance – would remain a key variable in the selection process, despite the increased attention for the value added of Dutch aid and for foreign policy considerations.

This said, a closer look at the entire set of criteria that have determined the selection of recipient countries demonstrates that the policy theory was less clear-cut than was to be expected given the dominance of the key criteria related

Table 4.3 Official Development Assistance allocated to partner and exit countries, 2004 (in thousands of euros)

	Sectoral support	Governance, human rights and peace-building	Environmental programme	Macro-economic support	Post-conflict reconstruction	Private sector development	Exit sectors
Partner countries							
Afghanistan	–	–	–	–	38,000	–	–
Albania	–	2,032	1,313	–	–	–	–
Armenia	–	247	–	4,700	–	–	–
Bangladesh	27,525	–	–	–	–	–	660
Benin	4,248	–	–	–	–	51	23
Bolivia	16,351	3,358	–	7,000	–	–	362
Bosnia-Herzegovina	–	15,831	–	–	–	–	–
Burkina Faso	19,187	–	–	19,342	–	762	168
Cape Verde	–	–	2,504	5,000	–	–	–
Colombia	–	3,362	9,509	–	–	–	–
Egypt	5,874	360	–	–	–	–	2,179
Eritrea	55	–	–	–	–	–	2,169
Ethiopia	21,858	–	–	–	–	2,580	15
Georgia	–	772	–	3,000	–	–	–
Ghana	28,999	–	–	16,500	–	–	–
Guatemala	2,000	2,744	4,985	–	–	–	–
Indonesia	2,338	26,984	–	–	–	–	–
Kenya	–	2,954	–	–	–	–	139
Macedonia	9,717	1,018	5,272	9,000	–	2,250	–
Mali	19,484	–	–	10,000	–	–	–
Moldova	–	1,310	6,582	–	–	–	1,170
Mongolia	–	–	3,231	18,000	–	–	126
Mozambique	13,747	–	–	–	–	4,445	4
Nicaragua	4,246	–	3,035	8,650	–	–	147
Pakistan	–	1,405	–	–	–	–	222
Palestinian Authority	–	9,174	–	–	–	–	–

Rwanda	1,541	–	–	–	405
Senegal	–	3,880	7,173	–	225
South Africa	15,042	9,651	–	–	658
Sri Lanka	2,638	4,063	2,104	206	17
Suriname	14,335	6,264	2,606	–	1,120
Tanzania	37,152	8,008	–	–	10
Uganda	2,409	6,823	14,591	1,721	146
Vietnam	11,764	–	21,800	–	348
Yemen	22,680	–	8,000	–	–
Zambia	34,049	–	–	2,409	–
Exit countries					
Angola	–	–	–	–	84
Bhutan	–	–	7,284	–	–
Brazil	–	–	2,547	–	–
Cambodia	–	1,263	–	–	–
China	–	561	8,501	–	1
Costa Rica	–	–	7,450	–	–
Ecuador	–	–	4,070	–	10
El Salvador	–	1,355	–	–	1
Honduras	–	2,408	–	–	7
India	24,174	–	3,549	–	2,034
Malawi	–	–	–	–	1,086
Nepal	–	1,095	2,211	–	–
Peru	–	–	5,003	–	8
Philippines	–	–	3,503	–	49
Sudan	–	–	–	11,197	–
Yugoslavia	–	–	–	–	9,758
Zimbabwe	–	73	–	–	176
Total	341,413	116,995	97,782	49,197	22,828	23,527
Percentage of total	42.8	14.7	12.3	6.2	2.9	3.0

Source: Ministry of Foreign Affairs 2005: 38–9.

to poverty, governance and policies. As was noted above (see note 4 of this chapter), straightforward application of governance and policy criteria would have resulted in the selection of a very small number of aid recipients. The use of additional criteria – such as the role of a country in upholding the regional rule of law, a country's relations with the Netherlands or the presence of a Dutch embassy – was understandable from the perspective of policy implementation, especially given the desire to retain a substantial bilateral aid programme. Inevitably, however, this approach was at odds with the logic of the policy theory that was elaborated to enhance aid effectiveness. The analysis of the policy-making process in this chapter has demonstrated that the criteria of governance and policy quality were not sufficiently capable of differentiating qualifying from non-qualifying countries, thus making the recourse to countries in the 'grey zone' inevitable. As the primary criteria offered insufficient guidance for the selection of such second-tier countries, secondary criteria played a large role in the choice of aid recipients beyond the few exemplary cases. The policy theory was weakened significantly as a result of the recourse to such secondary criteria.

The importance of governance and policy criteria, which had already been seriously qualified during Minister Herfkens' tenure, was reduced even further after the publication of Minister Van Ardenne's white paper *Mutual Interests, Mutual Responsibilities*. In responding to questions asked by the Standing Committee on Foreign Affairs, the minister emphasised that she was interested in

> the prospect of improvements in governance, including improvements in the operation of the private sector. We will therefore consciously remain present in a number of countries with 'substandard' governance, as it is felt that we can significantly contribute to processes of change and improvement. For instance, I am thinking of countries such as Georgia, Vietnam and Kenya, but also of Rwanda.
> (Standing Committee on Foreign Affairs 2003: 13)

By taking this position, the minister appears to have discarded de facto the governance and policy criteria for the selection of recipient countries.

A second striking feature of the policy theory, apart from the multitude of (secondary) criteria that had been applied, is the role of the poverty criterion. Despite the fact that various policy documents emphasised the importance of poverty for the selection of recipient countries, poverty had been operationalised as IDA (non-) eligibility. This implies that countries that qualified for IDA loans were automatically considered eligible for Dutch development assistance. Yet, the 'operational cut-off' ($925 per capita in 1997 and $865 per capita in 2002) is a relatively blunt instrument that distinguishes between relatively poorer and relatively richer developing countries, but it does not single out the least-developed or poorest countries. Policy making under Ministers Herfkens and Van Ardenne did not, however, take into account the differences in the degree of poverty *within* the group of IDA eligible countries. The point made by Michel

The Netherlands and recipient countries 65

van Hulten (1999: 431), less than one year after the presentation of the first ideas on selectivity, still seems valid: 'By adopting IDA's $925 cut-off, the Minister emasculated her own poverty criterion.'

The significance of the three key criteria in the policy theory behind country selectivity (poverty, good governance and good policies) was undercut even further by the size of the programmes that were included in the policy reorientation. In the first place, both Minister Herfkens and Minister Van Ardenne maintained separate country lists for specific bilateral aid programmes, such as the environmental policy and the GMV programmes (1998–2003) and the private sector programmes (1998 to date). During Minister Herfkens' tenure, the private sector programme was directed at a number of preferential countries and an additional set of 17 countries; since then, the number of eligible countries has increased to 31. To an important degree, countries that qualify for the private sector programmes are middle-income countries; these countries have not been screened with a view to the quality of their governance and policies.

In the second place, the budget for structural bilateral assistance has been relatively limited: in 2000 the budget was €435 million (or 12 per cent of total Dutch ODA), while the 2004 budget approximated €549 million, which was 14 per cent of ODA (Ministers of Foreign Affairs and Development Cooperation 2003: 48–9). Thus, while the key consideration for selectivity had been found in the presumed enhancement of aid effectiveness, the limitation of the Dutch selectivity operation to structural bilateral aid and the limited size of the budget seem to indicate that successive ministers for development cooperation have not been prepared to make major investments into the introduction of the selectivity principle.

4.4.2 Methodology

The analysis in this chapter has indicated that the methodology of the selection process provided little guidance for the ultimate selection of recipient countries by the Dutch government since 1998. Interviews with senior civil servants made it clear that high-level decision-makers had realised from the outset that the selection of recipient countries could not be made adequately on the basis of the key criteria, poverty and the quality of governance and policies. Several quotations from successive ministers and civil servants indicated that the application of these criteria would have produced too limited a list of recipients. This realisation brought the ministry to 'weigh' candidate countries 'on the hand' and to include certain countries that were underperforming with respect to the key criteria.

The analysis of the methodology in Section 4.2 has shown that the ultimate application of selection criteria in the 1998–2002 period could not be reconstructed to the full. This is caused, on the one hand, by the number of criteria that were applied in the selection process. On the other hand, the ministry's reliance on qualitative judgements – which were very often also subjective ones – has made complete reconstruction impossible. The fact that the selection process relied on a comparatively vague methodology and involved a high degree of political and bureaucratic discretion is, at the least, remarkable, as the avowed objective of selectivity was to use features that (co-)determine aid effectiveness.

The methodology that was applied for the selection of 36 partner countries under Minister Van Ardenne is evidently more transparent and comprehensible than the approach taken by her predecessor. Relevant policy documents and interviews with civil servants make it clear that the 2003 selection process focused on the elimination of a group of countries that had received less than a certain minimum of Dutch aid funds, had become relatively rich and/or had scored relatively badly in terms of the quality of governance and policies. The selection was limited to those countries that had been on one of the three country lists (for structural bilateral assistance, environmental policies, and good governance, human rights and peace-building). The categorical rule not to consider new countries for Dutch development assistance resulted in a rather technocratic selection process. The selection only involved the 49 countries that were receiving Dutch aid; as a result, there was no need to evaluate the performance of additional countries and compare these with existing recipients. The more fundamental question regarding the adequacy of Dutch aid (have those countries been selected where aid promises to be most effective?) was not asked because of the restriction of the selection process to countries that had already been recipients of Dutch aid.[16]

4.4.3 Implementation of the selection

Finally, some comments will be made about the implementation of the Dutch process of selecting aid recipients. First, the operationalisation of the poverty criterion will be discussed. Second, the focus will be on the criteria that were used to measure the quality of governance and policies. Finally, the discussion will concentrate on the selection process under Ministers Herfkens and Van Ardenne.

At several places in the chapter it has been noted that, for the purpose of the Dutch selection of recipient countries, the poverty criterion has been operationalised as the (non-)eligibility of developing countries for IDA loans. This approach has resulted in the application of a relatively imprecise instrument. IDA eligible countries were considered to be eligible for Dutch development assistance. The relative ranking of developing countries was not taken into consideration and, as a result, no explicit weighing of the least-developed and middle-income countries has taken place. Thus, the selection process failed to do justice to the relative needs of developing countries, expressed, for instance, by the income per capita. Alternative measurements of poverty, such as per capita income in purchasing power parity terms or the human development index, have not been used (see note 13 of this chapter), although there is broad agreement that such instruments capture dimensions of development that are neglected in conventional approaches to poverty.

The Netherlands and recipient countries 67

The decision to use IDA performance as an instrument to measure the quality of governance and policies is anything but uncontroversial. A good number of indicators that have been used to construct the CPIA index (see Chapter 3) reflect a view on governance and policy making that is associated closely with neo-liberal interpretations of the role of governments and markets. Indicators on inflation, macro-economic imbalances, fiscal policy, public debt, trade policy and exchange rate regime, financial stability, competitive environment for the private sector, and protection of property rights emphasise qualities of governance and policies that are connected directly with the so-called 'Washington Consensus' (Williamson 1997). Many critics doubt whether this type of variable is suitable for distinguishing developing countries with good governance and policies from those with bad performance, because this approach leads to a priori rejection of non-orthodox policy measures.

With respect to the selection process itself, the approach adopted by Minister Herfkens should be distinguished from that of her successor, Minister Van Ardenne. The former's approach aimed explicitly at enhancing aid effectiveness by selecting fewer recipient countries where the aid money was expected to have more impact in terms of poverty reduction. However, the failure to discriminate between the less and more needy among IDA eligible countries and the selection of several countries with an income level higher than the self-imposed threshold (such as Bolivia, Egypt, Macedonia and South Africa) cast serious doubt on the seriousness of the poverty criterion during the first phase of the selectivity process.

The selection process that was initiated by Minister Van Ardenne has not been in line with the declared intention to select countries on the basis of relative poverty and quality of governance and policies. Despite the Minister's claim that the selection of 36 partner countries shows 'a greater poverty focus' than previous lists, as some of the richer developing countries have been removed (Minister for Development Cooperation 2003c: 6), poverty does no longer seem to play an overriding role. As a result of the collapse of the list of preferential countries with the GMV and environmental policy lists, there is no longer a clear distinction between the type of countries involved and the type of assistance relationship. Relatively richer developing countries, which used to qualify only for specifically earmarked types of aid, are now theoretically eligible for general or specific budget support and sector-oriented support as part of the sector-wide approach. Countries that previously were part of the GMV and the environmental policy programmes are being treated differently from former preferential ('19+3') countries only with respect to the number of sectors that may be included in the aid relationship. In the 2003 selection process, it was decided that there should be no increase in the number of sectors targeted by Dutch assistance to the GMV and environmental policy countries.

Minister Van Ardenne's decision to de-emphasise the role of the governance and policy quality criterion is reflected in her attitude towards the group of GMV and environmental policy countries. The collapse of the three former lists into one list has brought the minister to consider all 36 countries – including those that, previously, were eligible only for the GMV and environmental policy programmes because of their underperformance in terms of governance and policies – full-fledged development assistance partners as of 2003.[17]

4.5 Conclusions

This chapter has analysed the introduction of the selectivity principle into Dutch development assistance policy by Minister Eveline Herfkens in 1998 and the ensuing implementation of the principle in the period between 1998 and 2007, under Minister Agnes Van Ardenne-Van der Hoeven. The review has made clear that the choice for selectivity, as well as for the more encompassing sectoral approach, has been thoroughly influenced by the international development policy environment.

At the introduction of selectivity, it was felt that the effectiveness of Dutch development assistance would be enhanced by choosing 19+3 countries on the basis of their policy and governance record, taking into consideration the relative poverty level of these countries. The 19+3, or preferential, countries would be the prime recipients of structural bilateral assistance, to be delivered through the Dutch embassies. Following the sectoral approach, the preferential countries were requested to choose two or three key sectors as focal points in the bilateral aid relationship. Despite the emphasis on selectivity, good policies and governance, three 'thematic' programmes were set up as instruments of bilateral cooperation. These programmes – on environment; human rights, peace-building and good governance; and private sector development – continued to channel substantial funds to developing countries.

During Minister Van Ardenne's tenure (2003–7), some major shifts were introduced into Dutch development assistance. The group of preferential countries was merged with two of the 'thematic' groups (environment, and human rights, peace-building and good governance) into a group of 36 partner countries. In addition to this change, the good governance criterion was deemphasised: instead of being an absolute requirement, governance quality was applied as a relative criterion. Countries would need to be demonstrating an 'improvement' of policies and governance in order to be considered eligible for Dutch development assistance.

The evaluation of the Dutch approach to country selectivity indicated that the policy theory that is embraced by the Netherlands, its methodology and the implementation of country selection suffer from several serious shortcomings. It was argued that the policy theory was weak, because the application of the primary selectivity criteria was unable to make a sufficient distinction between qualifying and non-qualifying countries, so that the ultimate selection was unduly influenced by secondary criteria. The reassessment of selectivity in 2003 seems even to have resulted in a de facto farewell to the criteria on governance and policy quality. Apart from the governance criterion, the role of the poverty criterion seems to have been less clear than was claimed by the successive ministers. As the income criterion for assistance was based solely on IDA eligibility, the Dutch minister for development cooperation had no means left to distinguish IDA eligible countries on the basis of their *relative* poverty. Finally, the size of the bilateral programme to which the selectivity logic was applied did not match the importance that was attached to governance and policy quality in the policy theory. The continuation of separate bilateral programmes that were not subject to country selectivity, as well as the absolute size of the funds for structural bilateral assistance leave the impression that selectivity was in fact less important than public rhetoric claimed it to be.

The methodology applied by the Netherlands in the two stages of country selection suffered from several problems. The method used in the first stage offered too little guidance to complete the selection. Additional criteria and more or less subjective judgements were used to arrive at the final group of recipient countries. The second stage of selectivity was primarily an elimination process among the countries that figured on several lists for bilateral assistance. As no new countries were considered for Dutch assistance, the selection process ended up being a rather technocratic affair.

The implementation of the selection process demonstrated that the poverty criterion did not occupy the role that was claimed by the successive ministers of development cooperation. In the first stage of selectivity, various countries were included to the '19+3' despite the fact that their per capita income level was over the IDA threshold. The collapse of various bilateral assistance programmes, some of which included a large group of middle-income countries, during the second stage led to a further decline of the significance of the income criterion. Moreover, the collapse of the bilateral programmes implied that several countries that had failed to make it to the list of preferential countries in the 1999–2002 period because of governance and policy weaknesses were included nevertheless among the 36 partner countries from 2003 onward.

5 The United States and the Millennium Challenge Account

5.1 Introduction

With around $19.7 billion allocated to Official Development Assistance (ODA), the United States was the world's largest bilateral donor in 2004. As ODA was only 0.17 per cent of its gross national income, the United States, in relative terms, was at the same time one of the least generous donors in the OECD's Development Assistance Committee (Organisation for Economic Co-operation and Development 2006a). On 14 March 2002, President Bush announced his plan for the so-called Millennium Challenge Account (MCA), which aimed at a gradual increase of the US budget for development assistance and should result in additional spending of $5 billion a year as of FY 2006. In a speech to the Inter-American Development Bank, Bush called the MCA 'a "new compact for development" that increases accountability for rich and poor nations alike, linking greater contributions by developed nations to greater responsibility by developing nations' (US Government 2002).

The introduction of the MCA needs to be understood against the background of the view, prevalent among US policy makers, that aid, first and foremost, is an instrument of foreign policy. The MCA was launched in the context of the sudden return to primacy of security considerations, caused by the sense of vulnerability that was propelled by the terrorist attacks of 11 September 2001 on New York and Washington, DC (Tarnoff and Nowels 2005: 2–4). The attention of the Bush administration for foreign aid was informed, to a large extent, by the assumption that exclusion and poverty provide a breeding ground for political radicalism and terrorism.[1] Following this logic, President Bush's National Security Strategy of September 2002 introduced development as one of the central objectives of US foreign policy: 'Including all of the world's poor in an expanding circle of development – and opportunity – is a moral imperative and one of the top priorities of US international policy' (US President 2002: 21).

In addition to the heightened sense of insecurity in the United States, the plan for the MCA seems also to have been inspired by a desire on the part of the Bush administration to emphasise that the United States, while waging a worldwide war on terror, was 'not focused solely on military action and that it want[ed] to play a positive nonmilitary role in low-income countries' (Radelet

2003: 14). The announcement of the MCA plans was timed so as to generate maximum publicity for the United States' renewed interest in development issues at the UN conference on 'Financing for Development' that would be held on 21–22 March 2002 in Monterrey (Mexico).

The MCA represented a break with the past in US foreign assistance in several ways. The announcement of a new aid initiative meant that the decrease in US funds for foreign assistance, which had been evident especially during the latter part of the 1990s, would come to an end (Tarnoff and Nowels 2005: 16, 33). The MCA was initiated to concentrate substantial aid flows on a small number of well-performing countries. This led to a reverse of the tendency of 'deconcentration' of US aid (Lancaster 2000: 29): the number of US aid recipients increased despite the overall reduction in US foreign assistance. Lancaster (2000: 29) estimated that, by 2000, 'only a handful of countries' (Bosnia-Herzegovina, Egypt, Israel, Jordan, Russia, the Ukraine, and the Palestinian Territories) received more than $100 million in bilateral US aid. Finally, the introduction of the MCA implied that foreign aid came back as an issue on the US political agenda. Since the mid-1980s, decisions on foreign assistance had been purely about the size of the aid budget and had been relegated to the Appropriations Committees of the US Senate and House of Representatives. The MCA initiative resulted in renewed attention for aid in the politically responsible bodies, the House International Relations Committee and the Senate Foreign Relations Committee (SFRC) (Lancaster 2000: 37–8).

In this chapter, the implementation of aid selectivity through the MCA United States is analysed. Section 5.2 discusses the political and institutional framework of US foreign aid, against the background of which the MCA has been introduced. Section 5.3 zeroes in on the MCA and analyses the policy process leading to its creation, as well as various components of the new aid mechanism. Section 5.4 provides an evaluation of the MCA approach to aid selectivity, and Section 5.5 presents the conclusions.

5.2 Foreign aid and governance: the US political and institutional framework

The introduction of the MCA, it was argued above, needs to be seen against the background of US policy makers' perception that foreign assistance may be a useful instrument of security policy, in particular aiming at the elimination of the breeding ground for anti-US terrorism. A US Agency for International Development (USAID) report, published around the same time as President Bush's 2002 National Security Strategy, worked out the implications of US security policy for foreign aid. The report argued that fostering development abroad serves US security interests, because such development would pre-empt threats and disasters, open new markets for US goods and services, lead to secure environments for US investment, create order and peace so that Americans can travel, study and do business, and can produce allies (US Agency for International Development 2002a: 2).

According to USAID, the following are the five core operational goals for US foreign aid:

- the promotion of transformational development, leading to changes in governance and institutional capacity, human capacity and economic structure;
- the strengthening of fragile states, in particular the strengthening of institutions, the management of conflict and the support of post-conflict reconstruction;
- humanitarian relief to countries affected by violent conflict, crisis, natural disasters or persistent poverty;
- the support of strategic states, in particular in the Middle East and Central Asia; and
- the attention for global and transnational issues and other special, self-standing concerns, such as HIV/AIDS and other infectious diseases, climate change, international trade agreements, human trafficking and counternarcotics (US Agency for International Development 2004: 14–15; US Agency for International Development 2006: 7–20).

These goals of US foreign assistance make clear that *development* is – and has been – only one among many other objectives. The United States has traditionally used its foreign aid as a tool to support its allies in parts of the world it considered strategically important, such as the Middle East and East Asia (Brainard 2003: 152–3).

Because of the many cross-pressures in the US foreign policy arena, US foreign aid has come to comprise many different programmes, which can be grouped into five major categories:

- bilateral development assistance (34.7 per cent of total foreign aid appropriations approved by the US Congress for FY 2005)
- economic aid supporting political and security objectives (21.8 per cent of foreign aid)
- humanitarian assistance (12.6 per cent)
- support for multilateral development projects (7.3 per cent)
- military assistance (23.6 per cent) (Tarnoff and Nowels 2005: 4–8).

Institutionally, most of US development assistance (the first and fourth categories above), which accounts for more than two-fifths of US foreign aid, has been managed by USAID. In 2004, the United States provided over $3.4 billion in official development assistance to 49 countries. Of all US aid recipients in 2004, only 22 received more than $34 million (or one per cent of US ODA), and the overall share of these 22 countries was 93.7 per cent of US spending on development assistance. A few countries (Afghanistan, the Democratic Republic of Congo, Ethiopia, Sudan and Uganda) received over 5 per cent of US development aid (Organisation for Economic Co-operation and Development 2006a); this particular choice of countries seems to have been heavily influenced by political motives.

The position of USAID mirrors the political use of foreign aid in the United States. The agency, set up in the 1960s to disengage development assistance from aid given for political and security reasons, has gradually become involved in many programmes – for instance, in Egypt and Colombia – that are not part of its original mandate (e.g. Radelet 2003: 5). In an attempt to strengthen the coordination of US foreign aid, Secretary of State Condoleezza Rice announced the appointment of a director of foreign assistance, who also serves as USAID administrator, in January 2006. This director of foreign assistance would be responsible for all foreign aid activities within the State Department and would coordinate with other US aid bodies, such as the Millennium Challenge Corporation (MCC) and the Office of the Global AIDS Coordinator (Rice 2006). In mid-2006, the new official presented the outlines of a new Foreign Assistance Framework that aimed at developing an overarching structure to organise the multitude of aid types of United States managed by different parts of the US government, including USAID and the MCC.[2]

The MCA was introduced by the Bush administration with the intention of concentrating substantial aid flows on well-governed developing countries. The introduction of the MCA reflected the conviction among US foreign policy makers that the quality of governance in developing countries would be critical for the success of the development policies implemented by these countries, and that governance quality should figure prominently in development assistance policies. The US government's views on governance quality were laid down in various USAID policy documents prior to the introduction of the MCA. As expressed by the US aid agency in its statement on foreign aid and the national interest, good governance should be seen a *conditio* sine qua non for development assistance, as '[n]o amount of resources transferred or infrastructure built can compensate for – or survive – bad governance' (US Agency for International Development 2002a: 6).

In the view of US government officials, good governance would not be an exclusive feature of the public sector. USAID explicitly made a connection between the nature of the political system and the functioning of the private sector, and stressed the centrality of the protection of property rights:

> [T]he prospects for development, and for effective development assistance, depend on the quality of governance – the way in which public power is exercised and public resources are managed and expended. Poorly performing states – those mired in poverty and illiteracy for decades – will not achieve sustainable development unless they dramatically improve governance. *Only when the rule of law ensures property rights and low transaction costs will domestic capital be invested productively and international capital flow in.* But corruption and weak rule of law will persist until voters have the power to remove governments that fail to perform – politically as well as economically.
> (US Agency for International Development 2002a: 42, italics added)

'Sound economic policies', which relate, in USAID's view, to good governance, have to do with the functioning of national markets, as well as with the

74 The US and the MCA

integration of developing countries in the world economy through trade and investment (US Agency for International Development 2002a: 56–64). Referring to the captions of two figures presented by USAID, 'greater freedom means greater integration with global markets' and 'market integrators grow faster' (US Agency for International Development 2002a: 60–1, Figures 2.2 and 2.4).

According to USAID, good governance is instrumental for democracy:

> For democracy to flourish over the long run, competent, transparent, and accountable government institutions are needed. Good governance provides security, operates according to reasonable standards of justice, and provides basic public services. Furthermore, democracy is more likely to be sustainable when it is held accountable by checks on its authority.
> (US Agency for International Development 2005: 5)

Democracy, apart from being valuable in and of itself, is also seen as central to US national security, as terror networks, which are defined as the 'primary' contemporary security threat, tend to flourish in 'failed states or weakly governed regions' (US Agency for International Development 2005: 5).

5.3 The Millennium Challenge Account

5.3.1 MCA's policy theory

The MCA approach to poverty reduction is grounded in an explicit macro- and micro-economic theoretical framework. The MCA's macro-economic approach was spelt out in a background paper published by the Bush administration in February 2003:

> The goal of the MCA is to reduce poverty by significantly *increasing the economic growth trajectory of recipient countries*. This requires an emphasis on investments that raise the productive potential of a country's citizens and firms and help integrate its economy into the global product and capital markets. Key areas of focus would include
>
> - agricultural development
> - education
> - enterprise and private sector development
> - governance
> - health
> - trade and investment capacity building.
>
> (US Government Background Paper, 'Implementing the Millennium Challenge Account', 5 February 2003 in US Department of State 2003: 28, italics added)

The micro-economic reasoning behind the MCA was summarised in a testimony before the SFRC by Treasury Under-Secretary John B. Taylor, who argued that poverty in many developing countries is caused by a failure to catch up with the industrialised world as a result of stagnant productivity growth. In Taylor's view, such stagnant growth is caused by three categories of impediments to investment and the adoption of technology. In the first place, poor governance leads to disincentives to invest in existing firms and start up new firms, which results in low degrees of capital formation and entrepreneurial activity. In the second place, weak health and education systems impede the development of human capital. Finally, restrictions on economic transactions (deriving from poor economic policies, state monopolies, regulation and the lack of trade openness) keep people from trading goods and services and adopting new technologies (Taylor 2003: 1–2).

The macro- and micro-economic logic behind its plans for development assistance brought the Bush administration to propose a new aid structure rather than add money to already existing US foreign aid programmes. In the administration's view, the MCA should not follow in the footsteps of established aid organisations, of which USAID was the most prominent. Rather, the MCA should reward 'good policies', which were summarised by President Bush as 'ruling justly, investing in their people, and encouraging economic freedom' (US President 2003). The incentives for developing countries to adopt the 'good policies' promoted by the United States were, according to Under-Secretary Taylor (2003: 2), that such policies:

- would, in and of themselves, lead to higher economic growth;
- would create an environment conducive to foreign and domestic investment; and
- would enhance the effectiveness of development assistance.

The MCA adopted the principle of aid selectivity and fully rejected the notion of conditionality (cf. Natsios 2003: 16), right from the start. The programme was meant to target the three impediments signalled by Taylor, phrased as follows by the White House:

> The funds into the MCA will be distributed to developing countries that demonstrate a strong commitment toward:
>
> - *Good governance.* Rooting out corruption, upholding human rights, and adherence to the rule of law are essential conditions for successful development.
> - *The health and education of their people.* Investment in schools, health care, and immunization provide for healthy and educated citizens who become agents of development.
> - *Sound economic policies that foster enterprise and entrepreneurship.* More open markets, sustainable budget policies, and strong support for development will unleash the enterprise and creativity for lasting growth and prosperity.
>
> (US Government 2002)

76 The US and the MCA

The MCA was contrasted with other development assistance programmes right from the start. According to MCC's first chief executive officer, Paul Applegarth, the MCA was based on six 'core structural components' (Applegarth 2004: 10). Apart from emphasising policy reform, he highlighted the programme's focus on sustainable growth, its result-orientation and the need for the permanent monitoring of progress. The programme would, Applegarth claimed, also be different because of the nature of the agreements between the United States and its MCA partners (the so-called 'MCA compacts'). Such agreements would be based on 'true partnership':

> Instead of telling donor countries what we want them to do or what they get their money for, we are going to ask the qualified nations what are your development priorities. The nations will own the programs from the start, and MCC will provide financial and implementation assistance to countries that are performing.
>
> (Applegarth 2004: 6)

Moreover, the MCA would stand out, in Applegarth's view, because of the requirement that recipient governments 'consult broadly' with 'non-governmental bodies, private businesses, and representatives of civil society, with all their skills, knowledge, interests and concerns' (Applegarth 2004: 10).

5.3.2 The legal framework

In order to implement the MCA and select well-performing developing countries, the Bush administration took the advice of an inter-agency steering committee[3] and proposed the creation of a new government organisation, the MCC. The corporation was established by law in the Millennium Challenge Act of 2003, as part of the agreement among both houses of Congress and President Bush on the 2004 budget (US Congress 2004: 209–24).

The inter-agency committee considered, but advised against, placing the MCA within the State Department or under the responsibility of USAID. Reasons for supporting MCC's independence from the State Department related to the department's inexperience in managing aid programmes, as well as the fear that the MCC would become susceptible to political influences and considerations. USAID was not considered to be the best home for the MCA, because this agency's outlook and approach was felt to be too traditional and bureaucratic, caused in part by close congressional oversight and interference (Nowels 2004: 20–1; Radelet 2003: 10).[4]

The discussion in Congress of the proposals made by the Bush administration led to quite some controversy about the issue of MCC independence. In May 2003, the SFRC adopted a bipartisan amendment, proposed by Senators Joseph R. Biden and Chuck Hagel, which aimed at bringing the MCC under the authority of the Secretary of State, who would appoint a coordinator from within the State Department. According to the senators, the creation of a new government body would counteract earlier decisions to integrate USAID with the State Department and would undermine the Secretary of State's leverage in issues of foreign assistance. The amendment met with strong opposition from the Secretary of State Colin Powell who said that he would recommend the president to veto the legislation if the Senate would stick to its position (Senate Foreign Relations Committee 2003: 2).

The Millennium Challenge Act eventually contained a compromise between the two extremes of creating a fully independent corporation and making the organisation subservient to the Secretary of State. The Act set up the MCC as an independent entity, headed by a chief executive officer (CEO), who would be appointed by the US president and confirmed by the Senate. The CEO was placed under the direct authority of the board of directors, members of which would be the Secretary of State (as chairperson), the Secretary of the Treasury, the administrator of USAID, the US Trade Representative, the CEO of the MCC, and four other individuals with relevant international experience[5] appointed by the president (US Congress 2004: 210–1).

The Millennium Challenge Act specified in detail which countries would be potential recipients of the new form of development assistance. In FY 2004,[6] all developing countries eligible for support from the International Development Association (IDA) and with a per capita income equal to or lower than IDA's historical cut-off ($1415 in 2004), could become so-called MCA 'candidate countries'. In the following fiscal year, all developing countries with an income below IDA's ceiling would qualify for candidate status. As of FY 2006, lower-middle-income countries (as classified by the World Bank) would also be candidates for MCA support and could receive up to 25 per cent of all MCA funds (US Congress 2004: 213–14).

According to the Millennium Challenge Act, 'eligible countries' – that is, countries that would be selected for actual MCA assistance – should be chosen on the basis of three central criteria, which were specified as follows in section 607(b):

> A candidate country should be considered to be an eligible country for purposes of this section if the Board determines that the country has demonstrated a commitment to
>
> 1 just and democratic governance, including a demonstrated commitment to
>   A promote political pluralism, equality, and the rule of law;
>   B respect human and civil rights, including the rights of people with disabilities;
>   C protect private property rights;
>   D encourage transparency and accountability of government; and
>   E combat corruption;
> 2 economic freedom, including a demonstrated commitment to economic policies that

>   A   encourage citizens and firms to participate in global trade and international capital markets;
>   B   promote private sector growth and the sustainable management of natural resources;
>   C   strengthen market forces in the economy; and
>   D   respect worker rights, including the right to form labor unions; and
> 3   investments in the people of such country, particularly women and children, including programs that
>   A   promote broad-based primary education; and
>   B   strengthen and build capacity to provide quality public health and reduce child mortality.
>
> (US Congress 2004: 214–15)

The act did not indicate in which way the MCC should select eligible countries, but specified that, apart from assessing to what extent developing countries meet the criteria, the board of directors should consider the 'opportunity to reduce poverty and generate economic growth in the country' in the light of available funds (US Congress 2004: 215).

In order to receive assistance under the MCA, developing countries need to sign an agreement with the United States (a 'Millennium Challenge compact') that 'establishes a multi-year plan for achieving shared development objectives'. A compact would contain, among other things, the specific objectives of the assistance programme, benchmarks to measure progress, an identification of the intended beneficiaries, a multi-year financial plan, a description of the contribution of other donors, and a description of the role of USAID[7] in the design, implementation and monitoring of the programme. In addition to these elements, lower-middle-income countries, which would be considered in a competition different from the one involving the low-income countries, should also specify their own financial contribution towards achieving the compact (US Congress 2004: 216–17). Developing countries that would hold promise but do not yet meet the criteria could be assisted by the MCC to become eligible for MCA support under the so-called 'threshold' programme, for which up to 10 per cent of the MCA funds would be available (US Congress 2004: 222).

5.3.3 The MCA budget

The budget requested by President Bush for the MCA in FY 2004 was $1.3 billion.[8] Congress appropriated $1 billion for the MCA in the Consolidated Appropriations Act 2004. SFRC Chairman Lugar expressed a more generally shared feeling that this reduction was 'not an expression of doubt about the MCA concept' but was based 'on the judgment that the MCA will require time to become established and may not be in a position to efficiently distribute the entire $1.3 billion request in the first fiscal year' (Lugar 2003b: 2).

The reduction of the MCA budget to lower levels than requested by the administration was repeated in subsequent years, thus leading to a much slower growth of the programme than anticipated by President Bush in 2002. In FY 2005, the funds appropriated by Congress were 60 per cent of the $2.5 billion budget requested, while the appropriations of FY 2006 stayed at 59 per cent of the $3 billion request. On the basis of deliberations in the US House of Representatives, an increase of the appropriations to $2 billion, or 67 per cent of the budget requested, may be expected in FY 2007 (see Table 5.1).

The funding approved by the US Congress fell seriously short of the minimum amount that, according to the MCC, would be necessary to fund MCA compacts in a substantial number of countries. The MCA was facing competition from spending on the reconstruction of Iraq and on the President's Emergency Plan for AIDS Relief (PEPFAR). The Appropriations Committee of the House of Representatives, moreover, advocated substantial cuts of the foreign affairs budget requested by President Bush in the light of the administration's own proposals to allow little or no growth in the funding of domestic programmes (Lugar 2004: 1; House of Representatives' Appropriations Subcommittee on Foreign Operations 2005: 2). As the foreign assistance programmes, in particular those related to development, have a much less vociferous constituency than domestic spending, MCA and other funds were slashed for reasons of political expediency (Fox and Rieffel 2005: 18–19).

The MCC emphasised its concern with MCA's effectiveness from the start of the programme. It was argued that the MCA should be 'among the largest providers of assistance in a country', in order to be 'an effective incentive for both eligible and threshold countries, command the attention needed for breakthrough country proposals, and help galvanize the political will essential to success' (Millennium Challenge Corporation 2004a: 7).

The MCC, in its budget justification for FY 2005, had issued the warning that 'a funding level of less than the requested $2.5 billion for FY 2005 will reduce the number of Compacts that the MCC will be able to finalize' (Millennium Challenge Corporation 2004a: 7).[9] Yet, Nita M. Lowey, the leader of the Democratic minority in the House Foreign Operations Subcommittee, indicated that, in her view, the failure of the MCC to spend much of its allocated funds during the first years of the corporation's existence, made the MCA budget an easy prey

Table 5.1 MCA's budget, 2004–7

Fiscal year	Administration's request (in billion dollars)	Congressional appropriations (in billion dollars)
2004	1.3	0.99
2005	2.5	1.49
2006	3.0	1.77
2007	3.0	2.00

Source: Millennium Challenge Corporation (2005b: 6); Center for Global Development (2006b).

Note
2007 Congressional appropriations are an estimate based on the appropriations agreed by the House of Representatives.

for cuts (House of Representatives' Appropriations Subcommittee on Foreign Operations 2005: 3). Similarly, Republican Chairman Henry J. Hyde of the House International Relations Committee said that 'the same observers who once received this initiative with such optimism now feel underwhelmed by the cautious pace and the modest scope of MCA writ large.... [I]t seems that we have more funding than program' (House of Representatives' Committee on International Relations 2005: 1–2).

5.3.4 MCA criteria

The MCC started its work, under temporary management, in February 2004. The first tasks of the corporation's Board of Directors were the identification of candidate countries and the formulation of the criteria and the methodology for determining the eligibility of developing countries for MCA support.

In line with earlier announcements, in March 2004, the MCC Board published 16 criteria for the selection of eligible countries (see Table 5.2, which sums up the indicators, categories and sources of data). Indicators were chosen on the basis of seven criteria: development by an independent third party; the use of objective and high-quality data; analytical rigour and public availability;

Table 5.2 Selection criteria of the Millennium Challenge Account

Ruling justly
1 Civil liberties (Freedom House)
2 Political rights (Freedom House)
3 Voice and accountability (World Bank Institute)
4 Government effectiveness (World Bank Institute)
5 Rule of law (World Bank Institute)
6 Control of corruption (World Bank Institute)

Encouraging economic freedom
1 Regulatory quality (World Bank Institute)
2 Inflation (IMF)
3 Fiscal policy (U.S. Embassies/IMF)
4 Days to starting a business (Private Sector Advisory Service, World Bank)
5 Until FY 2006: Country credit rating (Institutional Investor Magazine); since FY 2006: Cost of starting a business (Private Sector Advisory Service, World Bank)
6 Trade policy (Heritage Foundation)

Investing in people
1 Total public expenditure on health (World Health Organisation; supplemented, until FY 2007, by national government data)
2 Total public expenditure on education (UNESCO/national governments)
3 Immunisation (World Health Organisation)
4 In FY 2004: Primary education completion rate; since FY 2005: Girls' primary education completion rate (World Bank/UNESCO/OECD)

Source: Millennium Challenge Corporation (n.d.; 2006a).

Note
A full description of the indicators is given in Appendix D.

broad country coverage and comparability across countries; a theoretical link to economic growth and poverty reduction; amenability to policy measures; and consistency in results over time (Millennium Challenge Corporation n.d.: 1).

Developing countries are considered eligible for MCA assistance if they score above the median on at least half the indicators in each of the three policy categories and above the median on the corruption indicator.[10] In addition, countries need to have an inflation rate not higher than 15 per cent (Millennium Challenge Corporation 2005a: 10).[11] The MCA methodology stipulates that the assessment of country performance on the basis of the 16 indicators would be the 'predominant basis' for deciding about MCA eligibility, but that the MCC Board 'may exercise discretion in evaluating and translating the indicators into a final list of eligible countries' and 'may also take into account other data and quantitative information as well as qualitative information to determine whether a country performed satisfactorily in relation to its peers in a given category' (Millennium Challenge Corporation 2004d: 2).[12] Review of the indicators in subsequent years resulted in several changes to the selection criteria (Millennium Challenge Corporation 2004e: 2–3; Millennium Challenge Corporation n.d.: 9; see further Table 5.2).

In the preparation of its selection of eligible countries for FY 2007, the MCC Board adopted two indices of sustainable management of natural resources as 'sources of supplemental information' (Millennium Challenge Corporation 2006a: 2). The board had earlier expressed its interest in finding an indicator for natural resource management and had launched a 'public process', led by board member Christine Todd Whitman, to discuss the appropriateness of various possible measures with representatives from academia, the public and the private sectors and non-governmental organisations (NGOs). This process and the ensuing decision-making led to the inclusion of a natural resources management index and a land rights and access index in the MCC methodology (see Appendix D for details). The MCC Board expressed the intention of including the two natural resource management indices in the selection procedure for FY 2008 as part of the investing in people category (Millennium Challenge Corporation 2006a: 6).

5.3.5 *Country selection*

In February 2004, the MCC Board identified 63 developing countries as candidates for the MCA (Millennium Challenge Corporation 2004b: 2–3). Shortly after Paul V. Applegarth, a former Wall Street investment banker with experience in emerging markets, assumed office as MCC's CEO in May 2004, the MCC Board of Directors reported the countries that would be eligible for MCA support in the first year (FY 2004). A list of 16 eligible countries was published (see Table 5.3): Armenia, Benin, Bolivia, Cape Verde, Georgia, Ghana, Honduras, Lesotho, Madagascar, Mali, Mongolia, Mozambique, Nicaragua, Senegal, Sri Lanka and Vanuatu (Millennium Challenge Corporation 2004f: 1). Three countries (Cape Verde, Lesotho and Sri Lanka) were included in the list despite

Table 5.3 Eligible, threshold and compact countries, fiscal years 2004–6

Country	2004	2005	2006
Albania	T	–	T
Armenia	E	E	C
Benin	E	E	C
Bolivia	E	E	E
Burkina Faso	–	T	E
Cape Verde	E	C	C
East Timor	T	T	E
El Salvador	–	–	E
Gambia	–	–	E(S)
Georgia	E	C	C
Ghana	E	E	C
Guyana	–	T	T
Honduras	E	C	C
Indonesia	–	–	T
Jordan	–	–	T
Kenya	T	T	T
Kyrgyz Republic	–	–	T
Lesotho	E	E	E
Madagascar	E	C	C
Malawi	–	T	T
Mali	E	E	E
Moldova	–	–	T
Mongolia	E	E	E
Morocco	–	E	E
Mozambique	E	E	E
Namibia	–	–	E
Nicaragua	E	C	C
Paraguay	–	T	T
Philippines	–	T	T
São Tomé and Principe	T	T	T
Senegal	E	E	E
Sri Lanka	E	E	E
Tanzania	T	T	E
Uganda	T	T	T
Ukraine	–	–	T
Vanuatu	E	E	C
Yemen	T	T(S)	–
Zambia	–	T	T

Source: Millennium Challenge Corporation, various publications.

Notes
E – the country is eligible for an MCA compact; T – the country is eligible for the threshold programme; C – the country has signed a compact with the MCC; and S – the country's eligibility or threshold status has been suspended.

the fact that 'they were substantially below average on one indicator' each.[13] The measures that these countries had been taking to remedy the shortcomings were, according to the MCC Board, sufficiently convincing to accept them for MCA assistance (Millennium Challenge Corporation 2004f: 2). Bolivia, Georgia and Mozambique did not score above the median on at least half of the indicators in one of the three policy indicators or were below the median on corruption. Yet, these countries were grouped among the eligible countries because of positive trends in combating corruption and good performance on some of the other indicators (Millennium Challenge Corporation 2004f: 3).[14]

An analysis of the US Government Accountability Office (GAO), presented to the US Congress in April 2005, showed that six candidate countries met the MCA criteria in FY 2004 but had not been selected for inclusion in the MCA. The same finding was reported on ten candidate countries involved in the FY 2005 selection process. As the MCC is not required to justify its non-selection of countries, the GAO surmised that the corporation, in addition to seeing a score above the median on the corruption indicator as a sine qua non for MCA partnership, 'placed particular emphasis on three Ruling Justly indicators (political rights, civil liberties, and voice and accountability) in making its eligibility determinations' (House of Representatives' Committee on International Relations 2005: 51). In one or both of the first two years of the MCC's operations, Bhutan, China, Djibouti, Egypt, Swaziland and Vietnam met the MCA criteria but scored equal to or below the median on the three Ruling Justly indicators mentioned above. The GAO did not advance an explanation for the exclusion of the other countries: Burkina Faso, Guyana, Kiribati, Mauritania, Nepal, the Philippines and Tonga.

The MCC's report on the selection of eligible countries for FY 2006 contained a general statement on the reasons why some well-performing countries were not considered eligible. These reasons related to countries' commitment to fighting corruption and promoting democratic governance, their policies for the sustainable management of natural resources, the rights of people with disabilities in these countries, the MCA's opportunity to reduce poverty, promote economic growth and have a transformational impact in a country, and the availability of appropriated funds (Millennium Challenge Corporation 2005d: 2–3).

In addition to the 16 eligible countries listed above, the MCC selected seven countries for the 2004 threshold programme: Albania, East Timor, Kenya, São Tomé and Principe, Tanzania, Uganda and Yemen. This programme, for which the MCC can make available a maximum of ten per cent of MCA funds, was set up for the purpose of 'incentivizing policy reform'. Assistance to threshold countries, to be delivered in partnership with USAID, would be aimed at 'improving the specific performance indicators on which a Threshold Program country has failed to score higher than the median' (Millennium Challenge Corporation 2005a: 14).

In FY 2005, the criterion of IDA eligibility was dropped so that all developing countries with a per capita income equal to or less than the IDA historical cut-off of $1,465 in that year would qualify for MCA support. With this change of the criteria for MCA candidate status, the number of candidate countries accepted by the MCC increased to 66 (Millennium Challenge Corporation

2004c: 2–3). Morocco was the only country that was added to the list of eligible countries for FY 2005; all 16 countries selected for FY 2004 were re-endorsed by the MCC. Morocco was chosen despite the fact that the country scored low on the trade policy indicator. The MCC argued that the country had made sufficient progress in reducing tariff rates and non-tariff barriers in the period before selection to warrant inclusion in the list of eligible countries (Millennium Challenge Corporation 2004g: 2). Six countries (Burkina Faso, Guyana, Malawi, Paraguay, the Philippines and Zambia) were added to the threshold programme for 2005 (Millennium Challenge Corporation 2006c).

The preparations for FY 2006 were the beginning of the third phase in the life of the MCA. A new group of lower-middle-income countries – with per capita incomes between $1,575 and $3,255 in 2006 – was added to the 69 low-income candidate countries that had a per capita income of less than $1,575. In addition to these countries, the MCC selected a list of 29 lower-middle-income countries as candidates for MCA support (Millennium Challenge Corporation 2005c: 2–4).

In November 2005, the MCC selected 23 countries for MCA eligibility in FY 2006. Seventeen of these were low-income countries that were re-selected. In addition, four new low-income countries (Burkina Faso, East Timor, the Gambia and Tanzania) and two lower-middle-income countries (El Salvador and Namibia) were included. In December 2005, Armenia was warned that 'its eligibility may be re-examined if the trends in its "ruling justly" category continue to weaken' (Danilovich 2006: 2).

The number of threshold countries was increased for FY 2006. With the promotion of three countries (Burkina Faso, East Timor and Tanzania) to eligibility status, eight countries remained in the threshold programme: Guyana, Kenya, Malawi, Paraguay, the Philippines, São Tomé and Principe, Uganda and Zambia. Albania, which had been selected in 2004 but had been absent in the 2005 programme, Indonesia, Jordan, Kyrgyz Republic, Moldova and Ukraine were newly selected in November 2005. Yemen was removed as a result of underperformance (Millennium Challenge Corporation 2006c).

Following the rules of the Millennium Challenge Act, eligible countries are invited to submit programme proposals to the MCC, which may be building blocks for the conclusion of an MCA compact with the US government. The MCC's 2005 Budget Justification pointed out that

> the countries selected by the MCC's Board ... are not guaranteed assistance. Countries should maintain their performance on the selection indicators in order to preserve their status as MCA eligible. Most importantly, the quality of the initial proposal – including how well the country has demonstrated the relationship between the proposed priority area(s) and economic growth and poverty reduction – will likely determine how quickly the MCC can begin substantive discussions with a country on a Compact and influence the speed with which a Compact can be negotiated and the amount and timing of any MCA assistance approved by the Board.
>
> (Millennium Challenge Corporation 2004a: 5)

According to CEO Applegarth, the MCC had made significant progress in the first 15 months of its existence, despite the impression that few funds were committed during that period. He told the House International Relations Committee that the corporation, apart from committing about $110 million in the first compact that was signed in April 2005, had 'a pipeline' of proposals from eligible countries that would exceed the resources allocated to the corporation in fiscal years 2004 and 2005 'by at least a billion dollars' (House of Representatives' Committee on International Relations 2005: 6).[15]

In Applegarth's view, the MCC's 'role in the foreign assistance arena has yielded results even before spending money.... [T]he MCC does more than provide assistance; it disseminates and encourages democratic ideals.' In this context, Applegarth mentioned the fact that the governments of several eligible countries 'have consulted NGOs and the business sector for the first time', adopted anti-corruption legislation and improved the business environment (House of Representatives' Committee on International Relations 2005: 10–11). Many of MCC staff argue that the impact of the consultation requirement may actually be greater than the sheer size of the aid funds that are provided through the MCA, as the consultative process leads to the strengthening of institutions and civil society in the countries concerned. As one staff member commented, 'the outcome of the consultative process *is* development' (interviews, 28 September 2006).

5.3.6 MCA compacts and threshold programme

Soon after the decision-making on the first set of eligible countries had taken place, the MCC started to work on MCA compacts with the countries. MCC staff undertook missions to all eligible countries to instruct government officials and other interested parties about the MCC's procedures and requirements. The first MCA compact was signed with Madagascar in April 2005; subsequently, compacts were agreed upon with Honduras, Cape Verde, Nicaragua, Georgia, Benin, Vanuatu, Armenia and Ghana, totalling $2.061 billion by the end of 2006 (see Table 5.4). By September 2006, it was expected that new compacts would be concluded with El Salvador and Mali before the end of the year (interview, 28 September 2006).

The overall planning and implementation process of developing an MCA compact, as designed by the MCC, essentially goes through four stages: (1) proposal development; (2) due diligence; (3) compact negotiation; and (4) implementation (see Figure 5.1).

The first phase of the planning process (proposal development) ends with the writing of an 'Opportunity Memorandum', which 'describes the country's proposed MCC program, including an initial assessment of whether it has promise and effectively reflects basic MCC principles (poverty reduction, growth impact, consultative process, measurable results, etc.)' (Millennium Challenge Corporation 2005e: 3). The due-diligence phase that follows upon proposal development is intended for a review of the proposal by a 'transaction team', consisting of

86 The US and the MCA

Table 5.4 Signed Millennium Challenge Compacts, 2004–6

Country	Date of agreement	Duration of compact (in years)	Funds involved (in millions of US dollars)
Armenia	27 March 2006	5	235.7
Benin	22 February 2006	5	307.3
Cape Verde	4 July 2005	5	110.1
Georgia	12 September 2005	5	295.3
Ghana	1 August 2006	5	547.0
Honduras	13 June 2005	5	215.0
Madagascar	18 April 2005	4	109.8
Nicaragua	14 July 2005	5	175.0
Vanuatu	2 March 2006	5	65.7

Source: Millennium Challenge Corporation (mcc.gov/compacts/index.shtml).

MCC staff and technical experts. This phase is concluded with the completion of a consultation memorandum for the MCC's Investment Committee and the beginning of consultations with the US Congress. In the third phase (compact negotiation), the details of an MCA compact are negotiated with the country applying for MCA assistance. This phase results in the preparation of an 'Investment Memorandum', in which the proposed terms of the compact are described. The final proposed compact and annexes – 'the obligating agreement between MCC and MCC eligible countries' (Millennium Challenge Corporation 2005e: 3) – is sent to the US Congress before the MCC signs the compact. The implementation of MCA compacts (the fourth phase) is envisaged to take four to five years. All funds that are promised in these compacts are reserved by the MCC for the compact countries, which implies that they are not financed out of annual budgets that are subject to change in the Congress' appropriation process. The funds are disbursed 'as needed based on quantifiable benchmarks' (House of Representatives' Committee on International Relations 2005: 11).

Table 5.5 presents an overview of the allocation, by type of activity, of the funds committed to the compact countries. The table shows that roughly half of all MCA funds have been allocated to infrastructural programmes, most notably the construction or improvement of roads and ports. One-fifth of MCA funds has been allocated for spending on various agricultural programmes, ranging from irrigation to institutional support. Smaller percentages will be spent on market access and (agri-)business development, improvement of land tenure and property rights, financial sector development and credit schemes, among others for farmers, judicial reform, and general administrative and monitoring activities.

Early on in the MCC's operations, the corporation received criticism from various members of Congress for its emphasis on particular types of activities and their perceived bias in favour of some more-well-to-do parts of the population in the recipient countries. The MCA compact with Madagascar was criticised, for instance, because of its bias toward the financial sector and its lack of attention for health and education. Both in this case and in the case of the Hon-

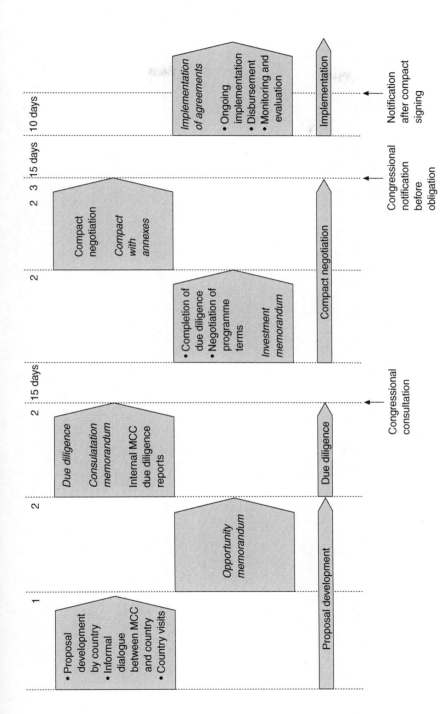

Figure 5.1 Stages of the MCA compact development process.

Note
At moment 1, the Transaction Team makes its recommendations; at moment 2, the Investment Committee makes recommendations to the CEO; at moment 3, the MCC Board decides.

Table 5.5 Millennium Challenge Compacts, allocation by type of activity (per cent)

Country	Infrastructure (roads and ports)	Agriculture and rural development	Market access, business development	Land tenure and property rights	Financial sector development, credit	Judicial reform	Administration, monitoring and evaluation	Total (in millions of US dollars)
Armenia	28.5	48.1	13.7	–	–	–	9.7	235.7
Benin	48.8	–	6.3	11.7	6.4	11.2	15.6	307.3
Cape Verde	71.6	9.8	6.5	–	–	–	12.1	110.1
Georgia	71.7	5.1	11.0	–	–	–	12.2	295.3
Ghana	36.7	41.3	–	–	10.7	–	11.3	547.0
Honduras	68.5	17.2	–	–	6.4	–	8.0	215.0
Madagascar	16.1	–	–	34.4	32.7	–	16.8	109.8
Nicaragua	53.0	–	19.2	15.1	–	–	12.6	175.0
Vanuatu	83.0	–	9.4	–	–	–	7.6	65.7
Total	49.5	19.5	6.4	4.9	6.2	1.7	11.9	2,060.9

Source: Millennium Challenge Corporation (www.mcc.gov/compacts/index.shtml).

Note
Figures may not add up to 100 per cent as a result of rounding.

duras compact, Congress members blamed the lack of civil society involvement and broader participation by the population for the bias. (House of Representatives' Committee on International Relations 2005: 3–4, 20–1, 91–4).

The MCA's 'second window', the so-called threshold programme, was intended to support countries that were close to eligibility for the MCA. Countries qualifying for this programme would generally have missed selection because of their score on one of the 16 MCA criteria. It was argued that countries, by participating in the threshold programme, would be able to implement certain policies to improve their weak rating on that criterion and, thus, become eligible for MCA support in the future.

By the end of March 2006, the proposals of six out of 18 threshold countries had received MCC Board approval, while three programmes were being implemented. The threshold programmes of Burkina Faso ($12.9 million), Jordan ($25.0 million) and Malawi ($20.9 million) are currently in the implementation phase, while programmes for Albania ($13.9 million), Paraguay ($37.1 million), the Philippines ($21 million), Tanzania ($11.2 million), Ukraine ($45.0 million) and Zambia ($24.3 million) were approved by the MCC Board in 2006. By September 2006, the conclusion of a threshold programme with Indonesia was expected in the foreseeable future (interview, 28 September 2006). Most threshold proposals focus on the introduction of anti-corruption programmes. The exceptions are Burkina Faso, which had proposed a programme to improve girls' primary education completion rates, and Jordan, which focused on the strengthening of municipal governance and the modernisation of its customs administration (Millennium Challenge Corporation 2006b: 2, 5; 2006c).

5.4 Evaluation

In this section, various aspects of the MCA's approach to aid selectivity are discussed and evaluated. The ensuing discussion focuses on, in particular: MCA's policy theory, the MCA methodology, the choice of selection criteria, and the role of the MCC.

5.4.1 Policy theory

The policy theory that informs the MCA centres around two elements. First, the MCA is grounded in the widely shared conviction that aid helps only in a conducive institutional and policy environment (see Chapter 2). Second, the MCA is based on the conviction that its objective – poverty reduction – is served best if aid is targeted on programmes that stimulate economic growth. The motto of the MCC, displayed prominently on the corporation's website, is 'Reducing Poverty Through Growth'.

The first element of the MCA's policy theory does not, in itself, distinguish the US approach from the cases of aid selectivity that were discussed in earlier chapters. The choice of *criteria* for MCA eligibility does, however, clearly set apart the US approach from the World Bank's and the Dutch selectivity policies.

The Millennium Challenge Act (see p. 77) has explicitly introduced a full set of political criteria ('just and democratic governance') along with a set of criteria related to 'economic freedom' and one to 'investments in the people'. In addition to this, the MCC's concern with institution-building and the strengthening of civil society indicates that the programme's objectives are not limited to economic growth, but are highly political. Somewhat surprisingly, the orientation of the MCC is much more political and seems to bear much less resemblance to the neo-liberal, technocratic outlook on 'good governance' that characterises the policies implemented by the World Bank and The Netherlands.

The MCA's exclusivity has led various observers to question the appropriateness of the programme's focus on a small number of developing countries, as it risks to 'condemn millions of Africans who have despicable governments' (Jesse Jackson in: House of Representatives' Appropriations Subcommittee on Foreign Operations 2005: 25). These critics of the MCA do not to have great faith in USAID's role in the non-MCA-eligible countries. The MCA's threshold programme is applauded by many, but its limited size, set at a maximum of 10 per cent of MCA funds, is often found to be insufficient. The group of threshold countries is potentially quite large, and their problems, related to institutional weaknesses and corruption, may be far too complex to be addressed successfully in relatively small institution-building threshold programmes.

The second element of the MCA's policy theory, which assumes a direct impact of economic growth on poverty reduction, has attracted quite some criticism, as well. The analysis in the previous sections has made it clear that MCA compacts tend to focus on large-scale investments that are supposed to have a growth-enhancing effect (see, in particular, Table 5.5). It seems that infrastructural programmes are in high demand among MCA's aid recipients. The MCA compacts place much less emphasis on the strengthening of education or the health sector, despite the fact that these are the primary targets of the Millennium Development Goals (MDGs). This feature of the MCA compacts has brought Herrling (2006: 2) to the observation that 'the MCC is cherry-picking the high and quick economic return projects to the detriment of longer yield return projects in education and health'. According to Herrling, the MCC's preference for large-scale investment may be the result of the corporation's focus on monitoring and accountability, which leads to a desire to select fewer programmes that guarantee a high return, rather than be occupied with a large number of smaller projects in the social sectors, the effects of which can be established much less easily. Over the years, various members of Congress and civil society groups have called for more explicit attention for the MDGs in the MCA because the chances would be higher that the poorest groups in developing countries benefit from spending on health and education than from infrastructural or general institutional reform programmes (e.g. House of Representatives' Committee on International Relations 2003: 45, 48, 66; House of Representatives' Appropriations Subcommittee on Foreign Operations 2005: 26).

Apart from the MCC's bias towards certain types of compacts, a more fundamental issue related to the apparent preference for large-scale infrastructural investments is whether these provide the most effective contribution to poverty reduction in the target countries, even if they would fuel economic growth. The recent debate in academic and policy-making circles about growth and poverty reduction has made it clear that the relationship between these two development objectives is less straightforward than is assumed by the MCC. Research has showed that certain conditions (most notably, policies targeting income redistribution) need to be met before growth benefits the poorest segments of society and that there is no spontaneous 'trickle down' of growth (e.g. Klasen 2004: 80–1).

5.4.2 Selection criteria and MCA methodology

Upon the introduction of the MCA, many commentators have applauded the boldness of the programme's methodology and selection criteria, as these could mean a break with the past of US development assistance policies. The establishment of the MCC was perceived as an attempt to compensate for the limited effectiveness of USAID and, in particular, to reduce the influence of Congress on day-to-day operations in the development assistance area. Radelet (2003: 2), among others, has repeatedly pointed out that congressional activity led to an 'elaborate web of legislation and directives' around the Foreign Assistance Act of 1961, which 'specifies a remarkable 33 goals, 75 priority areas, and 247 directives' as a result of amendments.

Ever since the programme's inception, the selection criteria and methodology of the MCA have attracted a fair amount of criticism. The discussion in the remainder of this sub-section focuses, first, on the MCA criteria, in particular the MCA's use of candidate country's income levels for candidate status and its application of the democracy and corruption indicators. With respect to the MCA methodology, this sub-section focuses on data accuracy, the reliance of the selection on median scores and the more general value of the indicators in the Ruling Justly category.

One of the most contested elements of the MCA approach is its procedure for the selection of candidate countries (see p. 77). Most notably, the decision has been criticised to include, as of FY 2006, lower-middle-income countries for MCA candidate status. Various issues have been raised in respect of the broadening of the category of MCA candidates. Some critics have pointed out that the inclusion of lower-middle-income countries would reduce the MCA funding that is available for the poor countries (e.g. Radelet 2003: 26). Moreover, it has been argued that middle-income countries generally have a significantly higher domestic savings rate than lower-income countries and have access to alternative financing through lending on international capital markets and through the World Bank (e.g. Radelet 2003: 26–7; McClymont 2003: 4–5). Finally, it was felt that the addition of middle-income countries to the group of MCA candidates might increase the weight of strategic and political considerations in MCC decision-making, as this group would contain several countries (such as Colombia, Egypt, Jordan and Turkey) that are generally regarded as strategically important to the United States (e.g. Radelet 2003: 27).

It was noted above that the MCA has been more 'political' in its selection of eligible countries than other examples of aid selectivity that have been discussed in this book. Several indicators used in the selection process are notable signs of the MCA's political orientation. In the first place, a cluster of three indicators (the Freedom House indices on civil liberties and political rights and the World Bank Institute's voice and accountability indicator) is used as a measure of the extent to which developing countries are governed democratically. In the second place, the World Bank Institute's control of corruption indicator is applied to measure the commitment of countries to fighting corruption.

The MCC has decided to use the corruption indicator as a sine qua non for MCA eligibility. Countries that do not score above the median on this indicator are not considered eligible for MCA support. In a report for the House of Representatives, the US Government Accountability Office has noted in 2005 that the three democracy indicators also seem to have acquired a de facto threshold role, in that countries scoring below the median on the three indicators are excluded from MCA funding (see p. 83). The seemingly covert use of the democracy indicators as a 'hurdle' has brought some commentators to the suggestion that, for reasons of transparency and accountability of the MCA process, it would be preferable if democracy would be treated as a sine qua non for eligibility rather than leave it to the discretion of the MCC Board to sift out countries that it considers insufficiently democratic (Herrling and Radelet 2005: 5; Palley 2003: 3; see Section 5.4.3).

The decision to treat corruption as a threshold indicator for MCA eligibility has equally been subject to much debate in Congress as well as among critical observers. The indicator that serves to measure the implementation of anti-corruption policies is taken from the World Bank Institute's database on *Governance Matters*. Two of the researchers who compiled this database have indicated that corruption data should be treated with great care and should probably not be elevated to the status of a threshold variable for MCA eligibility. World Bank Institute staff members Kaufmann and Kraay have cautioned against the uncritical use of the corruption indicator: 'it is important to emphasize that a simple "in-or-out" rule runs the risk of misclassifying some countries precisely because margins of error are not trivial.' Their analysis of the indicator showed that there are only few countries whose 90 per cent confidence interval is entirely above or below the median. As a result, the majority of countries run the risk of being 'mistakenly classified in the bottom half of the sample' (Kaufmann and Kraay 2002: 4–5).

The substantive issues of the choice of selection criteria are connected with some methodological issues. The potential problem of data accuracy and the issue of the margins of error that were discussed above in relation to the corruption indicator have more general applicability. The US Government Accountability Office has pointed out at least three 'difficulties' with the use of MCA indicators in the 2004 and 2005 selection process. In the first place, the margins of error for several indicators are such that a substantial number of countries may be misclassified. In the second place, missing data for certain indicators have significantly reduced the number of countries that could score above the median on those indicators. Finally, the scores on certain indicators appear to have clustered around the median to such a degree that these scores are less useful to distinguish good from worse performers (House of Representatives' Committee on International Relations 2005: 53).

A second methodological problem pertaining to the MCA approach concerns the use of the median as a cut-off point for eligibility. As the median distributes the observations into two halves, it will change very likely over time in any empirical distribution of policy-related variables. Countries run the risk of not being selected despite improving their performance, because their ranking is not so much dependent on their own *absolute* performance, but primarily on their relative performance vis-à-vis all other candidate countries (e.g. Radelet 2003: 46). Moreover, as Radelet (2003: 47) has pointed out, a median-based approach will limit the expansion of the MCA beyond a certain number of qualifying countries, since there will always be a substantial group of countries that miss the median despite improving their performance.

A final methodological problem that is related, first and foremost, to the indicators in the Ruling Justly category is that these are based on an aggregation of subjective judgements on the performance of political systems. The purpose of the data in the *Governance Matters* dataset of the World Bank Institute is not always very clear, nor is it uncontroversial whether they are an adequate reflection of the theoretical variables they are supposed to measure. Arndt and Oman (2006: 69) have pointed out that the *Governance Matters* data reflect a 'sample bias in favour of business-oriented perceptions'. A similar point may apply to the *Freedom House* indicators on political rights and civil liberties, the validity of which has been criticised in the House of Representatives because of the potential politically biased judgements of the organisation (House of Representatives' Committee on International Relations 2003: 29, 38).

5.4.3 The Millennium Challenge Corporation

The final issue that is discussed regarding the MCA and its implementation concerns the role and discretionary influence of the MCC. The discussion in the US Congress on the powers and institutional embedding of the MCC (see p. 77) made it clear from the outset that the creation of a separate government body to execute the programme, did not meet with unanimous enthusiasm in the foreign policy community. Issues that surfaced in the discussion about the position of the MCC were the dispersion of responsibilities for similar development assistance programmes over various bodies within the US government, the resulting problems with formulating a comprehensive and coherent US foreign aid strategy, and the MCC's discretionary authority with respect to the selection of eligible and threshold countries.

The proposal made by the Bush administration to set up a government corporation for the implementation of the MCA, separate from USAID, met with both approval and criticism. Although some argued that USAID had not proved to be a very effective and efficient foreign aid agency – to a large extent because it has been subjected to a multitude of congressional directives (see pp. 73, 76 and 91) – the creation of a separate organisation was not perceived as a step towards a more unified US foreign aid policy. Radelet (2003: 109), among others, has pointed out that the fragmentation of aid programmes across the executive branch 'risks significantly weakening [USAID] and starting a process of slow, painful withering' (cf. McClymont 2003: 6). Some argued in favour of establishing the MCC as an independent office within USAID. In connection to this, Democrat Congressman Tom Lantos proposed that an 'empowered USAID, not more bureaucracy, red tape, and foreign-aid balkanization, is what we need to make MCA a success' (House of Representatives' Committee on International Relations 2003: 3).

Critics who cautioned for the dispersion of foreign aid authority over different bodies, also brought up the lack of a comprehensive and coherent US foreign aid strategy. The existing situation of multiple assistance programmes (see p. 72 above), coupled with major proposals by the Bush administration on the MCA, the PEFPAR and the Middle East Partnership Initiative (MEPI), has created the fear that US foreign aid policy is getting more instead of less disjointed. In addition, US NGOs have pointed to problems with the coherence among various aspects of US foreign policy. In particular, they have noted the effects of economic and trade policies – resulting in subsidies for domestic producers of uncompetitive goods and protectionism vis-à-vis foreign products – that tend to undermine development assistance efforts (NGO Brief in House of Representatives' Committee on International Relations 2003: 50–1). At this moment, it is still too early to judge how successful the appointment of a Director of Foreign Assistance and the development of a Foreign Assistance Strategy to bring together and coordinate these different programmes will actually be.

Finally, the *Commitment to Development Index 2006*, compiled by the Center for Global Development, has indicated that the United States scores poorly on overall selectivity of aid: the United States ranks seventeenth among 21 donors, because a large share of its aid is allocated to less poor countries and there are many relatively undemocratic governments among US aid recipients (Center for Global Development 2006a: 2).

It was noted earlier in this chapter that the Millennium Challenge Act gives the MCC a certain degree of discretion to select countries for MCA eligibility (see p. 81). Several analysts have argued that certain decisions made by the MCC Board are very likely based on political considerations. In particular, decisions to include Georgia and Honduras among the eligible countries in 2004 (Radelet 2004: 5; Easterly 2006: 155) and to incorporate East Timor, Kenya and Yemen in the threshold programme of 2004 (Bhavnani *et al.* 2004: 2) and the Kyrgyz Republic in the programme of 2006 (Herrling 2006: 2) have been criticised for their apparent political bias. The desire to avoid political influences on MCC decision-making has led to a call for greater accountability and transparency of the corporation, for instance, by requiring full disclosure of all deviations from the MCA methodology to Congress (e.g. Herrling 2006; Schaefer and Pasicolan 2003).

5.5 Conclusions

This chapter has analysed the background and implementation of the MCA, a new initiative for development assistance that was announced by US President George W. Bush on the eve of the 'Financing for Development' conference in Monterrey in March 2002. The analysis of the 2002–6 period showed that the implementation of the MCA is lagging behind the original planning, which aimed at increasing the annual budget to $5 billion by 2006. The Iraq war and congressional dynamics have resulted in an allocation of $1.77 billion to the MCC in FY 2006, and probably not more than $2 billion in 2007.

The MCA has been designed as an aid programme that should benefit, first and foremost, those developing countries that have demonstrated 'good governance' in their political system and their economic and social policies. For the purpose of ranking countries, the MCC selected 16 quantifiable indicators in three rubrics ('ruling justly, encouraging economic freedom and investing in people'). Low-income countries – and, since FY 2006, also lower-middle-income countries – that scored above the median on at least half the indicators in each of the three categories would qualify for MCA assistance. In the years since its existence, the MCC selected between 16 and 23 countries as 'eligible' for MCA support. Another group of countries, which missed the target by one or two indicators, has been selected for a 'threshold programme' that should help them qualify for the MCA in the future. Until the end of 2006, nine MCA compacts have been signed, with a total value of just over $2 billion.

The evaluation of the MCA focused on three elements: the MCA's policy theory, its selection criteria and methodology, and the role of the MCC. With regard to the policy theory, the overriding political nature of the aims and objectives of the MCA is very interesting, in particular in the light of the much more technocratic and neo-liberal interpretation of governance that was found to characterise the World Bank's and Dutch selectivity approaches. At the same time, the MCA's highly selective character can be questioned, as developing countries that have improved their governance quality, but not yet reached the level desired by the MCC, will not be considered under this assistance programme. Further, the limited size of the MCA's threshold programme could mean that potential qualifiers will get too little support to improve institutional weaknesses and fight corruption. The dominance of economic growth in MCA's policy theory can be questioned, since research has found much less evidence for the contribution of economic growth to poverty reduction than is assumed by the MCC. In particular, the 'trickle down' of wealth to poorer groups appears to be highly contingent upon a set of additional policy conditions.

With respect to the MCA's selection criteria and its methodology, it was observed that the inclusion of middle-income countries among the candidates for assistance under the MCA is problematic, as this will reduce the funds available for the poorest countries. Moreover, the use of the various democracy indicators and the corruption indicator appear to be problematic. The three democracy variables, which appear to have served as de facto threshold indicators but have not

96 The US and the MCA

formally been accepted as such, give the MCC unwarranted discretion in specific selection decisions. The use of corruption as a threshold indicator has been criticised because of severe potential measurement problems. Further, the use of the median as a cut-off point for eligibility is unfortunate, because this parameter changes over time. Finally, it was observed that certain indicators, which are based on the aggregation of subjective judgements about political systems, may be biased in particular ways.

The role of the MCC is potentially to be applauded, as this agency is not subject to the kind of political restrictions that have traditionally hindered USAID. At the same time, the creation of yet another aid agency in the US government was felt to be a possible barrier to the formulation of a unified foreign assistance strategy. The discretionary powers of the MCC, which were also mentioned above, may enhance the possibilities for more politically motivated selection decisions.

6 Selectivity and good governance in the United Kingdom, Denmark and the European Union

6.1 Introduction

Chapters 3–5 discussed a series of cases where selectivity mechanisms for aid allocation had been introduced over the last decade. Although the instruments applied by the World Bank, the Netherlands and the United States were shown to be quite different, the common element of all three approaches was the belief that the effectiveness of development assistance would be enhanced if a substantial part of aid funds were to be allocated to developing countries that had introduced good policies and institutions ('good governance').

The discussion of the paradigm shift in development assistance, in Chapter 2, made it clear that the objectives, modalities and conditions of aid have undergone important change as a result of the renewed concern with aid effectiveness. The Millennium Development Goals (MDGs) have become a rallying point in the current development policy debate. Aid modalities such as sector-wide approaches, budget support and poverty reduction strategy papers (PRSPs) were heralded by many in the international development community. Selectivity of well-performing countries ('ex post conditionality') was advocated to get away from ineffective policy conditionalities.

Despite the general acceptance of the policy message that aid works in countries with good institutions and good policies, rather few countries and multilateral institutions have adopted country selectivity as an explicit principle in their assistance policies. Instead, many bilateral and multilateral donors have addressed the issue of governance in other ways and have started to implement programmes that differ considerably from the selectivity approaches described in the previous three chapters. In doing so, these donors have sometimes introduced particular forms of aid selectivity. A recent analysis of aid selectivity by two World Bank staff members indicates that the aid programmes of the International Development Association, the International Monetary Fund (the Enhanced Structural Adjustment Facility), the African Development Fund, the Netherlands, Denmark and the United Kingdom showed consistently high levels of selectivity between 1999 and 2002, while Norwegian aid and Swedish aid were selective during part of that period (Dollar and Levin 2004: 20). In general, the larger aid donors (such as the United States, Japan and the European

Union) turned out to be much less selective in aid allocation than the smaller ones.[1]

In this chapter, three alternative approaches to selectivity and good governance are discussed. Section 6.2 focuses on the development assistance policy of the United Kingdom and describes how considerations of aid effectiveness and the perceived need to work towards improved governance in developing countries have affected recent policy positions. Section 6.3 discusses the development assistance policies of Denmark, which has been one of the most generous providers of aid to developing countries since the 1980s, and focuses on its decision to select some 20 'programme countries'. Section 6.4 describes the policy of the European Union vis-à-vis developing countries. The discussion in this section zeroes in on the relationship between the European Union (EU) and its traditional 'clientele' – the former colonies in Africa, the Pacific and the Caribbean – and analyses the recent changes in the EU's common development policy, most notably its increasing selectivity in terms of socio-economic sectors. Section 6.5 concludes the chapter.

6.2 Assistance policies of the United Kingdom

The current British Labour government, headed by Prime Minister Tony Blair, has paid much attention to development assistance right from the start of its tenure in May 1997. Important institutional changes regarding development aid policy included changing the Overseas Development Administration, which had been part of the Foreign and Commonwealth Office, into the separate Department for International Development (DFID) and upgrading the status of the minister in charge to full cabinet status (Morrissey 2005: 161–3). Morrissey (2005) has pointed out that apart from the increase in funds that were made available for British development assistance, three major substantive changes were introduced by the Labour government. These changes already shone through in the White Paper that was presented by Clare Short, after having been in office for half a year (Secretary of State for International Development 1997).

In the first place, DFID started to place much emphasis on partnerships with developing countries aimed at poverty reduction, instead of focusing on the spending of aid funds and on the use of these to serve British economic interests (Morrissey 2005: 164). DFID emphasised the need to focus on the international development targets, the predecessor to the MDGs, as the basis for such partnerships (Secretary of State for International Development 1997: 36).

In the second place, the allocation of aid started to become more concentrated on fewer poor countries (Morrissey 2005: 170). Although by the financial year[2] 2005/6 DFID had country programmes in about 60 countries, only 23 countries in Africa, Asia and the Middle East were receiving more than £25 million annually in British aid. The aid allocated to these 23 countries accounted for 85.4 per cent of the total amount spent on country and regional programmes in the 2005/6 financial year, which in its turn was 43.9 per cent of total DFID spending (Department for International Development 2006a: 221, 224–5). Dyer *et al.*

(2003: 7) have calculated that aid flows to sub-Saharan Africa increased by 118 per cent and those to South Asia by 170 per cent in the period between 1997 and 2004, while aid to Eastern Europe and the former Soviet republics in Central Asia fell by 21 per cent and aid to the overseas territories decreased by 47 per cent. In a recent analysis of the history of British aid, Killick (2005: 673) has pointed out that UK assistance continues to have a 'persistently large share of Commonwealth country recipients'. Table 6.1 gives an overview of the major recipients in the UK's country aid programme in the financial year 2005/6.

In addition to concentrating aid on fewer recipients, DFID has increased its spending through new aid modalities. In the financial year 2005/6, so-called poverty reduction budget support (PRBS) accounted for 25 per cent of the UK's bilateral programme, an increase of 3 percentage points compared with the previous year (Department for International Development 2006a: 163). When compared with Morrissey's (2005: 172) estimate that budget support accounted for 15 per cent of bilateral aid in 2000, the current use of the new aid delivery mechanism shows a remarkable increase over previous years.

In the third place, DFID policies have demonstrated a deliberate move away from tied aid. By 2002, all aid was effectively freed of the condition that it be spent in the United Kingdom (Morrissey 2005: 174). The United Kingdom's

Table 6.1 Major recipients in the UK's country aid programme, 2005/6 (in thousands of pound sterling)

Country	Estimated outturn
India	248,000
Sudan	119,300
Bangladesh	119,000
Tanzania	110,000
Afghanistan	102,000
Pakistan	75,800
Uganda	70,600
Ghana	70,100
Nigeria	70,100
Iraq	64,800
Malawi	64,000
Ethiopia	63,700
Vietnam	55,000
Mozambique	54,800
Democratic Republic of the Congo	54,600
Kenya	50,200
Rwanda	46,000
Zambia	40,200
Zimbabwe	39,500
Sierra Leone	38,300
China	33,600
Nepal	32,000
South Africa	25,800

Source: Department for International Development 2006a: 224–5.

policy orientation on development assistance has also displayed more awareness of the international context, which showed in the attention for the coherence of development and economic policies, the functioning of international institutions and regimes (also referred to as 'global good governance', cf. Secretary of State for International Development 2006: 8) and the international coordination of donor policies (Morrissey 2005: 173–9).

The case of UK development policy resembles the increased emphasis on governance quality that has come to characterise most other bilateral and multilateral donors over the last decade. For DFID, good governance is the linchpin for successful poverty reduction. Hilary Benn, Secretary of State for International Development since October 2003, has phrased the emphasis of good governance in a recent White Paper as follows:

> Whether states are effective or not – whether they are capable of helping business grow, and of delivering services to their citizens, and are accountable and responsive to them – is the single most important factor that determines whether or not successful development takes place. Good governance requires: capability – the extent to which government has the money, people, will and legitimacy to get things done; responsiveness – the degree to which government listens to what people want and acts on it; and accountability – the process by which people are able to hold government to account.
>
> (Secretary of State for International Development 2006: 8)

Department for International Development's focus on partnership, its desire to establish 'mutual accountability' of donors and recipients of aid (a concept derived from the Paris Declaration on Aid Effectiveness, see High-Level Forum on Aid Effectiveness 2005) and its emphasis of good governance have resulted in a search for new arrangements with developing countries. Two interlinked approaches have been adopted to marry 'mutual accountability' with a good governance focus. On the one hand, the United Kingdom has come out with Development Partnership Arrangements with several developing countries. These arrangements seek to focus the aid relationship on targets that are in line with the MDGs, involve long-term engagement (up to ten years), and are explicit about the mutual responsibilities of the United Kingdom and the recipient country (Department for International Development 2003: 40).

On the other hand, DFID has developed a new philosophy on conditions for aid relationships. The department found it necessary to do so because it rejects old-style conditionalities but argues that '[d]eveloping countries need to know what aid they can expect when, and to be clear under what circumstances it can be withdrawn' (Secretary of State for International Development 2004: 1).

The outcome of the process of reconsideration of conditionalities was that DFID declared to be selective in its future aid relationships and would require the *ex ante* commitment of prospective partner countries to three objectives: '(a) poverty reduction and the Millennium Development Goals; (b) respecting human rights and other international obligations; and (c) strengthening financial management and accountability, which reduces the risk of funds being misused through weak administration or corruption' (Secretary of State for International Development 2005: 8). In case of a breach of the commitments, the UK response either could be to suspend or stop aid to the country concerned or could decide to change the form of aid delivery (for instance, away from the government to non-governmental channels) (Department for International Development 2006b: 12).

In order to monitor commitment to the three partnership objectives, DFID proposed a methodology, including a set of benchmarks. For the monitoring of the commitment to poverty reduction, DFID planned to agree with recipient governments a set of 'two or three benchmarks' on poverty reduction (Department for International Development 2006b: 6–7). The commitment to human rights and international obligations would be monitored by using various reports (including those drafted by the European Commission) on the human rights situation in the country (Department for International Development 2006b: 7–9). Monitoring of the commitment to strengthen financial management and anti-corruption policies would involve the use of 'partner countries' own data sources and/or other public financial management and accountability diagnostic studies' (Department for International Development 2006b: 9). According to DFID's Departmental Report 2006, the monitoring of the partnership objectives had resulted in the interruption, delay or suspension of aid in 11 cases during the 2005/6 financial year (Department for International Development 2006a: 159).

In addition to the monitoring of recipient countries' commitment to the three partnership objectives, the 2006 White Paper on International Development has announced the use of a new 'quality of governance' assessment to monitor whether governance is getting better or worse. The latter assessment would be used alongside the monitoring of the partnership objectives to determine the way in which UK aid is given. In cases where the assessment of governance is positive, the United Kingdom would have a preference for providing aid in the form of budget support. In cases where the governance assessment is less favourable, other aid modalities would be chosen. In countries where the government has not shown a clear commitment to poverty reduction, the United Kingdom would choose to work outside the government, through multilateral agencies, such as the United Nations, or non-governmental organisations (NGOs) (Secretary of State for International Development 2006: 24).

Department for International Development's approach of the issue of governance has, finally, led to an emphasis of so-called 'drivers of change'. The intention of the Drivers of Change approach is to get better information about the potential levers of better governance and poverty reduction in developing countries. The approach pays more attention to the political dynamics of good and bad governance than other programmes, which tend to be more technocratic in their outlook (Hulme and Chhotray 2006: 14). A summary statement of the Drivers of Change approach describes the philosophy behind the programme as follows:

'Drivers of Change' examines 'what is driving change' in the countries where DFID is active. This is to address the fact that, 'DFID and other donors find it easier to say "what" needs to be done to reduce poverty than "how" to help make it happen.' By better understanding *how change occurs* within specific contexts, it is hypothesised that DFID's programming decisions will be better equipped to respond to this 'how' question and help bring about pro-poor change. DoC therefore emphasises DFID's need to understand economic, political and social contexts, in other words, the application of political economy analysis to formulation of donor strategy and implementation.

(Warrener 2004: 1)

The Drivers of Change approach claims not to provide a blueprint to judge governance quality but rather to provide a set of key questions with the help of which actors, institutions and structural features can be identified that together determine the likelihood of change and the possibilities for applying change for poverty reduction (Department for International Development 2004: 2).

In general, there does not seem to be a publicly transparent mechanism for the allocation of UK development assistance across countries. A plausible hypothesis seems to be that British aid is allocated primarily to countries that are of importance to the United Kingdom (such as the former colonies that are part of the Commonwealth), with particular attention to those countries with the highest poverty incidence. This hypothesis is supported by the remarkable stability of major recipients of UK development assistance over the last decade. Despite the change from a Conservative to a Labour government, which induced a radical reorientation of British aid policy and a rapid increase of the budget for aid, many of the 23 major aid recipients in 2005/6 (listed in table 6.1) ranked among the top 20 recipients in 1994/5. Sixteen[3] of the 23 major aid recipients in 2005/6 received more than £15 million (or 1.5 per cent) of the United Kingdom's total bilateral aid budget in 1994/5. The share of these 16 countries in bilateral aid allocations was roughly 71 per cent in 1994/5 (Organisation for Economic Co-operation and Development 2002: 75).

Various documents provide indications of how allocation procedures have been applied in the past. The United Kingdom's country selection process has been informed by two targets that have been laid down in so-called Public Service Agreements (PSAs) between DFID and the Treasury Department (PSA 2003–6 and PSA 2005–8). The current targets in the PSA 2005–8 specify that DFID's aid programmes should induce progress towards the MDGs in 16 key countries in Africa and 9 countries in Asia, while the PSA 2003–6 focused on 16 African and 4 Asian countries (Department for International Development 2006a: 264–5). In addition to these country-related targets, goals have been set for the spending of at least 90 per cent of the United Kingdom's bilateral aid budget on low-income countries (Department for International Development 2006a: 267) and of £1 billion on Africa (Dyer *et al.* 2003: ii).

Selectivity and good governance 103

According to a 2003 review of aid allocation, four main considerations have influenced decisions regarding bilateral development assistance:

- the 'income poverty MDG' is seen as 'the main driver of resource allocation';
- the transfer of resources should be accompanied by the possibility to influence and promote change that makes effective use of aid;
- there is a desire to achieve greater focus and concentrated effort in aid delivery;
- aid should support good performers, 'while not overlooking countries in conflict or those with difficult policy environments' (Dyer *et al.* 2003: 5).

The review team arrive at the conclusion that '[r]ecent allocation decisions suggest DFID is moving towards responding to performance and needs, but tentatively' (Dyer *et al.* 2003: 15).[4]

6.3 Assistance policies of Denmark

Denmark has traditionally been one of the so-called 'like-minded donors' with regard to development assistance, alongside the other Nordic countries, the Netherlands and – at least since the 'Short-Blair' period – the United Kingdom. Denmark has consistently spent a fair proportion of its budget on development aid: at least since the 1980s, the country has met the target set by the United Nations General Assembly in 1970, to allocate at least 0.7 per cent of gross national product to official development assistance (Olsen 2005a: 185).

According to Olsen (2005a: 190–2), until the defeat of the social democratic party in the 2001 elections and the formation of a liberal–conservative coalition government, Danish aid policy has not been subject to much political debate. Olsen has argued that development assistance in Denmark has served to keep the 'political peace', with a substantial and relatively isolated 'epistemic community' in the civil service, development NGOs and the private sector as its main supporters. The Danish development community has built a common ideology in support of the country's aid effort. In part, the consensus on development assistance has been maintained by the use of aid funds for commercial interests, reflected, among other things, in 'tied' aid. Olsen (2005a: 190) has indicated that 'the Danish Government and the entire Danish policy community on aid have been strongly opposed' to movements to untie aid from spending in Denmark.

Roughly half of the Danish aid budget is spent on bilateral cooperation, while the rest is allocated to support multilateral organisations, as part of the Danish policy of 'active internationalism' (Olsen 2005a: 185, 188–9). Long before the current trends of concentration of development assistance had commenced, Denmark opted for a focusing of its aid on a limited number of countries as well as on specific sectors within its so-called 'programme countries'. During the 1990s, Denmark maintained a relationship with 20 programme countries which, in 1994, were receiving 64 per cent of bilateral aid (Olsen 2005a: 194). In its 2000 White Paper, the Danish aid agency, Danida, indicated that it would keep setting a maximum of 20 programme countries for reasons of capacity constraints and monitoring purposes (Danida 2000a: 71; Danida 2000b: 6).

Danida did also indicate, in its White Paper *Partnership 2000*, that the selection of Denmark's programme countries had not been and would not be based on criteria related to governance quality, despite the embrace of such criteria by other donors. Instead, the agency stipulated that

> [t]he selection of Denmark's 20 programme countries was guided by the criteria set up by the Folketing's Foreign Affairs Committee in 1989. On the basis of the overriding objective of poverty-oriented development co-operation, these criteria call for an assessment of, among other things, each country's economic and social stage of development, its development needs, the possibilities of meaningful dialogue and co-operation, especially on the promotion of democracy and human rights, the environment, the possibilities of involving women in the development process and Denmark's experience hitherto from bilateral development co-operation with the country in question. Finally, the criteria attach importance to the possibilities of involving the Danish business sector in the co-operation.
> (Danida 2000a: 70)

According to Danida, the real challenges for the Danish policy on country selection are how the fulfilment of the criteria by individual countries should be monitored, how Denmark should respond if a country were to experience a dramatic deterioration on one or more of the criteria, and which country should be selected in the place of an underperforming programme country (Danida 2000a: 71).

In 2004, 34 developing countries were receiving Danish aid, but only eight of these obtained more than 5 per cent ($24.7 million) of the budget for bilateral development assistance. Another five countries received between 1 and 5 per cent of the Danish bilateral aid budget (Organisation for Economic Co-operation and Development 2006a). The thirteen countries, which are listed in Table 6.2, together received over 95 per cent of Danish bilateral aid in 2004. Nine of the countries listed in Table 6.2 have been defined as programme countries. With the exception of Bhutan, all programme countries received more than 5 per cent of Denmark's bilateral aid funds.

In 2005, Danida announced its decision to include five additional countries in its bilateral programme: Bolivia, Ghana, Kenya, Nicaragua and Vietnam (Danida 2005: 20). Danida indicated that it would fund one or two sector programmes in these countries with aid budgets averaging $35 million (200 million Danish Kroner) annually between 2005 and 2010, and in some cases amounts up to $85 million (500 million Danish Kroner). In 2006, the Minister for Development Cooperation announced the selection of Mali as a programme country, with an allocation of $59 million in 2007 (Tørnæs 2006: 2).

In addition to focusing its aid efforts on a limited number of programme countries, Denmark was one of the first donor countries to introduce the concept of sector-wide approaches into its aid programme. The 1994 White Paper on

Table 6.2 Major recipients of Danish development assistance, 2004 (in thousands of US dollars)

Country	Disbursements
Programme countries	
Tanzania	93,930
Mozambique	67,420
Uganda	61,310
Bangladesh	45,670
Zambia	45,100
Nepal	34,250
Burkina Faso	32,840
Benin	32,200
Bhutan	18,400
Other countries	
Afghanistan	14,180
Cambodia	10,460
Niger	9,400
Malawi	4,720

Source: Organisation for Economic Co-operation and Development 2006a.

Danish aid policy, called *A World in Development*, embraced the sector-oriented mode as a major policy instrument for poverty reduction. In 2001 and 2002, approximately 45 per cent of the bilateral aid budget was spent on 'social infrastructure' (education, health, water and sanitation, and so on). Three 'crosscutting' concerns of Danish aid policy, introduced in the 1990s, were the participation of women in development, protection of the global environment and the sustainable exploitation of natural resources, and the promotion of democracy and the respect for human rights (Olsen 2005a: 196–7).

Recent Danish policy documents reaffirm the country's focus on poverty as the main inspiration for development cooperation (e.g. Danida 2000b: 10–11; Danida 2003: 4). The Monterrey Consensus and the United Nations' Millennium Declaration (see Chapter 2) serve as the new multilateral foundations for Denmark's policy. In the 2000 White Paper, the Danish government stressed the need to take a broader approach to development and focus not only on economic and social welfare but also on political dimensions:

> The opportunity for all individuals to engage democratically in the decision-making processes that have bearing on their own lives and the future of their countries is equally an integral aspect of human development. ... Denmark wishes to promote democratisation not only because democracy is a development policy objective in itself, but also because democracy promotes sustainable development oriented towards poverty reduction, the prevention of conflicts, respect for the equal participation of women and men, regard for the environment and respect for human rights. Denmark's development policy will promote good governance and administrative practices

free of corruption as an essential element in the creation of pro-poor growth and in fostering stable societies that possess effective mechanisms for peaceful resolution of conflicts.

(Danida 2000b: 32–3)

Danida's 2003 White Paper announced the allocation of approximately $85 million (500 million Danish Kroner) for programmes in the area of human rights, democracy and good governance for the 2004–9 period. These programmes would focus on anti-corruption programmes, support for free and fair elections, reform of the legal sector, support of free media and human rights organisations, and the strengthening of national parliaments and decentralisation. Another $71.5 million (425 million Kroner) was allocated for activities aimed at stability, security and the fight against terrorism (Danida 2003: 7–8). In 2006, the Danish minister for development cooperation announced the allocation of $85 million for 'new good governance activities' in the programme countries, aimed at strengthening public administration and creating a better and more reliable environment for private business (Tørnæs 2006: 4).

In line with the above, Danida's 2004 White Paper announced a new Africa policy and a wider Middle East initiative in an attempt to integrate policies aimed at poverty reduction, improved governance and democratisation (Danida 2004: 8–10). The Middle East programme would aim at strengthening democracy and human rights in several countries in North Africa and the Arab world. In particular, the initiative was meant to counter the 'threat from radical Islamists ... by a long-term and sustained effort to modernise and reform the Arab countries with a targeted partnership programme' (Danida 2005: 17).

6.4 Assistance policies of the European Union

The European Union's interest in development assistance developed out of the concern of its original six member states with their former colonies in Africa, the Caribbean and the Pacific.[5] The so-called Yaoundé and Lomé Conventions were the result of a strategy of 'collective clientelism', which produced 'a relationship in which a group of weak states combine in an effort to exploit the special ties that link them to a more powerful state or group of states' (Ravenhill 1985: 22). The Conventions aimed at establishing a relationship between the group of newly independent African, Caribbean and Pacific (ACP) countries and the former colonial states in Europe that combined elements of aid with trade facilitation. In particular, it was the EU's objective to strengthen the position of ACP countries in international trade by establishing a mechanism for the stabilisation of export earnings and granting the ACP countries preferential access to the European market (Olsen 2005b: 586).

After the end of the Cold War, the EU's outlook on development policy changed. In its external policy, the EU started to pay closer attention to the neighbouring states in Central and Eastern Europe and in the Mediterranean, as developments in these regions were increasingly felt to impact intra-EU relations. As a consequence of the EU's reorientation, countries on the Balkans and in other parts of Europe that had been dominated by the Soviet Union, as well as on the Mediterranean rim started to become increasingly important as recipients of EU assistance.

In 2000, the Lomé Convention was replaced by the Cotonou Agreement. The agreement, which was renewed in 2005, added several new elements to the EU's development policy vis-à-vis the 79 ACP countries. In particular, the Cotonou Agreement contained statements on anti-corruption measures, good governance, political dialogue, peace-building and conflict prevention. Moreover, the Cotonou Agreement included provisions for the creation of so-called Economic Partnership Agreements (EPAs) between the EU and individual ACP countries, which are supposed to be in place by 1 January 2008 and which should contain reciprocal instead of unilateral agreements on market access. According to the EU, the aim of the EPAs would be 'to help [the ACP countries] integrate with their regional neighbours as a step towards global integration, and to help them build institutional capacities and apply principles of good governance' (European Union 2006c). For the 49 least-developed countries, the European Union has removed all export restrictions, with the exception of arms, with the adoption of the 'Everything but Arms Initiative' of 2001 (European Union 2006c).

Two further innovations have been introduced into EU development policy since 2000. In the first place, the EU has attempted to formulate a set of common principles on development assistance. In November 2000, the European Council and the European Commission issued a declaration on development policy, which focused on poverty reduction as the 'principal aim' of EU development cooperation and called for the 'refocusing' of EU policies on a limited number of areas. The declaration mentioned six areas as key to this refocusing: the link between trade and development; regional integration and cooperation; support for macro-economic policies and the promotion of equitable access to social services; transport; food security and sustainable rural development; and institutional capacity building (European Union 2000: 3–6).

In December 2005, the European Council, Commission and Parliament reached agreement on the so-called 'European Consensus on Development'. The European Consensus emphasised the need to concentrate EU development assistance 'to ensure aid effectiveness'. Concentration would imply the selection of 'a strictly limited number of areas for action when Community aid is being programmed, instead of spreading efforts too thinly over too many sectors' (European Union 2006a: 11). The EU singled out the following areas, where it argued it had 'comparative advantages':

- trade and regional integration;
- the environment and the sustainable management of natural resources;
- infrastructure, communications and transport;
- water and energy;
- rural development, territorial planning, agriculture and food security;
- governance, democracy, human rights and support for economic and institutional reforms;

- conflict prevention and fragile states;
- human development; and
- social cohesion and employment (European Union 2006a: 11–15).

Like most aid policy documents, the European Consensus focuses on budget support as 'the preferred modality for support to economic and fiscal reforms and implementation of PRS' in countries where the structures allow such a form of aid (European Union 2006a: 17).

In the second place, the European Commission created the EuropeAid Cooperation Office to implement assistance policies funded by the EU budget and the European Development Fund (EDF). EuropeAid has been set up to act as a 'bridge' between the two central Directorates-General that deal with EU aid: the Directorate-General for Development (DG DEV) and the Directorate-General for External Relations (DG RELEX) (Richelle 2004). The EDF, which has existed since the start of the European Economic Community in 1958, has been separate from the overall EU budget and has been financed by the member states to supply aid to the ACP countries and the overseas countries and territories. In addition to the EDF, regular EU funds have been used for development assistance to countries in Asia and Latin America; these funds have generally been channelled through EuropeAid. Most aid flows to the Balkans and Turkey have been administered by other Directorates-General of the European Union (European Union 2006b).

The analysis of the general orientation of EU policy making on aid indicates that selectivity, in the EU context, is oriented more towards sectors than countries. The explanation of this tendency does not seem difficult: as a regional organisation in which external policy making is still dominated by intergovernmental practices and procedures, the selection of countries requires more or less general agreement. In such a political framework, negotiations on aid allocation easily end up as trade-offs between different favoured partner countries – an outcome that is still captured quite well by Ravenhill's (1985) concept of collective clientelism.

Although the European Union, for political reasons, has not used any explicit criteria for the selection of partner countries, the European Commission has nevertheless made attempts to build governance-related elements into aid relationships. A first step in this direction was the inclusion of so-called 'essential element' clauses, relating to the respect for fundamental human rights and democratic principles, into agreements between the EU and third countries since the beginning of the 1990s. On the basis of these clauses, the EU would consider 'a range of measures' in response to serious violations of human and the democratic order, including the alteration of the content of cooperation programmes, postponement of new projects and, in extreme cases, the suspension of cooperation (European Commission 2003: 8). Similarly, the Cotonou Agreement of 2000 contained articles that specified EU action in case of violations of human rights, democratic principles, the rule of law and good governance. Consultations would be a first step, termination of a partnership the last resort. The Commission indicated that it has acted on the 'essential element' clauses in 12 cases between 1995 and 2003, of which ten concerned ACP countries (European Commission 2003: 9).

In 2003, the European Commission presented a framework on governance and development that contained a distinction between three types of relations: 'difficult partnership', 'post-conflict' and 'effective partnership'. Each of these relations, the Commission argued, would require different approaches. In the case of difficult partnerships, which are 'characterised by a lack of commitment to good governance' (European Commission 2003: 20), alternative approaches to cooperation would have to be found, including the provision of humanitarian aid, collaboration with NGOs and civil society organisations, and political initiatives at the international and regional level. In 'extremely difficult partnerships' the only option would be to suspend cooperation entirely (European Commission 2003: 21).

In post-conflict situations, where state institutions are either non-functioning or non-existent, the priority would be reconciliation between parties involved in the conflict, the linking of relief to rehabilitation and development, and the provision of humanitarian aid. The aim of the approach would be to bring the authorities to address governance issues, which were at the root of the conflict in many cases (European Commission 2003: 24).

Effective cooperation partnerships, characterised by a commitment of the government to development objectives and internationally agreed targets, would call for close involvement of the European Union in supporting the adoption of 'adequate policies and pro-poor reform programmes' (European Commission 2003: 27). Concrete elements of EU development assistance in those cases could include: support of the strengthening of democratic processes, participation and the rule of law, support of human rights activities, and support of accountability, transparency and effectiveness of state institutions (European Commission 2003: 27).

Data indicate that European development assistance has traditionally been quite dispersed over a large number of recipients. The figures presented in Table 6.3 indicate that the ACP countries, as a group, are still the most important targets of assistance managed by EuropeAid. In 2005, the ACP countries were followed in importance by the Mediterranean countries, Asian countries, the Balkans, the Newly Independent States (former Soviet republics), Latin America and South Africa. Total allocations to the second most important group (the Mediterranean countries) were, however, not more than roughly one-third of the allocations to the ACP group.

Apart from the allocations of EU development assistance through EuropeAid, which are summarised in Table 6.3, the EU aid budget of 2005 contained over €1.8 billion in so-called 'official aid' (European Commission 2006a: 169). These funds were allocated, separate from EuropeAid, to a selection of more advanced developing countries (Cyprus, Malta and Slovenia) and countries in transition (primarily Bulgaria and Romania, which were candidates for EU membership).

110   *Selectivity and good governance*

Table 6.3 Regional breakdown of commitments of external assistance managed by EuropeAid and DG Enlargement, 2001 and 2005 (percentages of total allocation)

	2001	2005
Africa, Caribbean and Pacific (ACP)	35.4	44.2
Mediterranean, Near and Middle East (MEDA)	12.7	13.4
Asia	7.3	10.4
Western Balkans	12.7	6.5
Eastern Europe and Central Asia	7.7	6.4
Latin America	5.4	4.1
South Africa	2.2	1.9
Thematic	16.7	13.1
Total (in millions of euros)	5,568	8,027

Source: European Commission 2006c: 12.

Note
Due to different approaches to regional and country breakdown by the EU, the figures in this table are not fully comparable with those of Tables 6.4 and 6.5.

Analysis of the full list of aid recipients demonstrates that EU development assistance is very fragmented. The list of recipients included 136 developing countries and territories in 2005. Of all countries receiving EU aid, 27 received allocations of more than 1 per cent of the total budget for official development assistance (equivalent to €88.1 million or more, see Table 6.4). The sum of EU aid commitments to these countries amounted to a little over 50 per cent of total aid funds. In addition to these 27 recipients, 18 countries received allocations of 0.5 per cent or more of the EU aid budget. The share of the 45 countries in the total funds allocated in 2005 was 61.6 per cent. The remaining 91 developing countries together received allocations amounting to 38.4 per cent of EU aid funds (European Commission 2006a: 165–8).

Table 6.5 provides an overview of the sectoral orientation of EU external assistance, which is a good approximation of the way in which development aid is allocated. The figures on total external assistance indicate that almost 88 per cent of the aid funds is allocated to one of four sectors: social infrastructure and services (43.5 per cent), economic infrastructure and services (16.3 per cent), commodity aid and general programme assistance (16.9 per cent) and emergency assistance (10.0 per cent). Within these broad sectors, governance and civil society, transport and storage, and general budget support are important activities for EU assistance.

The breakdown of commitments per region indicates that the relative emphasis of sectoral allocations differs between the regions. Education has received relatively much attention in EU policies vis-à-vis Latin America, Asia, and Eastern Europe and Central Asia. Health programmes have targeted Asian countries above average. Programmes aimed at improving the economic infrastructure, in particular transport and storage, have been very pronounced in the ACP countries. Programmes targeting the production sector – most notably, the

Table 6.4 Major recipients of EU official development assistance, 2005 (in millions of euros)

Country	Commitments
Serbia and Montenegro*	314.01
Turkey*	286.83
Uganda	239.83
Afghanistan	224.48
Niger	209.27
Congo, Democratic Republic	199.10
Sudan	188.01
Bangladesh	186.92
Mozambique	183.53
Burkina Faso	183.52
Malawi	165.10
South Africa	154.33
Tanzania	146.11
Palestinian Territories	145.03
Morocco	141.76
Pakistan	140.75
Senegal	138.83
Mali	138.30
Haiti	134.80
Madagascar	134.45
Chad	131.58
Ukraine	129.74
Tunisia	120.30
Egypt	110.80
Croatia*	102.90
Ethiopia	95.63
Ghana	93.50

Source: European Commission 2006a: 165–8.

Note
* Assistance to this country was managed largely by EU Directorates-General not connected to EuropeAid, such as DG Enlargement.

industrial sector and trade policy and regulation – have been important for Latin America. General budget support programmes seem to have been targeted primarily on the ACP countries, while they were hardly or not at all used in the relationship with countries in Asia, Eastern Europe and Central Asia, Latin America and the other developing countries. In 2005, funds for emergency assistance have been allocated above average to Asia, which suffered from the tsunami in December 2004 and the earthquake in Pakistan in October 2005, and the Mediterranean and the Near and Middle East, where the European Union made large financial contributions to the reconstruction of Iraq.

Table 6.5 Sectoral and regional breakdown of commitments of external assistance managed by EuropeAid, 2005 (percentages of total allocation)

Sector	ACP	MEDA	Asia	EE/CA	Latin America	Other	Total
Social infrastructure and services, of which:	35.4	46.3	56.3	50.2	49.9	39.0	43.5
Education	6.2	6.8	15.1	11.0	15.6	–	7.6
Health	4.8	0.5	18.0	2.6	4.3	9.6	6.4
Water supply and sanitation	9.5	9.2	–	9.1	3.2	–	7.1
Government and civil society	13.2	15.7	17.0	19.2	10.1	9.4	14.5
Other social infrastructure	1.0	14.2	6.1	8.1	16.4	18.9	7.3
Economic infrastructure and services, of which:	23.0	11.6	2.1	21.5	17.6	0.1	16.3
Transport and storage	21.1	2.2	2.0	3.4	14.7	–	12.4
Production sectors	5.6	3.7	1.1	2.4	18.2	2.6	4.9
Multisector/crosscutting activities	5.2	4.9	5.4	14.9	6.9	6.1	6.4
Commodity aid and general programme assistance, of which:	25.3	15.1	6.9	6.9	0.9	1.3	16.9
General budget support	19.4	13.3	0.9	–	–	–	12.1
Food aid/food security assistance	5.9	1.8	6.0	6.9	0.9	1.3	4.8
Emergency assistance	5.1	16.9	25.9	–	2.9	11.6	10.0
Other/unallocated/unspecified	0.5	1.7	2.4	4.3	4.0	5.2	2.0
Total (in millions of euros)	3,873	1,109	919	582	347	670	7,500

Source: European Commission 2006a: 171.

Notes

The figures in this table include an estimated 3 per cent of Official Development Assistance. MEDA – Mediterranean and Near and Middle East; EE/CA – Eastern Europe and Central Asia.

6.5 Conclusions

This chapter has focused on several cases of aid donors that have decided not to adopt a country selection framework in their development assistance policies, despite their apparent agreement with the assumption that governance quality is important for developing countries, both for their prospects of development, and for aid effectiveness. The discussions in Sections 6.2–6.4 have made clear that the United Kingdom, Denmark and the European Union have introduced forms of aid selectivity that differ from the variants of ex post conditionality adopted by the World Bank, the Netherlands and the United States.

The discussion of the policies implemented by DFID in the United Kingdom indicated that British development aid has become rather selective, both in terms of the countries that are targeted and in terms of the aid modalities applied. Moreover, it was shown that the concern for governance quality has permeated British policy making on aid. The monitoring of governance in the countries that have been selected for an aid relationship with the United Kingdom appears to have become more important than the selection of countries per se. In particular, the introduction of three 'partnership objectives' (poverty reduction, respect for human rights and the strengthening of financial management and accountability) and the adoption of a separate governance quality assessment seem to offer DFID the possibility to respond fairly quickly to changes in the governance situation in the partner countries. Finally, the so-called 'Drivers of Change' approach would ideally give DFID the tools to identify which actors and institutions in developing countries may engage in political and social action that would benefit the poor.

Danish bilateral aid policies have been relatively stable since the first half of the 1990s. In that period, the Danish government decided to concentrate development assistance on a relatively small number of developing countries. The so-called 'programme countries' were selected on the basis of a set of criteria, which included development needs, democracy and human rights and the role of women in development. It was clear from the outset that opportunities for the Danish private sector weighed heavily on the selection of programme countries. The Danish aid agency Danida was at the forefront of the movement among donors to shift from project aid to sector-wide programmes. Denmark's selective approach to countries seems to have been matched by an equally selective orientation to sectors, as approximately half the funds for bilateral assistance have been spent in the social sectors, and a limited number of other activities (such as human rights, democracy and good governance, and women participation in development) were chosen.

The development assistance policy of the European Union can be located 'in the middle of the pack' in terms of aid selectivity, according to Dollar and Levin (2004: 12). The EU has traditionally concentrated its aid efforts on the former colonies of its member states in Africa, the Caribbean and the Pacific. Despite the increased political importance of other regions – most notably the Balkans, Eastern Europe and Central Asia, and the Mediterranean – allocations of EU

114 *Selectivity and good governance*

assistance have maintained a distinct ACP focus. As a multilateral organisation, the European Union needs to balance the political preferences and interests of its member states, and this feature may explain that aid has been allocated to a relatively large number of recipient countries. Despite the fact that there are important variations across regions, EU aid flows seem to be relatively concentrated in a few sectors: social infrastructure and services, economic infrastructure and services, commodity aid and general programme assistance, and emergency assistance.

The overall conclusion of this chapter is that selected bilateral and multilateral aid donors seem to have followed the trend towards greater aid selectivity that was analysed in Chapter 2. Although the United Kingdom, Denmark and the European Union have not adopted an explicit framework for country selectivity and aid allocation analogous to the cases discussed in Chapters 3–5, they have introduced particular selectivity measures with a view to enhancing aid effectiveness. The initiatives that were taken by the United Kingdom, Denmark and the European Union were shown to vary from the monitoring of recipient countries' progress on poverty reduction and the improvement of governance quality (as in the case of the United Kingdom's DFID) to the limiting of the number of recipient countries and/or targeted sectors within these countries to ensure proper implementation and management of aid relations (as in Danish and EU development policy) and the introduction of programmes to improve aspects of governance in the partner countries (in all three examples). The cases discussed in this chapter and those of the previous three chapters underline that allocation decisions about aid and, a fortiori, the decision to adopt aid selectivity criteria are ultimately highly political. The multitude of cases of limited aid selectivity (Dollar and Levin 2004) indicates that far fewer donor countries and organisations seem to have introduced measures to target development assistance at poorer and/or relatively well-governed countries than would be expected on the basis of the policy consensus that was signalled in Chapter 2.

7 Quantitative-empirical analyses of World Bank, Dutch and US aid selectivity

7.1 Introduction

This chapter represents a change in methodology, away from the policy analyses of the previous chapters, to quantitative-empirical analysis of the aid policies implemented by the World Bank, the Netherlands and the United States. The objective of the tests in this chapter is to find out whether, and to what extent, the claims made about aid selectivity at the policy level are borne out by empirical data. More concretely, the analyses presented in this chapter test whether it is possible to explain the choices made in World Bank, Dutch and US policies related to the selection of aid recipients and the allocation of aid on the basis of the criteria that had been introduced as part of the move towards greater selectivity (in particular, governance quality and poverty level). The findings from the analyses are important, as they serve as a test of the extent to which the policy rhetoric is matched by actual changes in day-to-day policy implementation.

The analyses in this chapter are reported following Neumayer's (2003: 2) important analytical distinction between the eligibility and level stages of aid allocation. Considerations of eligibility relate to the question: which countries are selected for particular aid programmes and which are not? In an analytical sense, the eligibility stage can be understood as the first phase of decision-making on aid selectivity. The level stage concerns the decisions on the actual allocation of aid funds over the selected aid recipients and can be seen as the second phase of decision-making.

This chapter reports the main findings of the analyses of World Bank, Dutch and US policies of aid selectivity. Section 7.2 discusses the details of the research design and methodology, as well as the data that are used in the empirical analyses. Sections 7.3–7.5 review the major findings of the quantitative analyses of the three cases that have been studied in previous chapters. Section 7.6 contains some conclusions that derive from the empirical analyses.

7.2 Research design and methodology

The policies targeting aid selectivity are of relatively recent date. Partly as a result of this, empirical studies focusing on this new trend in development assistance are still relatively scarce. Recent examples of studies that focus on the relationship between aid allocation and governance-related variables include the studies by Easterly (2002: 37–8), Hout (2002, 2007), Neumayer (2003), and Dollar and Levin (2004). Since the 1970s, a good number of studies have tried to explain the allocation of aid, and several of these have included democracy, corruption and political and civil rights as explanatory variables (for an overview, see Neumayer 2003: 21–9). Most of the latter studies, however, represent research agendas that are different from the current one, and their approach to explaining aid allocation is less relevant for this study.

The empirical tests reported in the following sections follow a design that takes on board some of the features of Neumayer's and Dollar and Levin's approaches. The analyses follow Neumayer in distinguishing the eligibility from the level stage of aid allocation. The approach adopted here is different from Neumayer's (2003: 33–50) in that it does not use panel data. Neumayer's study focused on the aid allocations of major donors between 1991 and 2000 and attempted to explain annual aid allocations by using lagged variables on governance quality, donor interests, recipient needs and a range of other features. The present study recognises that decisions on development assistance are typically made in annual budgetary cycles but argues that such annual decisions reflect more durable policy orientations that are the outcome of particular multilateral negotiations (as in the case of the World Bank's International Development Association (IDA)), government coalition agreements (as in the Netherlands) or executive–legislative interactions (as in the United States). For this reason, the current study focuses on country selections and aid allocations in clearly distinguishable policy periods. In the case of IDA, the relevant policy period is the 3-year replenishment round (in this case, IDA12 and IDA13, during 1999–2002 and 2002–5, respectively).[1] For the Netherlands, the appropriate policy period is that of particular coalition agreements (in this case, the agreements of the Kok and Balkenende governments, spanning 1998–2002, 2002–3[2] and 2003–7, respectively). The relevant policy period for the United States is largely determined by the duration of the president's tenure (in this case, the two periods of the Bush administration, starting with the adoption of the Millennium Challenge Act of 2003).

The current study also differs from Neumayer's in its choice of explanatory variables. Neumayer (2003: 44–8) opted for a model in which aid eligibility and aid allocation were regressed on several independent variables, including governance quality, recipient need and a range of donor interest indicators. The present analyses focus more explicitly on governance quality and poverty indicators and use only one variable for donor interest. In doing so, this study is closer to Dollar and Levin's (2004) analysis of policy and poverty selectivity of development assistance.

The quantitative analyses reported in the following sections have been performed using two variants of regression analysis. The choice for this estimation technique, which is in line with the large majority of studies in this area (see Neumayer 2003: 21–9), has been based on the fact that the data are measured at levels that are appropriate for the application of regression analysis. The variant used for the analyses of the eligibility stage of aid allocation is logistic regression, which is a technique that attempts to find a best-fitting model to represent the relationship between a binary dependent variable (with scores 0 and 1) and a set of independent variables. Logistic regression results in an estimate, applying the maximum likelihood method, of the overall fit of the specified model and of the relative importance of each of the explanatory variables (Hosmer and Lemeshow 1989). The analyses of the level stage have been performed with ordinary least-squares regression, which results in the estimation of a model consisting of variables measured at the ratio level.

The dependent variables in the analyses of the eligibility stage reflect whether developing countries from the low-income and lower-middle-income group (World Bank 2006) were considered eligible for assistance. In the case of the Netherlands and the US MCA, scores were assigned to the 113 developing countries on the basis of their eligibility (1) and non-eligibility (0) for assistance. A separate category was introduced for countries that are eligible for the MCA's threshold programme. In the case of the IDA, countries were assigned 0 if they had not been allocated any funds by IDA in the relevant policy periods.[3]

The dependent variables for the level stage analyses are the allocations of official development assistance to the 113 low-income and lower-middle-income countries, in millions of US dollars (in constant 2004 prices) as recorded by the OECD's Development Assistance Committee (Organisation for Economic Co-operation and Development 2006b). The variables have been entered into the analyses after logarithmic transformation, in order to correct the highly skewed distribution of the data. The data reflect the allocations over the policy periods mentioned above rather than the disbursed aid funds, since the former are felt to be more appropriate as a reflection of policy decisions. Actual disbursements may be influenced by various circumstances in the aid recipient countries, which are felt to be less relevant for the purposes of this study (cf. Neumayer 2003: 41–2).

The explanatory variables consist of four groups: variables measuring different aspects of governance quality, variables concerning relative poverty levels, a donor interest variable and a control variable. The values of all independent variables represent a time lag. Most of the variables have been introduced with a one-year lag, but some governance variables represent a two-year time lag as a result of limited data availability.

Since arguments centring on governance quality have been found to be fundamental to the debate about aid selectivity, a variety of indicators have been included in the present study. A first set of data on governance has been taken from the well-known, and widely used, *Governance Matters V* dataset compiled by the World Bank Institute (Kaufmann *et al.* 2006a). The dataset consists of measures on six aspects of governance quality that are available on a bi-annual or (as of 2002) annual basis. The following are the six indicators:

- *voice and accountability*: 'the extent to which a country's citizens are able to participate in selecting their government, as well as freedom of expression, freedom of association, and free media';

- *political stability and absence of violence*: 'perceptions of the likelihood that the government will be destabilized or overthrown by unconstitutional or violent means, including political violence and terrorism';
- *government effectiveness*: 'the quality of public services, the quality of the civil service and the degree of its independence from political pressures, the quality of policy formulation and implementation, and the credibility of the government's commitment to such policies';
- *regulatory quality*: 'the ability of the government to formulate and implement sound policies and regulations that permit and promote private sector development';
- *rule of law*: 'the extent to which agents have confidence in and abide by the rules of society, and in particular the quality of contract enforcement, the police, and the courts, as well as the likelihood of crime and violence';
- *control of corruption*: 'the extent to which public power is exercised for private gain, including both petty and grand forms of corruption, as well as "capture" of the state by elites and private interests' (Kaufmann *et al.* 2006b: 4).

These six indicators have been included in the analyses both separately and as one composite variable (calculated using principal components analysis).[4]

The second set of governance indicators has been derived from the *Freedom in the World* dataset, compiled by Freedom House (2006). Two measures – the political rights and civil liberties indices – have been used as indicators of the degree to which political and civil freedoms are respected in the developing countries' political systems. The scores of the two indices are reported on an annual basis and each have a minimum value of 7 and a maximum value of 1. Since there exists a significant conceptual overlap between the political rights and civil liberties indices, on the one hand, and the voice and accountability indicator, on the other, these two sets of indicators have been entered separately in the regression equations reported in Sections 7.3–7.5.

Two proxy variables have been used to measure relative poverty levels. The first, commonly used, variable is the developing countries' gross domestic product (GDP) per capita, measured in purchasing power parity and in US dollars in constant 2000 prices (World Bank 2006). In response to the equally common criticism that per capita GDP is an imperfect reflection of poverty levels and because this indicator does not provide information about the income *distribution* in countries, a second proxy variable has been introduced. The developing countries' score on the human development index, as calculated by the United Nation's Development Programme (UNDP), is taken as an indicator to reflect different aspects of development and deprivation of aid receiving countries (Norris 2005; United Nations Development Programme 2000, 2001, 2002, 2005).

Donor interest has been measured by taking the logged volume of exports from the aid donor (or, in the case of the World Bank, the volume of exports from all industrialised countries) to the developing countries in the sample (International Monetary Fund 2005).

Logged population size (World Bank 2006) has been used as a variable to control for population bias. As more populous countries can be expected, *ceteris paribus*, to receive higher absolute volumes of aid, the introduction of population size alongside the other independent variables serves to control for the possible population effect.

7.3 World Bank

The results of the regression analyses related to the allocation of aid by the IDA are reported in Tables 7.1 and 7.2. Table 7.1 contains the results on the eligibility stage, and table 7.2 reports on the level stage. In both cases, three equations have been estimated per policy period (1999–2001 and 2002–4). The first of each set of equations contains all indicators of the *Governance Matters V* dataset, alongside the data on relative poverty (GDP per capita and human development score), donor interest (logged exports) and the variable that controls for population bias (logged population size). The second equation in the group replaces the voice and accountability indicator from the *Governance Matters V* dataset with the political rights and civil liberties indicators from the *Freedom in the World Dataset*. The third equation in the series replaces all governance indicators with the composite governance indicator that was obtained with principal components analysis of the *Governance Matters V* dataset.

The results of the logistic regression analyses that are summarised in Table 7.1 lead to several interesting findings. In the first place, it should be noted that the equations explain between 50 and 72 per cent of the variance in the dependent variable; the values of the chi-square statistic indicate that all equations are significant. Over 82 per cent of aid recipients are classified correctly by the different equations, with equation 4 reaching a maximum of almost 88 per cent correctly classified cases.

The estimates of equations 1–6 demonstrate that the most important variable in the explanation of the selection of aid recipients by the IDA is GDP per capita. In all six cases, this variable is negative – indicating that countries with lower levels of wealth receive more loans and grants from IDA – and highly significant.

In only two other cases (equations 3 and 6) there is a second significant variable. In these equations, the governance component scores of the developing countries in the analysis contribute positively and significantly to the explanation of the IDA selection of recipient. The results on equations 1, 2, 4 and 5 indicate that the governance quality indicators from the *Governance Matters V* and the *Freedom in the World* datasets do not independently contribute to the explanation of IDA selectivity. This may be due to the fact that the effect of each of the individual variables is too diluted to show up as significant in the estimations, whereas their combined effect is strong enough to be recognised. In both equations 3 and 6, the governance component has a positive sign, indicating that developing countries that have better governance have a significantly higher chance to be included among IDA aid recipients.

Table 7.1 World Bank, eligibility stage

	1999–2001			2002–4		
	(1)	(2)	(3)	(4)	(5)	(6)
Voice and accountability	−0.119	—	—	—	—	—
Political stability	−0.130	−0.167	—	−0.488	−0.502	—
Government effectiveness	1.761	1.765	—	1.511	1.443	—
Regulatory quality	1.251	1.233	—	−0.547	−0.138	—
Rule of law	0.590	0.524	—	0.966	1.079	—
Control of corruption	−1.052	−0.898	—	0.017	0.083	—
Governance component score	—	—	1.298**	—	—	1.094**
Political rights	—	0.187	—	—	0.292	—
Civil liberties	—	−0.212	—	—	−0.721	—
GDP per capita	−0.002**	−0.002**	−0.002***	−0.001**	−0.001***	−0.001***
Human development score	1.771	1.888	0.297	3.822	3.883	3.194
Exports (log)	−1.388	−1.302	−0.504	−0.883	−0.580	−0.664
Population size (log)	0.746	0.692	−0.282	0.819	0.594	0.909
N	87	87	93	91	91	94
Correctly classified (per cent)	82.8	82.8	84.9	87.9	85.7	84.0
R^2	0.72	0.72	0.65	0.58	0.58	0.50
Chi-square	63.99***	64.22***	58.47***	46.56***	46.46***	40.16***

Notes
The coefficients reported are unstandardised regression coefficients; coefficients of constants are not reported.
*$p<0.10$; **$p<0.05$; ***$p<0.01$.

Human development scores are insignificant in all cases, and industrialised countries' exports also do not show up as an important explanation of IDA selections of aid recipients. For IDA, population size does not appear to be significant with respect to its decisions on the eligibility of countries for loans and grants.

The results summarised in Table 7.2, related to the levels of loans and grants allocated to developing countries by the IDA, lead to slightly different conclusions than those formulated above. The explanatory power of the six equations appears, on the whole, to be less (with R^2s ranging between 0.40 and 0.56) than of the previous set of equations. Nevertheless, the F values indicate that equations 7 to 12 produce significant estimates without exception.

As was the case in the estimates summarised in the previous table, per capita GDP appears the most constant predictor of aid levels allocated by IDA. This proxy for poverty indicates that poorer developing countries receive significantly higher amounts of support from IDA than developing countries that are better off. At the same time, countries' human development score does not figure among the significant variables, which suggests the conclusion that IDA decisions on allocation are informed more by the financial aspects of poverty than by the human development components of education and health.

In contrast to the equations on eligibility, all equations related to the level of IDA allocations contain one or more significant governance variables. Government effectiveness appears to have a positive effect in equations 7, 8, 10 and 11. Regulatory quality appears to have been a significant predictor in the IDA12 period, but has lost its role in IDA13. In the latter period, indicators of political democracy (voice and accountability in equation 10 and political rights in equation 11) seem to have played a larger role in IDA allocation decisions. These findings indicate that, in the IDA13 period, countries with better guarantees for popular influence on government have received significantly more assistance from IDA than countries with less democratic regimes. The impact of the governance component scores in equations 9 and 12 expresses the general tendency that developing countries with better governance overall have received more support in both the IDA12 and the IDA13 period.

In the case of IDA, economic interests of the major donors, reflected by the industrialised countries' exports to developing countries, seem to have had little or no impact. The conclusion may be that the multilateral character of the World Bank and its IDA offers few opportunities to the industrialised funders to influence aid allocations in one particular direction.

Population size appears to have a generally positive influence on IDA aid allocations, although this variable has shown up as insignificant in equations 8 and 9. The coefficients for population size in the six equations confirm the expected effect result that more populous countries receive more aid in absolute terms. The unstandardised regression coefficient for logged population size is, however, significantly less than one,[5] thus indicating that IDA aid to more heavily populated developing countries increases less than proportionally with population increase (cf. Neumayer 2003: 48).

Table 7.2 World Bank, level stage

	1999–2001			2002–4		
	(7)	(8)	(9)	(10)	(11)	(12)
Voice and accountability	0.013	—	—	0.276**	—	—
Political stability	−0.068	−0.072	—	−0.133	−0.131	—
Government effectiveness	0.249**	0.232*	—	0.261*	0.311*	—
Regulatory quality	0.230**	0.223*	—	−0.143	−0.101	—
Rule of law	0.016	0.020	—	†	†	—
Control of corruption	−0.097	−0.106	—	−0.003	−0.006	—
Governance component score	—	—	0.287***	—	—	0.215**
Political rights	—	0.018	—	—	−0.201**	—
Civil liberties	—	−0.052	—	—	†	—
GDP per capita	−0.879***	−0.902***	−0.881**	−0.778***	−0.782***	−0.771***
Human development score	0.123	0.120	0.072	0.102	0.104	0.128
Exports (log)	†	0.088	0.107	−0.207	−0.199	−0.175
Population size (log)	0.174**	0.121	0.106	0.308**	0.281**	0.365***
N	88	87	93	91	91	94
R^2 (adjusted)	0.40	0.55	0.51	0.56	0.55	0.51
F	13.33***	10.55***	19.74***	13.76***	13.28***	20.33***

Notes
The coefficients reported are standardised regression coefficients (beta-weights).
*$p<0.10$; **$p<0.05$; ***$p<0.01$.
† The variable has been removed because of high multicollinearity.

7.4 The Netherlands

The results of the regression analyses of Dutch country selectivity and aid allocation are reported in Tables 7.3 and 7.4, following the format chosen in the previous section. The analyses of the two stages of aid allocation lead to results that are roughly comparable to those obtained in the analysis of IDA selectivity.

The results summarised in Table 7.3 indicate that the overall explanatory power of the equations is much weaker in the more recent policy period (2003–4) than in the first period of aid selectivity (1999–2002). The percentage of explained variance in equations 13, 14 and 15 ranges between 39 and 47, and the chi-square statistics indicate that the estimates are highly significant. The percentage of correctly classified cases is well above 80 in all three equations. The estimates related to the 2003–4 period show that the overall strength of the estimates is much less: R^2s of equations 16, 17 and 18 are no higher than 0.27, and the percentage of correctly classified cases ranges between 66.7 and 71.1. The chi-square statistics of these equations have dropped considerably, and in one case (equation 16) the statistic is no longer significant. On the basis of these findings one may conclude that the deterioration of the models' explanatory power reflects the change in policy orientation in the Netherlands under the Balkenende governments. As was argued in Chapter 4, the adoption of the government white paper *Mutual Interests, Mutual Responsibilities: Dutch Development Cooperation En Route to 2015* (Minister for Development Cooperation 2003b) resulted in a merger of various separate lists, one of which was the governance-based list of 19+3 preferential countries, into one list of partner countries. The overall impact of governance quality on the composition of the list of partner countries has decreased considerably when compared to the earlier selection of preferential countries.

Table 7.3 indicates that the impact of poverty, as measured by countries' per capita GDP, has been very significant throughout the two policy periods. GDP per capita shows up as highly significant and negative in all equations. Human development considerations and economic interests, as represented by the Dutch export volume to individual developing countries, do not seem to have played an important role in decisions on the selection of aid recipients in the two periods. Population size appears to have had a negligible influence on the Dutch selection process.

The results in Table 7.3 seem to indicate that governance indicators have impacted aid selectivity in the Netherlands primarily during the tenure of the second Kok government (1998–2002). Equations 13 and 14 point to the influence of regulatory quality on Dutch aid selection in that period.[6] The individual governance quality indicators seem to have lost their explanatory power in the analysis of the countries selected by Minister Van Ardenne in the 2003–4 period. As in the case of the IDA, the governance component appears to have influenced the selection of aid recipients in both periods, reflected in the positive and significant coefficients of this variable in equations 15 and 18.

Table 7.4 contains a summary of the results obtained in the regression analyses of Dutch aid allocation (the level stage). These results indicate that,

Table 7.3 The Netherlands, eligibility stage

	1999–2002			2003–4		
	(13)	(14)	(15)	(16)	(17)	(18)
Voice and accountability	0.490	–	–	0.539	–	–
Political stability	−0.647	−0.555	–	−0.237	−0.339	–
Government effectiveness	1.506	1.494	–	0.914	1.218	–
Regulatory quality	1.827**	1.873*	–	0.177	−0.268	–
Rule of law	−0.929	−0.810	–	0.427	0.318	–
Control of corruption	1.534	1.395	–	0.256	0.538	–
Governance component score	–	–	1.405***	–	–	0.908***
Political rights	–	−0.081	–	–	0.135	–
Civil liberties	–	−0.065	–	–	−0.794	–
GDP per capita	−0.001**	−0.001**	−0.001**	−0.001**	−0.001***	−0.001***
Human development score	−0.388	−0.293	−1.438	3.403	3.705	3.915
Exports (log)	0.273	0.222	0.153	−0.040	0.059	−0.064
Population size (log)	1.060	1.012	1.207*	0.241	0.371	0.392
N	87	87	90	90	90	90
Correctly classified (per cent)	85.1	83.9	85.6	66.7	71.1	68.9
R2	0.47	0.46	0.39	0.21	0.27	0.20
Chi-square	32.53***	32.27***	26.66***	15.17	19.65**	13.78**

Notes
The coefficients reported are unstandardised regression coefficients; coefficients of constants are not reported.
*$p<0.10$; **$p<0.05$; ***$p<0.01$.

Table 7.4 The Netherlands, level stage

	1999–2002			2003–4		
	(19)	(20)	(21)	(22)	(23)	(24)
Voice and accountability	0.148	–	–	0.177	–	–
Political stability	–0.384***	–0.342***	–	–0.161	–0.179	–
Government effectiveness	0.101	0.094	–	0.074	0.107	–
Regulatory quality	0.347**	0.410***	–	–0.113	–0.135	–
Rule of law	–0.024	–0.019	–	0.126	†	–
Control of corruption	0.136	0.108	–	–	0.135	–
Governance component score	–	–	0.283***	–	–	0.079
Political rights	–	–0.246*	–	–	–0.212*	–
Civil liberties	–	0.168	–	–	†	–
GDP per capita	–0.590***	–0.566***	–0.440***	–0.462**	–0.474**	–0.440**
Human development score	0.229	0.199	0.059	0.159	0.177	0.146
Exports (log)	–0.132	–0.117	–0.078	0.168	0.157	0.157
Population size (log)	0.438***	0.395***	0.462***	0.275*	0.277*	0.303**
N	87	87	90	90	90	90
R^2 (adjusted)	0.38	0.39	0.25	0.17	0.18	0.18
F	6.33***	5.89***	6.92***	3.01***	3.21***	4.85***

Notes
The coefficients reported are standardised regression coefficients (beta-weights).
*$p<0.10$; **$p<0.05$; ***$p<0.01$.
† The variable has been removed because of high multicollinearity.

analogously to what was found above in the analyses of the eligibility stage, the explanatory power of the model is significantly reduced over time. This is reflected in the R^2s and F values, which are much lower in the case of equations 22, 23 and 24 than of equations 19, 20 and 21.

The regression coefficients of GDP per capita appear to be highly significant and negative in all equations of Table 7.4. This variable has exercised the strongest influence on aid allocations throughout both policy periods. This implies that the aid allocations to poorer developing countries tend to be higher than those to relatively wealthier countries. The human development score does not appear to have a significant impact. Thus, it is safe to conclude that allocation decisions seem to be informed primarily by the financial aspects of poverty, and not so much by the human development facets. Dutch economic interests, reflected in the logged export volume to developing countries, do not contribute significantly to the explanation of aid allocation. As in the case of IDA, population size has an impact on aid allocation. The size of the unstandardised regression coefficients leads to a similar conclusion as in the previous section: more populous developing countries receive more aid from the Netherlands, but aid increases less than proportionally with population increase.[7]

Various governance indicators seem to have influenced Dutch aid allocations in the 1999–2002 period. The impact of these indicators has been almost absent in the 2003–4 period. Equations 19 and 20 indicate that political stability and regulatory quality contributed significantly to the explanation of aid levels. Political stability has a negative impact, implying that aid was allocated more than proportionally to countries where unconstitutional changes of government and political violence are likely to occur. The impact of regulatory quality, which was also clearly visible in the analyses of the 1999–2002 eligibility stage, is positive, meaning that countries with market-friendly policies tended to receive more aid than countries with policies that were less conducive to private sector development. According to equation 20, the political rights indicator exerted a negative influence on allocations in the 1999–2002 period. This implies that countries that showed more respect for the political rights of their citizens tended to get more Dutch aid than countries with worse reputations in this area. The positive coefficient of the governance component in equation 21 confirms the strong overall impact of governance considerations on Dutch aid allocations during the second Kok government.

The analyses pertaining to the second policy period (2003–4) demonstrate that the impact of governance-related variables had decreased dramatically over time. The influence of considerations related to governance quality is apparent only in equation 23, where the political rights indicator is barely significant at the 0.10 level. As was noted above, in relation to the eligibility stage, the policy shift marked by the merger of the list of preferential countries with thematic lists in 2003, has clearly had an impact on the importance of governance considerations in aid allocation decisions. The introduction of the unified list of 36 partner countries in 2003 has implied the de facto emasculation of the governance criterion in Dutch development cooperation policy.

7.5 The United States

Using the same style of presentation as in previous sections, the results of the regression analyses of US country selectivity and aid allocation are reported in Tables 7.5 and 7.6. As a result of the recent introduction of the MCA, the analyses differ from previous ones in some important respects. In the first place, Table 7.5 presents the findings from analyses in which MCA eligibility and eligibility for the MCA threshold programme are regressed on the governance, poverty, donor interest and population size variables. Further, Table 7.6 analyses the allocations made by US Agency for International Development (USAID) in 2003 and 2004 and the allocations announced in the MCA compacts (2004–6). Some of the findings reported below are in line with the conclusions about the policies of the IDA and the Netherlands, but some indicate that the United States occupies a position in the international development landscape that is slightly different from other donors.

The left-hand side of Table 7.5 contains the estimates related to MCA eligibility (equations 25, 26 and 27). The models estimated appear to be relatively strong, as between 83 and 87.8 of all cases are classified correctly, the R^2s range between 0.55 and 0.65 and the chi-square statistic is highly significant. The results emphasise the importance of GDP per capita for the explanation of MCA eligibility. None of the other three basic variables (human development score, logged exports and logged population size) appear to contribute much to the overall result.

The impact of governance-related variables is clearly noticeable in the three equations related to MCA eligibility. In equation 25, voice and accountability takes in a prominent position among the governance indicators. The coefficient indicates that political participation, the presence of a free press and freedom of expression have had important impact on the decisions of the Millennium Challenge Corporation (MCC) to select countries for possible inclusion in the MCA. Rather surprisingly, government effectiveness also shows up as a significant variable with a negative sign. This counterintuitive finding may be explained by the existence of an interaction effect between voice and accountability and government effectiveness: countries selected for MCA eligibility tend to offer better prospects for popular participation and influence, but these countries also had less effective government apparatuses.[8] Control of corruption, which is close to the 0.10 significance level in equation 25, appears as an important variable in equation 26, thus confirming the importance attached to this issue in the MCA. Equation 27 shows the positive and significant impact of the governance component when this is introduced instead of all other indicators of governance quality.

The right-hand part of Table 7.5 contains the estimates related to eligibility for the MCA's threshold programme. The logic behind this programme was altogether different from that of the MCA compacts. The differences between the two programmes are illustrated quite well by the coefficients of equations 28, 29 and 30. On the whole, GDP per capita plays a much less prominent role

Table 7.5 The US Millennium Challenge Account, eligibility stage

	MCA eligibility, 2004–6			Threshold eligibility, 2004–6		
	(25)	(26)	(27)	(28)	(29)	(30)
Voice and accountability	2.905***	—	—	0.708	—	—
Political stability	0.607	0.743	—	−0.084	−0.100	—
Government effectiveness	−2.396*	−1.198	—	0.695	0.796	—
Regulatory quality	1.307	0.857	—	2.603*	2.441*	—
Rule of law	1.365	0.735	—	0.576	0.249	—
Control of corruption	3.406	3.823*	—	−4.397**	−4.123*	—
Governance component score	—	—	2.991***	—	—	0.283
Political rights	—	−0.804	—	—	−0.976	—
Civil liberties	—	−0.281	—	—	0.799	—
GDP per capita	−0.001***	−0.001***	−0.001***	0.000	−0.001	−0.001**
Human development score	7.627	7.606	4.886	6.710	8.497*	8.569**
Exports (log)	0.150	0.284	0.282	−0.514	−0.785	0.006
Population size (log)	−0.259	−0.533	−1.039	0.488	0.503	0.231
N	90	90	94	90	90	94
Correctly classified (per cent)	87.8	86.7	83.0	84.4	83.3	85.1
R^2	0.65	0.64	0.55	0.31	0.35	0.13
Chi-square	49.26***	48.56***	41.69***	17.41*	19.90**	7.13

Notes
The coefficients reported are unstandardised regression coefficients; coefficients of constants are not reported.
*$p<0.10$; **$p<0.05$; ***$p<0.01$.

in the explanation of threshold eligibility than in other estimates. In equation 28 and 29, this variable is not significant (the p values are 0.16 and 0.11, respectively). Equation 30, which results in a non-significant solution overall, contains a negative and significant effect of GDP per capita. In equations 29 and 30, the human development score of countries is significant and positive, indicating that developing countries with higher human development levels stand a better chance in selection for the MCA threshold programme.

The threshold programme was intended, in the first place, to assist countries that failed to qualify for MCA eligibility with improving certain governance features. The discussion in Chapter 5 has shown that most countries in the threshold programme have introduced measures that intend to reduce corruption. The significant and negative coefficients of control of corruption in equations 28 and 29 bear witness to the programme's focus on corruption, as selected countries tend to score low on the corruption variable. Finally, the significant and positive coefficient of regulatory quality seems to indicate that developing countries with market-friendly policies have a higher probability of participation in the MCA threshold programme.

Table 7.6 presents the estimates related to the allocations to the MCA compact countries since 2004 (equations 34, 35 and 36). In order to place the analysis of the selectivity initiative in a somewhat broader perspective, MCA allocations are compared with the allocations of general (that is, non-MCA) US development assistance in the years since the adoption of the Millennium Challenge Act of 2003 (equations 31, 32 and 33). The majority of these funds are managed by the USAID.

The estimates summarised in the left-hand side of Table 7.6 show that the three equations explain 31 per cent of the variance in US aid allocated in 2003 and 2004. The F values indicate that the model estimates are highly significant. The poverty level of aid recipient countries appears to have played a dominant role in the allocation of US assistance. Human development scores are non-significant, indicating that the financial aspects of poverty have dominated in US aid policy. For a major economic power as the United States, population size appears to play a much less important role in the determination of aid allocations. In contrast to the practices of smaller aid donors such as the Netherlands, the amounts allocated to aid recipients by the United States are virtually unrelated to the size of the population. Interestingly, US economic interests (measured as logged exports) are highly significant as predictor of aid allocations to developing countries. In the 2003–4 period, the size of aid funds could be understood, in part, as a function of the export interests in the recipient countries.

The indicators of governance quality do not appear to have played a central role in decisions about US aid allocations in the 2003–4 period. The estimates in Table 7.6 demonstrate that political stability is the only governance-related variable that had a significant influence on the amount of aid allocated to developing countries. As in the case of Dutch aid allocations between 1999 and 2002 (equations 19 and 20), developing countries where the likelihood of unconstitutional

Table 7.6 The US Millennium Challenge Account and USAID, level stage

	USAID, 2003–4			MCA, 2004–6		
	(31)	(32)	(33)	(34)	(35)	(36)
Voice and accountability	0.124	–	–	0.294**	–	–
Political stability	−0.371***	−0.373***	–	0.045	0.053	–
Government effectiveness	0.208	0.214	–	†	†	–
Regulatory quality	0.061	0.086	–	−0.196	−0.156	–
Rule of law	†	†	–	†	†	–
Control of corruption	−0.115	−0.109	–	0.220	0.225	–
Governance component score	–	–	−0.012	–	–	0.262**
Political rights	–	−0.094	–	–	−0.256*	–
Civil liberties	–	†	–	–	†	–
GDP per capita	−0.425***	−0.435***	−0.403***	−0.475***	−0.473***	−0.463***
Human development score	−0.037	−0.026	−0.047	0.322*	0.312*	0.284
Exports (log)	0.366**	0.373**	0.471***	0.132	0.139	0.089
Population size (log)	0.024	0.020	0.114	−0.152	−0.183	−0.228
N	90	90	94	90	90	94
R2 (adjusted)	0.31	0.31	0.31	0.09	0.09	0.08
F	5.53***	5.49***	9.28***	2.15**	2.13**	2.70**

Notes: The coefficients reported are standardised regression coefficients (beta-weights).
*$p<0.10$; **$p<0.05$; ***$p<0.01$.
† The variable has been removed because of high multicollinearity.

political changes and political violence was higher tended to receive more aid from the United States than more stable countries.

The estimates related to the allocations in the MCA compacts lead to quite different conclusions about the orientation of aid. The estimates in equations 34, 35 and 36 need to be treated with caution as the proportion of explained variance is quite low in all three cases (the R^2s are below 0.10), although the F values indicate that the solutions are significant at the 0.05 level.

The constant element in the equations on the MCA allocations as compared to USAID's allocations in the previous years is that GDP per capita has a significant and negative influence. Also in the case of the MCA, poorer developing countries tend to receive more aid than relatively wealthier ones. At the same time, the human development score is shown to have a significant and positive influence in two out of three estimates (equations 34 and 35), implying that the MCA favours countries with better human development records.

The claims made by the MCC that aid is allocated on the basis of performance, and not according to considerations of foreign policy or US economic interests, are supported by the insignificance of the coefficients of logged exports. In contrast to the allocations made in 2003 and 2004, economic interests do not appear to have played an important role in decisions on the MCA compacts.

The estimates lend some support to the MCC's claim that its aid programme is based, first and foremost, on judgements about governance quality. The coefficients of two variables (voice and accountability, and political rights) indicate that the MCC allocates aid funds with a clear view to countries' record on political participation, freedom of the press and citizens' rights. Apart from these variables, the control of corruption, which is almost significant, has a positive influence on the allocation of MCA compact funds. The governance component score seems to capture the combined effects of the two governance indicators in equation 36. Its positive and significant coefficient indicates that countries that perform better in terms of the governance component get larger allocations from the MCA.

7.6 Conclusions

The analyses reported in this chapter aimed to test to what extent the choices made by World Bank, Dutch and US policy-makers on the selection of recipient countries and the allocation of aid can be explained on the basis of the central criteria that are part of the policy theories of the different donors. Three major sets of indicators were used in the logistic and multiple regression analyses of the eligibility and level stages in the policies of the World Bank, the Netherlands and the United States: recipient-needs indicators related to relative poverty and human development levels (GDP per capita and human development score), one donor-interest indicator (exports to low-income and lower-middle-income countries) and three clusters of governance indicators (the six indicators in the World Bank's *Governance Matters* dataset, the indicators on political rights and civil liberties in the *Freedom in the World* dataset compiled by Freedom House, and a composite indicator created on the basis of the *Governance Matters* data). Population size was introduced into all equations to control for the possible bias in the aid decisions of donors towards larger countries.

The analyses of the World Bank's lending policy have indicated that the Bank's choice of eligible countries can be explained quite well with the use of the indicators in the various regression models. The results are similar for both periods in the analyses (1999–2001 and 2002–4). Recipient needs, measured by GDP per capita, appeared to have a major impact on country selection, which implies that poorer developing countries have been selected as the main targets for IDA support. Of all other explanatory variables, the composite governance score was the only one that contributed significantly to the explanation, indicating that developing countries with higher average governance scores tend to have a much higher probability to be selected for IDA loans and grants than countries that perform worse.

The results of the analyses of IDA allocations are roughly similar to the ones related to country eligibility. IDA allocations can be explained quite well with reference to recipient needs and governance quality. On the whole, donor interests (measured as industrial countries' exports to low-income and lower-middle-income countries) do not seem to play a role in IDA decision-making. Generally speaking, countries with lower average wealth levels appear to receive more loans and grants from the World Bank's soft loan window. Various governance indicators were shown to have a positive impact on IDA allocation, signalling that IDA loans and grants are distributed with an eye to governance performance.

The analysis of Dutch country selection decisions produced results that are highly similar to the ones on IDA eligibility. This is hardly surprising given the adoption of central elements of the World Bank's evaluation framework by successive Dutch ministers for development cooperation. As in the case of IDA eligibility, the selection of developing countries for Dutch bilateral assistance reflected a preference for poorer countries with a higher average level of governance quality. Interestingly, regulatory quality, which can be interpreted as a sign of market-friendly policies, has shown up as an important determinant of country selection in the first period of Dutch aid selectivity (1999–2002).

The explanation of Dutch decisions on aid allocation appears to be quite different in the two phases of selectivity. Allocations made during the first phase can be understood relatively well against the background of recipient needs and governance quality. As in the case of the selection of recipient countries, poorer and better-governed developing countries were favoured over wealthier countries with lower levels of governance quality. At the same time, the adoption of market-friendly policies and political stability also appear to have had considerable influence on Dutch aid allocations during the first selectivity phase. In this phase, countries that demonstrated a more market-friendly attitude received noticeably more aid from the Netherlands than countries with policies that were less conducive to the private sector. Also, developing countries that were faced with serious problems of political stability, as well as those that showed more respect for the political rights of their citizens, tended to be favoured in terms of the aid allocated to them. Results of the analyses related to the second phase of aid selectivity show that governance considerations have been well-nigh absent in decisions on the allocation of development assistance. The change of attitude towards governance quality during the tenure of Minister Agnes van Ardenne seems a plausible explanation for the reduced impact of governance indicators in this period.

The analyses related to US development assistance are in many ways comparable to those on the World Bank and the Netherlands, although there are some important differences. Overall, recipient needs, reflected in GDP per capita, appear the overriding factor in the selection of countries for the MCA. MCA eligible countries were selected primarily from among the poorer developing countries. Average governance quality appeared to have a positive influence, implying that eligible countries tend to have higher levels of governance quality. Certain features of the political system, such as political participation and freedom of expression (captured in the voice and accountability variable), seem to have been crucial in the MCA selection process – this is a finding that supports arguments, reported in Chapter 5, about the de facto threshold character of political democracy in the MCA framework. The selection of countries for the MCA's threshold programme seems to have taken place on the basis of a very different logic. Recipient needs appear to have played a much less important role in this programme than in decisions on MCA eligibility. Market-friendly policies and corruption have been reported as the most important explanatory factors, which may lead to the conclusion that countries in the threshold programme are primarily those that place much emphasis on private-sector development but face problems of corruption. As the MCA threshold programme is intended to help countries reduce corruption and other governance problems, the important role of these variables seems plausible.

The allocation of US development assistance by USAID and other aid agencies (2003–4) and by the MCC (2004–6) is based primarily on relative poverty levels in the developing world. Interestingly, pre-MCA allocations demonstrate the centrality of US economic interests, measured by the level of US exports to low-income and lower-middle-income countries. Developing countries that are important in terms of US exports tended to receive relatively more US development assistance in the 2003–4 period than less prominent countries. As in the case of Dutch development assistance, US aid was allocated more than proportionally to politically unstable developing countries in 2003 and 2004. Despite the overall weakness of the explanation of MCA allocation levels, the analyses show interesting differences with pre-MCA development assistance. In particular, the prominence of political variables (voice and accountability, political rights and, to a lesser extent, control of corruption) and average governance scores are noteworthy.

8 Conclusion

8.1 The challenge of aid selectivity

The adoption of the aid selectivity principle in development assistance policies since the late 1990s was based on a distinctly political motivation. The international development community had been faced with widespread doubts about the effectiveness of aid and witnessed the decline of budgets allocated to development assistance. Several initiatives were taken in response to the prevalent scepticism about aid. At the global level, in such institutions as the Organisation for Economic Co-operation and Development and the United Nations, proposals were made to reassess the core objectives of development assistance policies. These proposals ultimately led to the general acceptance of the Millennium Development Goals (MDGs) in the first few years of the new millennium. At the same time as the aims of development assistance were being rethought, the instruments of development aid were the subject of intense scrutiny in policy circles. Ideas about new aid modalities and new forms of conditionality came out of the debate about instruments.

Aid selectivity, in terms of objectives, instruments and recipients, became a keyword in aid policies as of the beginning of this century. Country selectivity figured very prominently among the new concepts for development assistance. Researchers at the World Bank developed a 'powerful narrative' (Court and Maxwell 2006: 17; see Chapter 2) that gained currency among policy-makers. Building on the generally shared conviction that 'aid does not buy policy reform', World Bank researchers Burnside and Dollar (1997) argued that new forms of conditionality had to be found. Using increasingly popular ideas developed by the new institutional and information-theoretic economists, policy-makers started to argue that aid works but only in countries with good governance and good policies. This laid the foundation for the introduction of so-called 'ex post' conditionalities, which would not depend on promises by governments about future policy changes as they would be based on the past performance of developing countries in terms of (primarily economic) policy making and the operation of economic, social and political institutions.

This book has focused on three major cases of aid selectivity, implemented by the World Bank, the Netherlands and the United States. In many respects, these three cases represent relatively 'pure' examples of ex post conditionality, as policy-makers in all three instances have justified their decisions with direct reference to Burnside and Dollar's policy 'narrative'. The three examples have been chosen also because they offered the possibility to bring out the strengths and weaknesses of the new approach quite clearly. The discussion in Chapter 6 has demonstrated that other donors besides the World Bank, the Netherlands and the United States have taken up important elements of the selectivity agenda, but that their approach has been significantly different from the cases studied in this book. In the policies of the other donors, components of the agenda of aid selectivity have been adapted and embedded in their existing approaches to development assistance.

In this final chapter, several important themes that have come up in the policy analyses and empirical tests in earlier chapters are discussed. The attempt here is to draw out some general concerns related to the background and implementation of country selectivity, as these may have wider significance for the debate on the role of governance criteria in development assistance policies. This chapter inevitably glances over some of the differences between specific problems inherent in the various selectivity programmes, as these have been discussed extensively in Chapters 3, 4, 5 and 7.

The remainder of this chapter raises several issues that are related to the policy theory underpinning aid selectivity, the methodologies that have been applied and the implementation of selectivity policies. The following sections deal with the mechanism that is assumed to connect governance quality to aid effectiveness; the economistic and neo-liberal bias in the definition of 'good' governance; the deeper causes of 'bad' governance; the concentration of the methodology on quantifiable governance features; the focus on the selection aspects of the policy frameworks; the indeterminate nature of selection on the basis of governance quality; and the relative importance of poverty reduction.

8.2 Governance quality and aid effectiveness

The argument underpinning the move towards country selectivity in development assistance policies derived, to a large extent, from empirical analyses on the impact of governance and (economic) policies on aid effectiveness (Burnside and Dollar 1997; World Bank 1998). Despite fierce criticism levelled at the methodology of the studies and the validity of their conclusions by academic researchers, the relationship between governance quality and aid effectiveness became almost a dogma in certain policy-making circles.

It is highly plausible that the findings in the World Bank studies resonated well in the development policy community because they supported intuitively held understandings about the impact of bad governance on development. The general argument that bad governance is not conducive to effective spending of development assistance funds could easily be substantiated with reference to cases of serious abuse of aid monies, such as Mobutu Sese Seko's Zaire, Nicaragua under the Somoza dynasty and the Philippines during the reign of Ferdinand Marcos.

136 *Conclusion*

The claim that countries with very poor governance should receive little or no development assistance can thus be backed up almost effortlessly with data and examples detailing how aid funds have been misspent. In its *Assessing Aid* report, however, the World Bank went much further and asserted that there is an almost *linear* relationship between the quality of governance and policies, on the one hand, and aid effectiveness, on the other. The central message of the report (also quoted in Chapter 2) was that '[a]mong countries with similar poverty levels but different policy regimes, more finance should go to the countries with better management' (World Bank 1998: 16).

It is highly doubtful whether the impact of governance should be assumed to have a linear-like impact on aid effectiveness. On theoretical grounds, it is much more plausible to assume that political arbitrariness, corruption, violence and a bad business environment will stifle social and economic activities if these cross a certain threshold level. People are able to cope with a certain degree of uncertainty in their environment. If uncertainties reach the level that investments and property are being threatened and people can no longer live normal lives, people's relative valuation of the present and the future will be changed dramatically. It is very unlikely that foreign assistance, if given to countries faced with circumstances of extreme uncertainty and threats, will have a positive contribution to development.

Rather than applying a linear logic to development assistance and relying on indicators that express relative governance performance, development agencies should define the conditions under which they would no longer be prepared to support particular countries. The corollary is that they should develop the monitoring capacity to judge whether the conditions for the continuation of a development aid relationship are still met, or whether other means should be used to support people whose livelihoods are being threatened, for instance by using non-governmental aid channels.

8.3 Definitions of governance

The issue of the conceptualisation of governance is directly connected to the problem of the relation between governance quality and aid effectiveness, which was discussed in the previous section. Aid agencies that have implemented selectivity policies usually also adopted definitions of governance developed by the World Bank. It was argued in Chapter 3 that the understanding of governance issues in World Bank circles has been heavily influenced by neo-liberal precepts of market-oriented reform. The Bank's Country Policy and Institutional Assessment (CPIA) was and still is dominated by considerations related to economic management and structural policies, while issues of democracy, political participation, the rule of law and human rights are completely absent in this evaluation tool of country performance.

The neo-liberal bias of the CPIA, which is also applied by donors such as the Netherlands, has two important implications. In the first place, the concept of governance that transpires in the CPIA is overly economistic and leads to an overexposure of the implications of 'governance' performance on economic growth and the economic effects of aid. There is broad agreement nowadays that development is more than simply growth of GDP per capita and at least should include aspects of health and education (as in the human development understanding of the term), as well as pay attention to the distribution of wealth. More alternative conceptions of development also refer to, less easily quantifiable, notions of community development, social participation and self-reliance.

In the second place, the equation of 'good governance' with certain types of institutions (in particular, more market- and property-oriented ones) and of 'good policies' with orthodox monetary, fiscal, debt and trade policies leads to a bias against institutions and policies that do not conform to the post-Washington Consensus. Heterodox approaches, which are, for instance aimed at the maintenance of general standards of welfare or the self-sufficiency of a country in terms of food or energy production, will easily be cast aside as examples of 'bad policy' (cf. Pronk 2001: 625). Cuba, which occupied the 52nd position in the 2005 Human Development Index (United Nations Development Programme 2005: 219), is an example of a country that has achieved good social results with policies that would be considered out of bounds by the World Bank.

Instead of buying in to the governance concepts developed by the World Bank, development assistance agencies would be well advised to apply a multi-dimensional definition of governance. Such a definition should comprise the more political dimensions of governance (participation, democracy, human rights) and should avoid equating good with orthodox economic policies. Also, the economistic fallacy of equating development with economic growth should be avoided in order to acknowledge the diversity of objectives of public policy making.

8.4 Causes of 'bad' governance

In Chapter 3, it was argued that the prevailing policy theory on aid selectivity does not pay sufficient attention to the complex interrelationship between development level and governance quality. In particular, the policy theory shows too little awareness of the fact that governance quality in poorer developing countries may generally be lower because these countries do not have sufficient financial means or human capital to upgrade their governance structures. According to this logic, governance quality may itself be at least as much a *result of* economic development as it is a condition for development (cf. Doorenspleet 2005: 87–111; Burkhart and Lewis-Beck 1994). For this reason, the focus on governance quality as a precondition for aid and a potential criterion for country selection may at the least be ill-founded and at the most be counterproductive (see further in Section 8.6).

In addition to the above, another characteristic of developing countries may give rise to wrongly focused policy conceptions. Although governance plays a central role in contemporary development assistance policies, there is a lack of attention for the structurally disadvantaged political position of developing countries. In an attempt to analyse the causes and consequences of *political underdevelopment*, Moore (2001: 387) has argued that 'the states of the South are different from those of the North because they emerged into an international environment already dominated by the relatively rich and powerful Northern states.' Over the past several centuries, the states in industrialised countries managed to maintain close links with society and, as a result, came to play an important role in the economic development of these countries. In many developing countries, however, the state and society stayed disconnected, and the state failed to become an engine of development. In a good number of cases, it became quite the contrary of a developmental state and turned out to be a predatory institution.

One of the main challenges of development policy in the early twenty-first century is the re-establishment of the positive relationship between the state and society in developing countries, so that the state would be enable to play a proper role in development. The current trend of selectivity in development assistance policies, which sees aid as a reward for good governance, may actually lead to the failure of states in developing countries to transform and, thus, runs the risk of making such policies self-defeating.

8.5 Methodology and quantification

Current approaches to aid selectivity tend to rely on quantitative measurements of governance quality. The three cases of aid selectivity that were discussed in this book offer as many examples of the attempt to quantify governance performance. In most cases, quantification is desired for reasons that are, in themselves, quite valid. Donor agencies argue that rational and transparent policy making requires the development of instruments that lead to a clear distinction of good, mediocre and bad performance.

This being said, it is highly doubtful whether the almost exclusive reliance on quantitative indicators will ever lead to sound governance-oriented policies. Several methodological and operational features of the governance quality measures can be mentioned in this regard. In the first place, the need to have data available on a broad range of developing countries produces a focus on a limited number of formal characteristics of politics and policy making. To mention but one well-known example, cross-country assessments usually pay more attention to the fact that elections are being held and that multiple parties take part in those elections than to the nature of political competition and the less easily visible impediments in the political system that restrict political opponents to stand up against incumbent political functionaries.

In the second place, the methods of collection and interpretation of data by aid agencies can lead to problems. The issue mentioned by Kanbur in relation to the World Bank's application of the CPIA (see Chapter 3) is worth recalling in this context, as his point has more general validity. According to Kanbur, the views of aid agencies represent the interests of the industrialised donor countries, which do not necessarily run parallel to those of the aid-receiving developing countries. Moreover, aid agencies have vested interests in certain programmes, and their interpretation of the data on governance may well be influenced by these interests (Kanbur 2005: 8).

In addition to these methodological problems, previous chapters have brought out several operational difficulties linked to the use of quantitative governance indicators. One important issue in this regard is the subjective nature of certain variables. The routine that is used by the World Bank in its assessment of policies and institutions (leading to the CPIA scores) relies heavily on judgements by members of country teams (see Chapter 3). Despite the benchmarking process to which all judgements on developing countries are subjected, the resulting scores are still the reflection of (inter-)subjective assessments that partly reflect the underlying values embedded in the Bank's organisational culture (cf. Miller-Adams 1999: 6). In a similar vein, the indicators of the *Governance Matters* dataset are, to a large extent, based on judgements that may reflect a business-oriented bias (Arndt and Oman 2006: 69).

Another operational problem that appeared to characterise various governance indicators discussed in previous chapters relates to the inability of indicators to distinguish usefully among good, mediocre and bad performers. In the real world, countries tend to cluster around the median score of the distribution of most governance indicators, while only few are located at the positive or negative extremes. The resulting inability of aid agencies to select well-performing countries solely on the basis of governance scores transpired in all three case studies reported in Chapters 3–5. As a result of its inability to distinguish good performers, the International Development Association (IDA) took recourse to increasing the weight of the governance factor as compared to the previously used governance discount. Decision-makers in the Netherlands, when faced with a similar problem, opted for 'weighing' countries 'on the hand', while the Millennium Challenge Corporation (MCC) used the discretionary powers it had obtained in the Millennium Challenge Act of 2003 to select countries that it considered promising despite the fact that they missed qualification by one or several indicators.

If governance concerns are to be taken seriously in development assistance policies, more in-depth analyses of political and social trends in developing countries should be made that are less vulnerable to the problems mentioned above. The analytical framework of the Drivers of Change approach, which has been set up by the United Kingdom's Department for International Development (see Chapter 6), seems a promising way to identify trends in governance and may be more useful than the quite formalistic approach that has been used to date by most other aid donors. The drawbacks of the Drivers of Change approach, which relate to its labour intensity, costs and required country expertise, may be overcome if donor countries would effectively coordinate and harmonise their efforts in this area.

8.6 Bias towards selection

The currently dominant methodological approach to aid selectivity has resulted in a bias towards selection instead of programmes aimed at improving governance. In addition to the issue raised in Section 8.4 – where it was noted that the reliance of aid selectivity on governance quality may lead to the adoption of an incorrect policy theory – the problem that the introduction of aid selectivity may produce the wrong type of policies focused on in this section.

Many scholars have pointed out that the types of institutions and norms of behaviour that are commonly seen as expressions of 'good governance' by the donor agencies have been the result of long-term change in the presently industrialised countries. The political, social and economic institutions in these countries are the product of complex social and political battles and generally reflect the settlement of conflicts among contending socio-economic groups (cf. Moore 2001). Many developing countries have not experienced such battles; their social, political and economic systems have been shaped instead by colonial history and decolonisation and more often than not reflect the interests of dominant groups whose power depends on access to land or other resources and/or some traditional form of legitimacy. In these circumstances, various manifestations of 'bad governance', such as patronage, clientelism and corruption, may be connected intimately to the absence of a clear prospect of development (cf. Chabal and Daloz 1999: 156).

It may be argued that aid agencies that take governance issues seriously would focus less on the selection of good performers than on the 'lifting up' of mediocre or bad performers. Pronk (2001: 627) has drawn attention to the paradox that is connected to many aid selectivity policies: 'To use aid as a reward for good development governance may indeed be justified under certain circumstances, but often such conditions can only be met with some outside help.' Countries and agencies that have adopted aid selectivity policies do certainly show an awareness of the need to assist developing countries with improving their governance structures, but on the whole they have only made limited funds available for this purpose. Thus, the activities of the World Bank's Poverty Reduction and Economic Management (PREM) Network, the Dutch programme of institutional strengthening and the MCC's threshold programmes have stayed relatively limited in size.

8.7 Indeterminacy of governance quality

In addition to the inability of governance indicators to distinguish clearly between countries with varying levels of governance quality (as indicated in Section 8.5), the selection process is influenced by the fact that governments have multiple objectives in their foreign policies. As a result, decisions on recipient countries are often affected by different considerations. A study by Alesina and Dollar (2000) on the motives of countries to give foreign aid provides evidence that a multitude of considerations jointly determine aid allocation decisions. Political and strategic motives resulted, in the period between 1970 and 1994, in aid flows that were heavily biased to former colonies and political allies, in particular. As a consequence of the importance of other considerations than governance quality, Alesina and Dollar (2000: 55) concluded that 'bilateral aid has only a weak association with poverty, democracy, and good policy'.

The indeterminacy of governance quality as a motive to support developing countries with aid was also observed in the empirical analyses reported in Chapter 7. The analyses of the eligibility stage of aid selectivity in the case of the IDA, the Netherlands and the United States indicated that, at most, 72 per cent of the variance in the dependent variable (selection or non-selection) could be explained (see equations 1 and 2 in Table 7.1). This implies that the variables included in the equations could not explain 28 per cent of the variance. In many other cases, the percentage of explained variance turned out to be much lower, reaching a low of 17 to 18 per cent in the case of the Dutch selection of aid recipients in the 2003–4 period (see equations 16–18 in Table 7.3).

The results obtained in the quantitative-empirical analyses of Chapter 7 indicate that, even in the cases where governance quality and per capita gross domestic product (GDP) did have a significant effect, the central variables in the aid selectivity discourse need to be supplemented by others in order to arrive at a convincing explanation of aid selectivity. Policy-makers would no doubt argue that they want to maintain certain discretion in deciding on the countries they wish to support. They are certainly right in claiming their freedom of manoeuvre from a substantive, policy-oriented point of view. At the same time, if policy-makers obtain too much leverage when choosing aid recipients, the role of the policy theory that they have created themselves will rapidly lose credibility. If the discretion to deviate from the policy guidelines becomes too great, policy-makers will ultimately face the situation of the emperor without clothes in Andersen's famous fairy tale: they may pretend to have a policy theory of aid selectivity, but the multiplicity of other considerations would render the theory devoid of any content.

8.8 The importance of poverty reduction

The discussion in Chapter 2 has made it clear that poverty reduction has occupied a central position in debates about development assistance since the mid-1990s. The new global targets formulated for development assistance (the MDGs) and some new instruments (most notably, the Poverty Reduction Strategies) have placed much emphasis on poverty reduction. The introduction of aid selectivity has been legitimised primarily in terms of aid effectiveness; it is by no means clear, however, how aid selectivity or enhanced aid effectiveness would contribute to poverty reduction. At least two observations can serve to illustrate this point.

The issue of poverty has not been central to the World Bank's analysis of governance quality and aid effectiveness. The studies that were instrumental in relating governance quality to aid effectiveness focused on the impact of

Conclusion

governance, policies and aid, and possible interactions among these variables, on *economic growth* (Burnside and Dollar 1997: 11; World Bank 1998: 121–3). The conclusions about aid selectivity have, thus, not been based on possible poverty-reducing impacts of governance and policies.

Further, the discussions in Chapters 3–5 have indicated that the implementation of selectivity policies has been based on the average wealth of developing countries by focusing on their per capita GDP but has not included poverty-related indicators. Middle-income countries with large groups of poor people – of which Brazil is probably the best example – have in these approaches been treated equally to countries with comparable average income levels but overall much more equal distributions of wealth.

The relative neglect of the issue of poverty in policy making may appear odd in an era where poverty reduction is so high on the agenda of development assistance. The focus on economic growth may, however, be understandable given the nature of current thinking about development, in which trickle-down mechanisms have come to occupy a more prominent position than in the past. The discussion of the MCA in Chapter 5 illustrated this point quite well. At the same time, there are signs that certain development assistance agencies are seriously paying attention to the poverty reduction agenda that resulted from the adoption of the MDGs. The cases of the World Bank's introduction of results measurement in IDA14 – although still without implications for IDA allocations (see Section 3.3) – and the inclusion of progress towards the MDGs in 25 aid-receiving countries in the United Kingdom's Public Service Agreement for 2005–8 (see Section 6.2) signal that some agencies are relaxing their focus on economic growth and take certain forms of poverty reduction more seriously. As is usually the case with development assistance, it will probably take quite some time before this reorientation will have general applicability.

Appendix A
Interviews

Karina I. Blanco: Programme Assistant, Department of Operations, Millennium Challenge Corporation

Joan Boer: former Deputy Director-General for International Cooperation, Netherlands Ministry of Foreign Affairs (until 2003); currently Permanent Representative to the Organisation for Economic Co-operation and Development (OECD)

Rui Coutinho: Adviser, Operations Policy and Strategy, World Bank

Stephen B. Gaull: Country Director, Department of Operations, Millennium Challenge Corporation

Peter van de Geer: former Adviser to the Director-General for International Cooperation, Netherlands Ministry of Foreign Affairs (2001–4); currently Head of the Central America and Caribbean Division of the Directorate for the Western Hemisphere, Netherlands Ministry of Foreign Affairs

Paul Litjens: Head of the West Africa Desk, Netherlands Ministry of Foreign Affairs

Freek Keppels: former Deputy Head and ODA Coordinator, Budget Office, Department of Financial and Economic Affairs, Netherlands Ministry of Foreign Affairs (2000–4); currently Deputy Head of the Weapons Control and Export Policy Unit of the Directorate for Security Policy, Netherlands Ministry of Foreign Affairs

Amy J. Kirschenbaum: Programme Assistant, Department of Operations, Millennium Challenge Corporation

Valeria R. McFarren: Programme Assistant for Latin America, Department of Operations, Millennium Challenge Corporation

Richard A. Morford: Managing Director for Donor and Multilateral Relations, Department of Policy and International Relations, Millennium Challenge Corporation

Anne Pence: Special Advisor, Department of Operations, Millennium Challenge Corporation

Alicia Phillips Mandaville: Development Policy Officer, Department of Policy and International Relations, Millennium Challenge Corporation

Frederik van Bolhuis: Lead Economist, Resource Mobilisation, World Bank

Appendix B
The Country Policy and Institutional Assessment (CPIA)

1 1999–2004

The Country Policy and Institutional Assessment method that was introduced in 1998 and used during IDA12 and IDA13 (1999–2004) consisted of four items and twenty components (International Development Association 2003b).

1.1 Economic management

1 Management of inflation and macro-economic imbalances
   Assesses whether a country has a consistent macro-economic programme (in terms of exchange rate, monetary and fiscal policy) that addresses inflation and internal and external balances.
2 Fiscal policy
   Assesses the size of the fiscal balance and the composition of government spending to assess their compatibility with adequate provision of public services for economic growth, favourable macro-economic outcomes and a sustainable path of public debt.
3 Management of public debt (external and domestic)
   Assesses whether a country can manage its public debt, external and domestic, and service it now and sustainably into the future. Two separate, but linked dimensions, of equal weight, are debt service capacity and debt management capacity.
4 Management and sustainability of the development programme
   Assesses the degree to which the management of the economy and the development programme reflect technical competence; sustained political commitment and public support; and participatory processes through which the views of stakeholders can be heard and inform government decision-making. A high score is given when all three dimensions are satisfactory; a low score when there is weak performance on any one dimension.

1.2 Structural policies

5 Trade policy and foreign exchange regime
   Assesses how well the policy framework fosters trade and capital movements.

6   Financial stability
    Assesses whether the structure of the financial sector, and the policies and regulations that affect it, are conducive to diversified financial services to be provided in a context of integrity and with a minimal risk of systemic failure. The key, and equally weighted, dimensions for assessment are competition policies, legal regime and regulatory regime. The size of the economy is taken into account as appropriate.
7   Financial sector depth, efficiency and resource mobilisation
    Assesses to what extent the policies and regulations affecting financial institutions foster the mobilisation of savings and efficient financial intermediation. The key, and equally weighted, dimensions for assessment are monetary and credit policies, tax policies and ownership policies.
8   Competitive environment for the private sector
    Assesses whether firms face competitive pressures to behave efficiently or be forced to exit. Factors inhibiting competition are direct regulation by the state, the reservation of significant economic activities for state-controlled entities, or administrative procedures. The existence and effectiveness of anti-trust measures may be a criterion that is more relevant for middle-income countries.
9   Goods and factor markets
    Assesses the policies that affect the efficiency of goods markets and factor markets for labour and land.
10 Policies and institutions for environmental sustainability
    Assesses the extent to which economic and environmental policies contribute to the incomes and health status of the poor, by fostering the protection and sustainable use of natural resources and the management of pollution.

1.3 Policies for social inclusion/equity

11 Gender
    Assesses the extent to which a country has created laws and policies, and institutions to enforce them, that promote equal access for males and females to productive and economic resources (e.g. employment), human capital development opportunities (e.g. in education and health), and equal status and protection under the law (e.g. freedom from discrimination on the basis of sex in both the private and the public spheres).
12 Equity of public resource use
    Assesses the extent to which the pattern of public expenditures and revenues favours the poor, based on available poverty analysis, public expenditure reviews (PERs), and other relevant analyses, as well on the country-owned Poverty Reduction Strategy, or, if not available, informed judgement based on existing information and analysis.
13 Building human resources
    Assesses the programmes and policies that affect access to and quality of health care and nutrition services; access to and quality of education, training and literacy; and prevention of HIV/AIDS and other communicable diseases.

14 Social protection and labour
    Assesses the extent to which government policies for social protection and labour market regulation reduce the risk of becoming poor and assist those who are poor to mitigate and cope with further risk to their well-being. Programmes and policies the effects of which are assessed include regulation that minimises segmentation and inequity in the labour market; protection of basic labour standards; social safety nets; community-driven development projects; and active labour market programmes such as public works or job training.
15 Monitoring and analysis of poverty outcomes and impacts
    Assesses both the quality of systems to monitor poverty outcome/impact indicators and their use in formulating policies. The indicators include impact indicators such as income poverty, inequality, malnutrition and other indicators of well-being, and outcome indicators on the access to, use of and satisfaction with public services.

1.4 Public sector management and institutions

16 Property rights and rule-based governance
    Assesses the extent to which private economic activity is facilitated by an effective legal system and a rule-based governance system in which property and contract rights are reliably respected and enforced.
17 Quality of budgetary and financial management
    Assesses the extent to which there are (a) a comprehensible and credible budget, linked to policy priorities, which are in turn linked to a poverty reduction strategy; (b) effective financial management systems to ensure that incurred expenditures are consistent with the approved budget, that budgeted revenues are achieved and that aggregate fiscal control is maintained; (c) timely and accurate fiscal reporting, including timely and audited public accounts and effective arrangements for follow-up; and (d) clear and balanced assignment of expenditures and revenues to each level of government.
18 Efficiency of revenue mobilisation
    Assesses the overall pattern of revenue mobilisation – not only the tax structure as it exists on paper, but revenues from all sources as they are actually collected.
19 Quality of public administration
    Assesses the extent to which civilian central government staff members (including teachers, health workers and police) are structured to design and implement government policy and deliver services effectively. The key dimensions for assessment, which are equally weighted, are policy coordination and responsiveness; service delivery and operational efficiency; merit and ethics; and pay adequacy and management of the wage bill.

Table B1 Categories and judgements on the CPIA, 1999–2004

Score	Judgement
1	Unsatisfactory for an extended period
2	Unsatisfactory
3	Moderately unsatisfactory
4	Moderately satisfactory
5	Good
6	Good for an extended period

Source: IDA (2003b).

20 Transparency, accountability and corruption in the public sector
Assesses the extent to which (a) the executive can be held accountable for its use of funds and the results of its actions by the electorate and by the legislature and judiciary and (b) public employees within the executive are required to account for the use of resources, administrative decisions and results obtained.

All components contributed 5 per cent to the overall CPIA score. The components were rated on a scale ranging from 1 to 6, allowing intermediate scores of 2.5, 3.5 and 4.5. The scores reflected the judgments that are given in Table B1.

2 Since 2005

The CPIA method that was introduced in 2004 and is used since 2005 consists of four items and sixteen components (World Bank Operations Policy and Country Services 2004a).

2.1 Economic management

1 Macro-economic management
Assesses the quality of the monetary/exchange rate and aggregate demand policy framework. A high quality policy framework is one that is favourable to sustained medium-term economic growth. Critical dimensions are: a monetary/exchange rate policy with clearly defined price stability objectives; aggregate demand policies that focus on maintaining short and medium-term external balance (under the current and foreseeable external environment); and avoid crowding out private investment.
2 Fiscal policy
Assesses the short- and medium-term sustainability of fiscal policy (taking into account monetary and exchange rate policy and the sustainability of public debt) and its impact on growth. This component covers the extent to which (a) the primary balance is managed to ensure sustainability of the public finances; (b) public expenditure/revenue can be adjusted to absorb shocks if necessary; and (c) the provision of public goods, including infrastructure, is consistent with medium-term growth.

Appendix B

3 Debt policy
Assesses whether the debt management strategy is conducive to minimise budgetary risks and ensure long-term debt sustainability. The component evaluates the extent to which external and domestic debt is contracted with a view to achieving/maintaining debt sustainability and the degree of coordination between debt management and other macro-economic policies.

2.2 Structural policies

4 Trade
Assesses how the policy framework fosters trade in goods. The overall score on this component is a weighted average of two dimensions: trade restrictiveness (0.75) and customs/trade facilitation (0.25).
5 Financial sector
Assesses the structure of the financial sector and the policies and regulations that affect it. Three dimensions, of equal weight, are covered: (a) financial stability; (b) the sector's efficiency, depth, and resource mobilisation strength; and (c) access to financial services.
6 Business regulatory environment
Assesses the extent to which the legal, regulatory and policy environment helps or hinders private business in investing, creating jobs and becoming more productive. Three dimensions, of equal weight, are measured: (a) regulations affecting entry, exit and competition; (b) regulation of ongoing business operations; and (c) regulation of factor markets (labour and land).

2.3 Policies for social inclusion/equity

7 Gender equality
Assesses the extent to which countries have enacted and put in place institutions and programmes to enforce laws and policies that (a) promote equal access for men and women to human capital development opportunities; (b) promote equal access for men and women to productive and economic resources; and (c) give men and women equal status and protection under the law. All three dimensions are of equal weight.
8 Equity of public resource use
Assesses the extent to which the pattern of public expenditures and revenue collection affects the poor and is consistent with national poverty reduction priorities. The public expenditure dimension contributes two-thirds towards the overall rating.
9 Building human resources
Assesses the national policies and public and private sector service delivery that affect access to and quality of (a) health and nutrition services, including population and reproductive health; (b) education, early child development programmes, training and literacy programmes; and (c) prevention and

treatment of HIV/AIDS, tuberculosis and malaria. All three dimensions are of equal weight.
10   Social protection and labour
Assesses government policies in the area of social protection and labour market regulation, which reduce the risk of becoming poor, assist those who are poor to better manage further risks, and ensure a minimal level of welfare to all people. This component consists of five, equally weighted, indicators: (a) social safety net programmes; (b) protection of basic labour standards; (c) labour market regulations; (d) community-driven initiatives; and (e) pension and old age savings programmes.
11   Policies and institutions for environmental sustainability
Assesses the extent to which environmental policies foster the protection and sustainable use of natural resources and the management of pollution, using multi-dimensional criteria (i.e. for air, water, waste, conservation management, coastal zones management and natural resources management).

2.4 Public sector management and institutions

12   Property rights and rule-based governance
Assesses the extent to which private economic activity is facilitated by an effective legal system and rule-based governance structure in which property and contract rights are reliably respected and enforced. The assessment is performed on four, equally weighted, dimensions: (a) the legal basis for secure property and contract rights; (b) predictability, transparency and impartiality of laws affecting economic activity, and their application by the judiciary; (c) difficulty in obtaining business licences; and (d) crime and violence as an impediment to economic activity.
13   Quality of budgetary and financial management
Identical to component 17 of the 1999–2004 CPIA.
14   Efficiency of revenue mobilisation
Assesses the overall pattern of revenue mobilisation – not only the tax structure as it exists on paper, but revenues from all sources as they are actually collected. Revenue mobilisation is rated on the basis of two, equally-weighted, dimensions: (a) tax policy and (b) tax administration.
15   Quality of public administration
Identical to component 19 of the 1999–2004 CPIA.
16   Transparency, accountability and corruption in the public sector
Assesses the extent to which the executive can be held accountable for its use of funds and the results of its actions by the electorate and by the legislature and judiciary, and the extent to which public employees within the executive are required to account for the use of resources, administrative decisions and results obtained. This component consists of three, equally-weighted dimensions: (a) the accountability of the executive to oversight institutions and of public employees for their performance; (b) access of civil society to information on public affairs; and (c) state capture by narrow vested interests.

Appendix B

The four items contribute 25 percent each to the overall CPIA score; within each item, all components receive equal weight. The components are rated on a scale ranging from 1 to 6, allowing intermediate scores of 1.5, 2.5, 3.5, 4.5 and 5.5. The scores reflected the judgments that are given in Table B2.

Table B2 Categories and judgements on the CPIA, since 2005

Score	Judgement
1	Very strong
2	Strong
3	Moderately strong
4	Moderately weak
5	Weak
6	Very weak

Source: World Bank Operations Policy and Country Services (2004a)

Appendix C
IDA borrowers, by per capita income, 1999

$100–400	$400–500	$500–600	$600–700	$700 and over
Angola	Armenia	Azerbaijan*	Congo, Republic	Albania
Bangladesh	Haiti	Bhutan	Georgia	Bolivia
Benin	India*	Cameroon		Cape Verde†
Burkina Faso	Pakistan*	Guinea		Cote d'Ivoire
Burundi	Nicaragua	Indonesia*		Djibouti
Cambodia		Lesotho		Dominica†*
Central African Rep.		Senegal		Grenada†*
Chad		Zimbabwe*		Guyana
Comoros				Honduras
Eritrea				Kiribati†
Ethiopia				Maldives†
The Gambia				Macedonia*
Ghana				Samoa†
Guinea-Bissau				Solomon Islands
Kenya				Sri Lanka
Kyrgyz Republic				St. Lucia†*
Laos				St. Vincent and
Madagascar				the Grenadines†*
Malawi				Tonga†
Mali				Vanuatu†
Mauritania				
Moldova				
Mongolia				
Mozambique				
Nepal				
Niger				
Nigeria*				
Rwanda				
São Tomé and Principe				
Sierra Leone				
Sudan				
Tajikistan				
Tanzania				
Togo				

continued

Appendix C

$100–400	$400–500	$500–600	$600–700	$700 and over
Uganda				
Vietnam				
Yemen				
Zambia				

Source: IDA 2001b.

Notes:
* blend countries; † small island exception.
Not available: Afghanistan, Democratic Republic of Congo, Bosnia and Herzegovina, Liberia, Myanmar and Somalia.

Appendix D
Selection criteria of the Millennium Challenge Account

The selection criteria of the Millennium Challenge Account are subdivided into three categories and sixteen indicators (Millennium Challenge Corporation n.d.).

1 Ruling justly category

1 Civil liberties
   Measures country performance on freedom of expression and belief, association and organisational rights, rule of law and human rights, personal autonomy, individual and economic rights and the independence of the judiciary.
   Score from an evaluation by a panel of experts convened by Freedom House on a 7-point scale, with 1 representing 'most free' and 7 representing 'least free'.
2 Political rights
   Measures country performance on the quality of the electoral process, political pluralism and participation, government corruption and transparency, and fair political treatment of ethnic groups.
   Score from an evaluation by a panel of experts convened by Freedom House on a 7-point scale, with 1 representing 'most free' and 7 representing 'least free'.
3 Voice and accountability
   Measures country performance on the ability of institutions to protect civil liberties, the extent to which citizens of a country are able to participate in the selection of governments, and the independence of the media.
   Index constructed by the World Bank Institute from up to 20 different polls and surveys, depending on availability in countries, each of which receives a different weight, depending on their estimated precision and country coverage.
4 Government effectiveness
   Measures country performance on the quality of public service provision, civil services' competency and independence from political pressures, and the government's ability to plan and implement sound policies.

154 *Appendix D*

Index constructed by the World Bank Institute from up to 19 different polls and surveys, depending on availability in countries, each of which receives a different weight, depending on their estimated precision and country coverage.

5   Rule of law

Measures country performance on the extent to which the public has confidence in and abides by rules of society, incidence of violent and non-violent crime, effectiveness and predictability of the judiciary, and the enforceability of contracts.

Index constructed by the World Bank Institute from up to 22 different polls and surveys, depending on availability in countries, each of which receives a different weight, depending on their estimated precision and country coverage.

6   Control of corruption

Measures country performance on the frequency of 'additional payments to get things done', the effects of corruption on the business environment, 'grand corruption' in the political arena and the tendency of elites to engage in 'state capture'.

Index constructed by the World Bank Institute from up to 21 different polls and surveys, depending on availability in countries, each of which receives a different weight, depending on their estimated precision and country coverage.

2   Encouraging economic freedom

1   Regulatory quality

Measures country performance on the burden of regulations on business, price controls, the government's role in the economy, foreign investment regulation and many other areas.

Index constructed by the World Bank Institute from up to 15 different polls and surveys, depending on availability in countries, each of which receives a different weight, depending on their estimated precision and country coverage.

2   Inflation

Measures the government's commitment to sound monetary policy and private sector growth.

Figure expresses the most recent 12-month change in consumer prices.

3   Fiscal policy

Measures the government's commitment to prudent fiscal management and private sector growth.

Figure expresses the overall budget deficit divided by GDP, averaged over a 3-year period, provided by the recipient government and cross-checked with other sources.

4   Days to starting a business

Measures government regulations that impact the business climate, specifically the number of days necessary to start a new business.

Figure expresses the median duration, in calendar days, that a particular company needs to open a new business, as assessed by local lawyers and other professionals.

5   Cost of starting a business
Measures government regulations that impact the business climate, specifically the cost of starting a new business.
Figure expresses the costs for a particular company, as a consequence of all generic official procedures, time investment and paid-in minimum capital requirements involved in the starting up of an industrial or commercial business.
Until FY 2006, country credit rating was used as indicator of a country's risk of default, measured on the basis of semi-annual surveys of bankers' and fund managers' perceptions (Millennium Challenge Corporation 2004c: 6).

6   Trade policy
Measures a country's openness to international trade based on average tariff rates and non-tariff barriers to trade.
Score on a 5-point scale calculated by the Heritage Foundation from World Bank data on weighted average tariff rates (weighted by imports from the country's trading partners).

3 Investing in people

1   Total public expenditure on health
Measures the government's commitment to investing in the health and well-being of its people.
Figure expresses health expenditures consistent with the IMF definition, on the basis of health data reported by national governments or by the World Bank's *World Development Indicators*.

2   Total public expenditure on primary education
Measures the government's commitment to investing in primary education.
Figure expresses primary education expenditures consistent with the IMF definition, on the basis of primary education expenditure data reported by national governments or by the World Bank's *World Development Indicators*.

3   Immunisation
Measures the government's commitment to providing essential public health services and reducing child mortality.
Figure expresses the average of DPT3 and measles immunisation rates for the most recent year available, as reported by the World Health Organisation.

4   Girls' primary education completion rate
Measures the government's commitment to investing in basic education for girls in terms of access/enrolment and retention.
Figure, calculated by the World Bank, UNESCO and OECD, expresses the number of female students that have successfully completed their last year of primary school divided by the total number of female children of official graduation age.

156 *Appendix D*

In FY 2004, primary education completion rate was used as the (gender-blind) second education-related indicator (Millennium Challenge Corporation 2004c: 6).

Indices of sustainable management of natural resources

In the preparation of the selection for fiscal year 2007, the MCC Board adopted two indices of sustainable management of natural resources, one on natural resources management, the other on land rights and access. The natural resources management index, developed by research centres at two US universities (Columbia and Yale), is a measure of environmental health and protection and consists of four indicators: eco-region protection (a government's commitment to habitat preservation and biodiversity protection), access to improved water, access to improved sanitation and infant mortality (Millennium Challenge Corporation 2006a: 3). The land rights and access index is composed of three indicators that are produced by the International Fund for Agricultural Development (IFAD) and the World Bank's International Finance Corporation, respectively: access to land, days to register property and the costs of registering property (Millennium Challenge Corporation 2006a: 4–5).

Appendix E
Low-income and lower-middle-income countries in the analyses

Afghanistan
Albania
Algeria
Angola
Armenia
Azerbaijan
Bangladesh
Belarus
Benin
Bhutan
Bolivia
Bosnia and Herzegovina
Brazil
Bulgaria
Burkina Faso
Burundi
Cambodia
Cameroon
Cape Verde
Central African Republic
Chad
China
Colombia
Comoros
Congo, Democratic Republic of
Congo, Republic of
Cote d'Ivoire
Cuba
Djibouti
Dominican Republic
Ecuador
Egypt, Arab Republic of
El Salvador
Eritrea
Ethiopia
Fiji
Gambia, The
Georgia
Ghana
Guatemala
Guinea
Guinea-Bissau
Guyana
Haiti
Honduras
India
Indonesia
Iran, Islamic Republic of
Iraq
Jamaica
Jordan
Kazakhstan
Kenya
Kiribati
Korea, Democratic Republic of
Kyrgyz Republic
Lao People's Democratic Republic
Lesotho
Liberia
Macedonia, Former Yugoslav Republic of
Madagascar
Malawi
Maldives
Mali
Marshall Islands
Mauritania
Micronesia, Federal States of
Moldova
Mongolia
Morocco
Mozambique
Myanmar
Namibia
Nepal
Nicaragua
Niger
Nigeria
Pakistan
Papua New Guinea
Paraguay
Peru
Philippines
Romania
Rwanda
Samoa
São Tomé and Principe
Senegal
Serbia and Montenegro
Sierra Leone
Solomon Islands
Somalia
Sri Lanka
Sudan

Suriname
Swaziland
Syrian Arab Republic
Tajikistan
Tanzania
Thailand
Timor-Leste

Togo
Tonga
Tunisia
Turkmenistan
Uganda
Ukraine
Uzbekistan

Vanuatu
Vietnam
West Bank and Gaza
Yemen, Republic of
Zambia
Zimbabwe

Notes

3 The World Bank and performance-based allocation

1 The World Bank's ideas have a direct influence on the work of the Asian, African and Inter-American Development Bank and European Bank for Reconstruction and Development (Santiso 2003: 7). This has brought one observer to characterise the relationship among the organisations as striking 'mimetic processes' (Miller-Adams 1999: 20). The regional development banks are not analysed in this chapter, although they have more or less advanced systems of performance-based allocation, modelled on the World Bank's system.

2 The terms *lending* and *loans* are used in this chapter in accordance with World Bank practice, according to which 'loans' include credits and IDA grants (World Bank 2004a, note 1). Grants have increasingly played a role in IDA commitments. In IDA13, estimates were that between 18 and 21 per cent of available IDA funds would be distributed as grants. Certain percentages of funds could be made available as grants in the case of IDA-only countries (i.e. countries without access to IBRD loans), in relation to HIV/AIDS projects in IDA-only and blend countries, for natural-disaster reconstruction and for post-conflict reconstruction (International Development Association 2002a: 79).

3 Interestingly, in this report the World Bank indicated that '[j]udgements of performance are already routinely made for purposes of IDA allocation and in assessing creditworthiness. This involves judgments about the quality of development management as it relates to growth and to poverty reduction.... There is *no need for additional criteria to reflect concerns with governance:* merely the effective and consistent application of existing criteria based on a greater awareness of the importance of issues of governance for development performance' (World Bank 1991: 19).

4 The Comprehensive Development Framework (CDF) was launched officially in January 1999 and was endorsed as the basis for all of the World Bank's work in 2001. The principles of the CDF are long-term holistic vision, country ownership, country-led partnership and results focus. This approach implies that development strategies should not focus only on short-term macro-economic stability but should aim at social and structural improvements, in particular targeted at the poor. The development priorities should be established by the developing country concerned, in a process involving stakeholders within and outside of the government and in partnership with external donor agencies. Development performance should be measured not by inputs and outputs but by outcomes in terms of the quality of life and productivity of people in developing countries (World Bank 2001: 5; 2003: 1–12; 2004c). In terms of its development targets, the CDF is 'aligned' with the global emphasis on poverty reduction, as expressed in the Millennium Development Goals (World Bank 2001: 1). The CDF is not itself a development strategy, and its implementation has taken place through other means, such as the Poverty Reduction Strategy (PRS) process and the

160 *Notes*

formulation of World Bank Country Assistance Strategies (CASs). The World Bank's Strategic Framework has phrased this relationship as follows: 'IDA countries, both those eligible for HIPC and others, prepare Poverty Reduction Strategy Papers (PRSPs) – which encapsulate a country's own vision of its development priorities. Building on CDF principles, PRSPs help us, in turn, to prepare our CASs – including the program of lending and non-lending products to be used in supporting the country's agenda. The CDF/PRSP process has been welcomed by clients and partners, and is ideally tailored for discussion of division of labor – thus ensuring consistency of programs and reducing overlap' (World Bank 2001: 8; cf. Hatcher 2003: 641).

5 In the rest of this chapter, the World Bank Operations Evaluation Department is referred to as OED.
6 IDA operations are usually sub-divided into 3-year periods relating to the replenishment of IDA funds. As IDA is providing concessionary, long-term loans (lasting for up to 50 years) to the least developed countries, the funds need to be replenished on a regular basis.
7 The CPIA and its indicators are described in Appendix B.
8 See Appendix C for an overview of IDA eligible countries.
9 The portfolio performance score is often referred to as the ARPP (Annual Review of Portfolio Performance) score.
10 The calculations made in 2002 for fiscal years 2004–6 showed a larger difference of population-weighted annual allocations per capita. According to the IDA (2003a: 8), the ratio between the top and lowest quintiles would be 5.0.
11 As specified by the World Bank Operational Manual, '[t]he appropriateness of providing development policy lending to a country is determined in the context of the Country Assistance Strategy.... The expected total volume or share of development policy lending for a borrower is determined in the CAS, taking the following factors into consideration: (a) the country's financing requirement, given the actions necessary to achieve the expected results of the program, the costs of the program, the size and disbursement profile of the Bank's lending program, and other financing available; (b) for IDA borrowers, the country's relative allocation of available concessional resources ... (c) the borrower's overall debt sustainability, based on an assessment of the expected impact of development policy program on the debt condition of the country; (d) the country's absorptive capacity; and (e) country performance triggers [policy conditions] for CAS lending scenarios' (World Bank 2004a: para. 3 and 4).
12 The intention in IDA13 was to enhance the link between performance-based allocations and the CASs: 'the CAS base case three-year lending envelope is expected to reflect the most recent performance-based allocation norm. If there is a significant deviation from the norm, then this should be explained in the CAS' (International Development Association 2001b: 9; 2002a: iv–v). Given the fact that IDA allocations are not made public, it is not possible, at this stage, to determine whether the abovementioned difference between allocations and commitments has become less distinguished since 2000.
13 India, Indonesia and Pakistan – as well as Nigeria under IDA12 – were the so-called *capped* blend countries, as these countries would have taken the bulk of IDA funds on the basis of their population size if no limits had been set to their allocations. As the IDA (2003c: 4) has signalled, 'it should be noted that these countries are underfunded vis-à-vis the PBA allocations, leaving important opportunities for alleviating poverty underfunded.'
14 The eligibility criterion was operationalised by establishing two categories that qualify for assistance: countries with a high impact (cases where 2–5 per cent of the population had been killed, 5–15 per cent of the population had been displaced and destruction of infrastructure had taken place at a regional scale) and countries with a

very high impact (cases where more than 5 per cent of the population had been killed, more than 15 per cent of the population had been displaced and infrastructure had been destroyed almost entirely) (interview, 3 June 2005).
15 As the scores of 1 and 6 related to the protracted existence of unsatisfactory and good performance, and post-conflict support would not normally go beyond a period of three years, these scores were not used in the PCPI.
16 Henceforth, this task force is referred to as Task Force on LICUS.
17 In the light of this, OED Director-General Picciotto (2002: 10) stressed that 'development indicators should go beyond the measurement of inputs ... monitoring indicators should allow tracking of progress toward the MDGs – as well as the intermediate objectives embedded in country programs'.
18 The only change that was implemented was the reduction of the governance factor from six to five components, as a result of the elimination of the fourth component, management and sustainability of the development programme (see Appendix B). Calculations on the effect of changes in the governance factor revealed that removal of the exponent of 1.5 would reduce the factor's impact on allocation from 66 to 59 per cent. It was argued that the removal of the exponent, 'while further reducing the volatility of the ICP [IDA Country Performance] rating, would also significantly affect the resulting country allocations in favor of weaker performing countries' (International Development Association2004d: 4).
19 Grants are available exclusively for IDA-only countries. Two transitional countries (Kosovo and Timor-Leste) have temporary access (during IDA14) to grants, as well as eligible post-conflict countries with large and protracted arrears (International Development Association 2005b: 3–4).
20 The same clause is present in Article V, section 6 of the Articles of Agreement of the IDA.
21 On the basis of the allocation formula, a doubling of per capita income leads to a decrease of per capita allocations of less than 10 per cent.

4 The Netherlands and the selection of recipient countries

1 I would like to thank Dirk-Jan Koch for his substantial input into this chapter, which is largely based on our joint report for the Policy and Operations Evaluation Department of the Dutch Ministry of Foreign Affairs (Hout and Koch 2006).
2 This and the subsequent quotes from Dutch have been translated by the author.
3 The Dutch Minister for Development Cooperation is a so-called 'minister without portfolio'. This means that there is no separate ministry or budget for development cooperation: development assistance is managed by the directorate-general for international cooperation of the Ministry of Foreign Affairs and its budget is part of the overall foreign affairs budget (although development cooperation accounts for approximately two-thirds of the non-EU-related budget for foreign affairs). Because of this ministerial status, the minister for development cooperation is a member of the cabinet. Only during the short-lived first government led by Jan Peter Balkenende, development cooperation was under the responsibility of a state secretary (deputy minister), a position then occupied by the later minister Agnes van Ardenne-van der Hoeven.
4 According to high-ranking civil servants in the directorate-general for international cooperation, it had been clear from the outset of the selection process that it would be impossible to include only countries with 'impeccable records' of policy and governance quality, since the list would not have contained more than six or seven countries. As considerations of capacity on the Dutch side required the selection of 15–20 structural aid recipients, the decision was made to select additional countries from the 'grey' zone between good and bad performers. The additional countries would need to be ones that had scored relatively well on the indicators of policy and governance quality (interview, 10 December 2003).

162 Notes

5 This list of criteria was used for the 'country screenings' that were submitted by the Dutch embassies in 1998 and later years (see further on p. 58).
6 In response to a Parliamentary question, the minister estimated this limited period to last for five years (Standing Committee on Foreign Affairs 1999: 25).
7 It proved to be impossible to determine which considerations had ultimately determined the selection of the preferential countries. A well-placed civil servant indicated that both rounds of country selection (1998–9 and 2003) had been processes in camera, which had not led to the production of extensive policy memoranda (interview, 22 December 2003).
8 The Palestinian Authority was added to the thematic programme on governance, human rights and peace-building (the GMV programme).
9 In addition to the funds mentioned here, a number of preferential countries and five transition countries from Eastern Europe and the former Soviet Union received the so-called 'macro-oriented programme assistance'. This form of assistance is not earmarked for specific sectors or projects and includes balance of payments support, general budget support, cofinancing of structural adjustment programmes and debt relief. The amount of macro-oriented programme assistance allocated in 1999 was €353 million (Minister for Development Cooperation 2000: 3, 5). In order to decide which countries qualify for this kind of assistance, the ministry has developed a methodology that focuses on eight different criteria in four clusters (judgement of the multilateral organisations and quality of the policy dialogue, macro-economic policies, good governance and institutional capacity, and social development and policies) (Minister for Development Cooperation 1999d: 7).
10 When answering questions in Parliament about the prominent role of World Bank indicators, Minister Herfkens argued that 'the system as applied by the World Bank is preferred because there is no alternative that meets the criteria of depth, consistency and empirical basis. This is not to say, however, that no charges can be levelled at the organisation's lack of transparency and its lack of attention for governance and institutional aspects.... Also, this does not imply that the country selection process was based predominantly on World Bank data; these data have been used as the best information available' (Standing Committee on Foreign Affairs 1999: 106).
11 The first Balkenende government was the result of the elections of May 2002, which produced a landslide victory for the *Lijst Pim Fortuyn* (LPF), the political grouping that was led by populist Pim Fortuyn, who got killed a week and a half before the elections. The government resigned in October 2002, after having been in office for less than three months, as a result of a conflict between two LPF Ministers. Agnes van Ardenne, at the time State Secretary for Development Cooperation, stayed on in the caretaker government that was appointed after the resignation of the first Balkenende government. It is a convention that a caretaker government does not initiate new legislation or major new policies.
12 In an interview (10 December 2003), one senior civil servant argued that the merger of the three separate lists into one implied a major policy reversal, as the poorest countries no longer take in a special position among potential aid recipients. In the minister's opinion, however, the new list of partner countries shows 'a greater poverty focus than the previous 19+3, environmental policy, and good governance, human rights and peace-building lists, because several relatively rich developing countries have been removed from the list' (Minister for Development Cooperation 2003c: 6).
13 According to civil servants, an alternative operationalisation of the poverty criterion (income per capita on the basis of 'purchasing power parity') had been considered, but was ultimately rejected because this would create discontinuities with the country selection process of 1998. Other considerations involved the fact that such alternative operationalisations are not commonly used by the international donor community and the expectation that they would lead to a less clear-cut distinction between qualifying and non-qualifying countries (interview, 22 December 2003).

14 In a letter to Parliament of 12 December 2003, the criteria on the need for aid and value added were subsumed under one heading (Minister for Development Cooperation 2003c: 5).
15 The criteria are: poverty reduction strategy and political commitment for poverty reduction policies (cluster: poverty reduction); macro-economic (stabilisation) policies and conduciveness for entrepreneurship/structural reform policies (cluster: economic ordering); public finance management and basic conditions for good governance (cluster: good governance); and quality of the policy dialogue and harmonisation and alignment (cluster: policy dialogue).
16 A so-called 'zero-base' approach had been rejected forthwith because of the costs that would be involved in the termination of existing programmes in underperforming countries and the establishment of new programmes in well-performing countries (interview, 18 June 2004).
17 A civil servant who was involved in the 2003 selection round commented that the inclusion of countries in the GMV and environmental policy lists during Minister Herfkens' tenure had not automatically implied that they received less in bilateral aid than the group of '19+3'. According to this civil servant, the GMV and environmental policy lists already comprised full-fledged partner countries, but they could not be called such, given the good governance rhetoric.

5 The United States and the Millennium Challenge Account

1 Some US politicians, such as Republican Senator Richard G. Lugar, Chairman of the Senate Foreign Relations Committee, have taken a much stronger view, which was not fully embraced by the Bush administration: 'In my judgment, the primary goal of American foreign assistance must be to combat terrorism. In some cases this requires military and economic aid to key allies in the war on terrorism. But our foreign assistance also must be aimed at broader objectives that aid in the fight against terrorism over the long run. These include strengthening democracy, building free markets, and encouraging civil society in nations that otherwise might become havens or breeding grounds for terrorists. We must seek to encourage societies that can nurture and fulfil the aspirations of their citizens and deny terrorists the uncontrolled territory and abject poverty in which they thrive' (Lugar 2003a: 1).
2 The Foreign Assistance Framework that was presented in July 2006 is a reworking of the approach put forward in USAID's Policy Framework of January 2006 (US Agency for International Development 2006: 10–11). The new framework (Director of Foreign Assistance 2006) differentiates between five categories of countries (rebuilding, developing, transforming, sustaining partnership and restrictive) and five policy objectives (peace and security, governing justly and democratically, investing in people, economic growth and humanitarian assistance). On the basis of the categorisation of countries and the policy objectives, specific foreign assistance programme areas are defined that should be included in country strategies.
3 This committee was composed of representatives from the National Security Council, the Office of Management and Budget, the Department of State, USAID and the Department of the Treasury (Nowels 2004: 5).
4 Radelet has argued that USAID operations have been influenced negatively by the multiplicity of development and foreign policy objectives that were formulated by the US Administration and Congress: 'one of the purposes of establishing USAID as an independent agency was to separate development assistance from political and security-based aid. Over the years, however, USAID's focus has blurred, as it was asked to provide assistance in post-conflict situations, support democracy building, and implement the kinds of political and security-based programs it was meant to avoid, such as its current programs in Egypt and Colombia' (Radelet 2003: 5).
5 The four individuals should be selected from lists of candidates submitted by,

164 *Notes*

respectively, the majority and minority leaders of the House of Representatives and the Senate.
6 The US fiscal year runs from 1 October of the previous calendar year and ends on 30 September of the year with which it is numbered.
7 Section 615 of the Millennium Challenge Act specifies the relationship between the MCC and USAID as follows: 'The Chief Executive Officer shall consult with the Administrator of the United States Agency for International Development in order to coordinate the activities of the Corporation with the activities of the Agency.... The Administrator of the United States Agency for International Development shall seek to ensure that appropriate programs of the Agency play a primary role in preparing candidate countries to become eligible countries' (US Congress 2004: 222). In a testimony before the House International Relations Committee in March 2003, USAID Administrator Andrew Natsios (2003: 21) reported that USAID 'welcome[s] the MCA as the strongest possible commitment by the Administration to making development a core element of our foreign policy.... [It] gives USAID the opportunity to clarify its role and better focus its activities within the context of a coordinated US development strategy.... MCA, due to its strict criteria, will only assist a limited number of countries. That leaves the large majority of the developing world to USAID and other agencies and actors.... USAID has been reviewing its portfolio to determine the best way to organize itself both to support the mission and operations of the MCC and to fulfil our mandate to help a wider range of developing countries. In addition to providing support that may be needed in MCA countries, we believe that USAID should focus activities on four broad groups of countries: (1) countries that just miss getting into the MCA; (2) the mid-range performers with the will to reform; (3) failed or failing states that need post-conflict, transition or humanitarian assistance; and (4) countries requiring assistance for strategic national security interests.'
8 The administration's request for $1.3 billion in FY2004 led to some discussion in the Committee on International Relations of the House of Representatives as initial documents on the MCA (for instance, US Agency for International Development 2002b) had presented a budget estimation of $1.7 billion for FY2004 (House of Representatives' Committee on International Relations 2003: 25).
9 In his testimony before the House Foreign Operations Subcommittee, CEO Applegarth indicated that the MCC was considering, by April 2005, the funding of compact proposals to a value of about $3 billion, not including Morocco's 'fairly large' proposal (House of Representatives' Appropriations Subcommittee on Foreign Operations 2005: 6).
10 The criteria are not applied to countries that are subject to legal provisions that prohibit US foreign assistance. Such legal provisions apply to potential candidates that are major drug-transit or drug-producing countries, have experienced a coup d'état against an elected government, or are subject to prohibitions under the Appropriations Act. For FY 2004, 12 countries were excluded from MCA support for legal reasons: Burma, Burundi, Cambodia, Central African Republic, Cote d'Ivoire, Guinea-Bissau, Liberia, Serbia, Somalia, Sudan, Uzbekistan and Zimbabwe (Millennium Challenge Corporation 2004b: 3–4).
11 The maximum rate of inflation was changed from 20 to 15 per cent in the methodology for FY 2005 (Millennium Challenge Corporation 2005a: 10).
12 The methodology for FY 2004 specified several sources of 'supplemental data and qualitative information', such as: the State Department's assessment of a country's respect of the rights of people with disabilities, the treatment of women and children, worker rights and human rights; Transparency International's Corruption Perception Index; expert views on deforestation, conservation of land and marine resources, land tenure institutions, the protection of threatened and endangered species, and citizens' access to sanitation (Millennium Challenge Corporation 2004d: 2–3).
13 Cape Verde scored low on the trade policy indicator, but was judged to be eligible

because of the country's reduced dependence on import tariffs as a result of the introduction of a value added tax system, and because of its efforts to become a member of the World Trade Organisation. Lesotho underperformed with regard to the indicator on the number of days to start a business. Yet, the country was accepted for the MCA because of the introduction of new policy measures that encourage new business formation and because of its good overall performance in the economic freedom category and the other two categories. Sri Lanka scored well below the median on fiscal policy but was accepted for eligibility because of the country's reduction of its budget deficit and its decreased reliance on non-concessional borrowing (Millennium Challenge Corporation 2004d: 2).

14 The MCC Board argued that the quantitative indicators failed to reveal that the three countries witnessed major improvements in the period immediately prior to the selection process for the MCA (March–May 2004). With respect to Bolivia, the board referred to the introduction of anti-corruption measures by the new government since October 2003. Georgia was felt to have made substantial progress in the Ruling Justly category with introducing, among other things, an anti-corruption bureau, a single treasury account for all government revenue, and new government procurement legislation. Mozambique was commended for its anti-corruption efforts – reflected in a relatively favourable position on Transparency International's corruption index – and the increase of general and girls' primary school enrolment rates in the 1995–2000 period (Millennium Challenge Corporation 2004d: 3). One MCA staff member argued that the MCC Board 'gambled' in the case of Georgia and was willing to take the risk that changes would not materialise (interview, 26 September 2006).

15 The actual total of commitments of the first nine compacts (see Table 5.3) represented roughly four-fifths of the budget allocations for fiscal years 2004 and 2005.

6 Selectivity and good governance in the United Kingdom, Denmark and the European Union

1 According to Dollar and Levin's analyses, the Dutch aid programme was highly selective during most of the period under investigation. The data on 2002 show, however, a sharp decrease in selectivity on the part of the Netherlands. As the data used by Dollar and Levin relate to the 1999–2002 period, the impact of the Millennium Challenge Account has not been assessed.
2 The United Kingdom's financial year runs from 1 April in one year to 31 March in the next.
3 These countries are (in the order of magnitude of their 1994/5 allocations): India, Zambia, Bangladesh, Uganda, Malawi, Pakistan, China, Zimbabwe, Kenya, Ethiopia, Rwanda, Mozambique, Tanzania, Ghana, Nepal and South Africa.
4 The review team has also expressed its preference for moving to an 'allocation process [that would be] a balance between both decision rules and discretion, allowing judgements to be applied' (Dyer *et al.* 2003: 6). The team recommended that DFID 'should move more explicitly to directing bilateral aid to countries in need and with good policy environments' (Dyer *et al.* 2003: 16). Potential criteria in an allocation model could be poverty (measured as gross national income per capita), population size, policy and performance (potentially to be measured with the CPIA) and DFID performance (the impact of DFID programmes on wider country development). Other factors that the team recommends to adjust the model-based allocation outcomes are an assessment of developing countries' prospects to meet the six core social sector MDGs, the economic vulnerability of aid recipients, other donor flows and post-conflict indicators (Dyer *et al.* 2003: 16–20).
5 Throughout this section, the term 'European Union' is used to mean both the European Union proper, which was established in the Treaty of Maastricht, and the European Community that existed prior to 'Maastricht' and lives on as part of the EU.

166 *Notes*

7 Quantitative-empirical analyses of World Bank, Dutch and US aid selectivity

1 Since the World Bank fiscal year does not run parallel to the calendar year, the analyses relate to 1999–2001 and 2002–4.
2 The first Balkenende coalition government is not analysed as a separate policy period in Section 7.4. In the first place, the government collapsed due to internal tensions after having been in office for a few months only. In the second place, the policies on development assistance adopted by the later Balkenende governments can be seen as a continuation of those started during the first period.
3 Countries were classified on the basis of actual allocations rather than on the basis of their so-called IDA eligibility, as the latter is based on per capita income only. Among the IDA eligible countries are certain countries that are considered eligible for IDA loans and grants but did not receive funds because of governance-related considerations.
4 The first principal component captured, on average, 68.2 per cent of total variance. The component loadings are, on average, high to very high, thus confirming that there is a meaningful underlying dimension of governance quality that can be used in the following analyses.
5 These coefficients range between 0.18 (equation 9) and 0.60 (equation 12).
6 This result is also reported in Hout (2002).
7 In the case of the Netherlands, the unstandardised coefficients range between 0.40 (equation 22) and 0.70 (equations 19 and 21).
8 Such an interaction effect was indeed established. When the separate influence of voice and accountability and government effectiveness was removed and replaced with an interaction effect, the resulting regression coefficient was -4.022 ($p=0.036$). This finding supports the interpretation given here.

Bibliography

Abonyi, G. (2004) 'Toward a Political Economy Approach to Policy-Based Lending', *International Public Management Journal*, 7(1): 101–31.
Alesina, A. and Dollar, D. (2000) 'Who Gives Foreign Aid to Whom and Why?' *Journal of Economic Growth*, 5(1): 33–63.
Alexander, N. (2004) *Judge and Jury: The World Bank's Scorecard for Borrowing Governments*. Online, www.servicesforall.org/html/otherpubs/judge_jury_scorecard.shtml (accessed 2 March 2005).
Applegarth, P. (2004) *Testimony before the Committee on International Relations of the House of Representatives*, Hearing on Implementation of the Millennium Challenge Act, Serial No. 108–13, 19 May. Online, www.house.gov/international_relations (accessed 26 January 2006).
Arndt, C. and Oman, C. (2006) *Uses and Abuses of Governance Indicators*, Paris: Development Centre of the Organisation for Economic Co-operation and Development.
Bachrach, P. and Baratz, M.S. (1962) 'Two Faces of Power', *American Political Science Review*, 56(4): 947–52.
Bauer, P. (1991) *The Development Frontier: Essays in Applied Economics*, London: Harvester Wheatsheaf.
Bhavnani, R., Lucas, S. and Radelet, S. (2004) *2004 MCA Threshold Program: A Comment on Country Selection*. Online, www.cgdev.org/doc/commentary/2004%20MCA%20Threshold%20Program1.pdf (accessed 30 March 2005).
Bøås, M. and McNeill, D. (2004) 'Ideas and Institutions: Who is Framing What?', in M. Bøås and D. McNeill (eds) *Global Institutions and Development: Framing the World?* London: Routledge.
Booth, D. (1985) 'Marxism and Development Sociology: Interpreting the Impasse', *World Development*, 13(7): 761–87.
Brainard, L. (2003) 'Compassionate Conservatism Confronts Global Poverty', *Washington Quarterly*, 26(2): 149–69.
Burkhart, R. and Lewis-Beck, M. (1994) 'Comparative Democracy: The Economic Development Thesis', *American Political Science Review*, 88(4): 903–10.
Burnside, C. and Dollar, D. (1997) *Aid, Policies and Growth*, World Bank Policy Research Working Paper 1777, Washington, DC: World Bank.
Burnside, C. and Dollar, D. (2004) *Aid, Policies, and Growth: Revisiting the Evidence*, World Bank Policy Research Working Paper 3251, Washington, DC: World Bank.
Cammack, P. (2002) 'Neoliberalism, the World Bank, and the New Politics of Development', in U. Kothari and M. Minogue (eds) *Development Theory and Practice: Critical Perspectives*, Houndmills: Palgrave.

168 Bibliography

Cammack, P. (2004) 'What the World Bank Means by Poverty Reduction, and Why it Matters', *New Political Economy*, 9(2): 190–211.

Center for Global Development (2006a) *Commitment to Development Index 2006 Country Report: United States*, Washington, DC: Center for Global Development. Online, www.cgdev.org/doc/cdi/2006/country_reports/USA2006.pdf (accessed 16 August 2006).

Center for Global Development (2006b) *MCA Monitor*. Online, www.cgdev.org/section/initiatives/_active/mcamonitor/about_mca#time (accessed 22 August 2006).

Chabal, P. and Daloz, J.-P. (1999) *Africa Works: Disorder as Political Instrument*, Oxford: James Currey.

Clague, C. (1997) 'The New Institutional Economics and Economic Development', in C. Clague (ed.) *Institutions and Economic Development: Growth and Governance in Less-Developed and Post-Socialist Countries*, Baltimore: Johns Hopkins University Press.

Collier, P. (2000) 'Conditionality, Dependence and Coordination: Three Current Debates in Aid Policy', in C.L. Gilbert and D. Vines (eds) *The World Bank: Structure and Policies*, Cambridge: Cambridge University Press.

Collier, P. and Dollar, D. (1999) *Aid Allocation and Poverty Reduction*, World Bank Policy Research Working Paper 2041, Washington, DC: World Bank.

Court, J. and Maxwell, S. (2006) *Policy Entrepreneurship for Poverty Reduction: Bridging Research and Policy in International Development*, States and Societies Seminar Paper, 7 March, The Hague: Institute of Social Studies.

Craig, D. and Porter, D. (2006) *Development beyond Neoliberalism? Governance, Poverty Reduction and Political Economy*, London: Routledge.

Dalgaard, C.-J. and Hansen, H. (2001) 'On Aid, Growth and Good Policies', *Journal of Development Studies*, 37(6): 17–41.

Danida (2000a) *Partnership 2000: Denmark's Development Policy – Analysis*. Online, www.eldis.org/static/doc10777.htm (accessed 19 September 2006).

Danida (2000b) *Partnership 2000: Denmark's Development Policy – Strategy*. Online, www.eldis.org/static/doc10775.htm (accessed 19 September 2006).

Danida (2003) *World of Difference: The Government's Vision for New Priorities in Danish Development Assistance, 2004–2008*, Copenhagen: Ministry of Foreign Affairs.

Danida (2004) *Security, Growth – Development: Priorities of the Danish Government for Danish Development Assistance, 2005–2009*, Copenhagen: Ministry of Foreign Affairs.

Danida (2005) *Globalisation – Progress through Partnership: Priorities of the Danish Government for Danish Development Assistance, 2006–2010*, Copenhagen: Ministry of Foreign Affairs.

Danilovich, J.J. (2006) *Keynote Speech*, conference hosted by the American Enterprise Institute to mark the second anniversary of the MCC, 23 January. Online, www.mca.gov/public_affairs/speeches/012306_JDD_2nd_anniversary_AEI.shtml (accessed 3 February 2006).

Department for International Development (2003) *Departmental Report 2003*, Cm 5914, London: The Stationery Office.

Department for International Development (2004) *Drivers of Change*, Public Information Note. Online, www.gsdrc.org/docs/open/DOC59.pdf (accessed 20 September 2006).

Department for International Development (2006a) *Departmental Report 2006*, Cm 6824, London: The Stationery Office.

Department for International Development (2006b) *Implementing DFID's Conditionality Policy*, Policy Division Info Series 092. Online, www.dfid.gov.uk/pubs/files/draft-implementing-conditionality.pdf (accessed 19 September 2006).

Department for the United Nations and International Financial Institutions, Netherlands' Ministry of Foreign Affairs (2004) *Handreiking Track Record [Guidelines Track Record]*, The Hague: mimeo.

Deputy Director-General for International Cooperation (2002) *Internal Memorandum 144/02*, 26 September, The Hague: mimeo.

Development Assistance Committee (1996) *Shaping the 21st Century: The Contribution of Development Co-operation*, Paris: Organisation for Economic Co-operation and Development.

Development Assistance Committee (2001) *The DAC Guidelines: Poverty Reduction*, Paris: Organisation for Economic Co-operation and Development.

Development Committee (2006) *Strengthening Bank Group Engagement on Governance and Anticorruption*, DC2006-0017. Online, www.worldbank.org/html/extdr/comments/governancefeedback/gacpaper.pdf (accessed 16 October 2006).

Dijkstra, G. (2006) *The Shift to Budget Support in Foreign Aid: New and Old Challenges*, Economics Research Seminar Paper, 2 February, The Hague: Institute of Social Studies.

Dollar, D. and Levin, V. (2004) *The Increasing Selectivity of Foreign Aid, 1984–2002*, World Bank Policy Research Working Paper 3299, Washington, DC: World Bank.

Doorenspleet, R. (2005) *Democratic Transitions: Exploring the Structural Sources of the Fourth Wave*, Boulder: Lynne Rienner.

Dyer, N., Beynon, J., Butler, M., De, S., Landymore, P., Porter, C., Richards, S., Smart, M., Speight, M. and Turner, R. (2003) *Strategic Review of Resource Allocation*, Discussion Paper, London: Department for International Development.

Easterly, W. (2002) *The Cartel of Good Intentions: Bureaucracy versus Markets in Foreign Aid*, Working Paper No. 4 (Revised version, May 2002), Washington, DC: Center for Global Development.

Easterly, W. (2006) *The White Man's Burden: Why the West's Efforts to Aid the Rest Have Done So Much Ill and So Little Good*, New York: Penguin.

Easterly, W., Levine, R. and Roodman, D. (2003) *New Data, New Doubts: Revisiting 'Aid, Policies, and Growth'*, Working Paper No. 26, Washington, DC: Center for Global Development.

Ellerman, D. (2005) 'Can the World Bank Be Fixed?', *Post-Autistic Economic Review*, 33: 2–16. Online, www.paecon.net/PAEReview/issue33/Ellerman33.htm (accessed 16 January 2006).

European Commission (2003) *Governance and Development*, Communication from the European Commission to the European Council, the European Parliament and the European Economic and Social Committee, COM(2003)615 final.

European Commission (2006a) *Annual Report 2006 on the European Community's Development Policy and the Implementation of External Assistance in 2005*, Luxemburg: Office for Official Publications of the European Communities.

European Commission (2006b) *Governance in the European Consensus on Development: Towards a Harmonised Approach within the European Union*, COM(2006)421 final. Online, www.europe-cares.org/africa/docs/COM(2006)421_EN.pdf (accessed 20 November 2006).

European Commission (2006c) *Highlights – Annual Report 2006 on the European Community's Development Policy and the Implementation of External Assistance in 2005*, Luxemburg: Office for Official Publications of the European Communities.

170 Bibliography

European Union (2000) *Development Policy of the European Community – Statement by the Council and the Commission*. Online, ec.europa.eu/comm/development/body/publications/docs/EU_com_Dev_policy_en.pdf#zoom=100 (accessed 28 September 2006).

European Union (2006a) 'The European Consensus on Development', Joint Statement by the Council and the Representatives of the Governments of the Member States Meeting within the Council, the European Parliament and the Commission, *Official Journal of the European Union*, 24 February, C46/01: 1–19.

European Union (2006b) *Managing Community Aid*. Online, europa.eu/scadplus/leg/en/lvb/r12002.htm (accessed 9 October 2006).

European Union (2006c) *Overviews of the European Union Activities: Development*. Online, europa.eu/pol/dev/overview_en.htm (accessed 16 October 2006).

Fine, B. (2001) *Social Capital versus Social Theory: Political Economy and Social Science at the Turn of the Millennium*, London: Routledge.

Fine, B. (2003) 'Neither the Washington nor the Post-Washington Consensus: An Introduction', in B. Fine, C. Lapavitsas and J. Pincus (eds) *Development Policy in the Twenty-First Century: Beyond the Post-Washington Consensus*, London: Routledge.

Fox, J.W. and Rieffel, L. (2005) *The Millennium Challenge Account: Moving toward Smarter Aid*, Brookings Working Paper, Washington, DC: Brookings Institution. Online, www.brook.edu/views/papers/20050714rieffel.htm (accessed 28 February 2006).

Freedom House (2006) *Freedom in the World Country Ratings, 1972–2006*. Online, www.freedomhouse.org/uploads/fiw/FIWAIIScores.xls (accessed 25 October 2006).

Gastil, R.D. (1990) 'The Comparative Survey of Freedom: Experiences and Suggestions', *Studies in Comparative International Development*, 25(1): 25–50.

Gelb, A., Ngo, B. and Ye, X. (2004) *Implementing Performance-Based Aid in Africa: The Country Policy and Institutional Assessment*, Africa Region Working Paper No. 77, Washington, DC: World Bank.

Gilbert, C.L. and Vines, D. (2000) 'The World Bank: An Overview of Some Major Issues', in C.L. Gilbert and D. Vines (eds) *The World Bank: Structure and Policies*, Cambridge: Cambridge University Press.

Gore, C. (2004) 'MDGs and PRSPs: Are Poor Countries Enmeshed in a Global–Local Double Bind?', *Global Social Policy*, 4(3): 277–83.

Guillaumont, P. and Chauvet, L. (2001) 'Aid and Performance: A Reassessment', *Journal of Development Studies*, 37(6): 66–92.

Gwin, C. (2002) *IDA's Partnership for Poverty Reduction: An Independent Evaluation of Fiscal Years 1994–2000*, Washington, DC: World Bank Operations Evaluation Department.

Hansen, H. and Tarp, F. (2000) 'Aid Effectiveness Disputed', in F. Tarp (ed.) *Foreign Aid and Development: Lessons Learnt and Directions for the Future*, London: Routledge.

Hansen, H. and Tarp, F. (2001) 'Aid and Growth Regressions', *Journal of Development Economics*, 64(2): 547–70.

Harriss, J. (2001) *Depoliticizing Development: The World Bank and Social Capital*, New Delhi: LeftWord.

Hatcher, P. (2003) 'Le Modèle de développement intégré: Vers une harmonisation des orientations stratégiques de l'aide au développement', *Canadian Journal of Development Studies*, 24(4): 635–51.

Haver Droeze, F. (2003) *Selectivity and Allocation Policies for Dutch Bilateral Aid*, The Hague: Policy Planning Department, Ministry of Foreign Affairs.

Bibliography 171

Hermes, N. and Lensink, R. (2001) 'Changing the Conditions for Development Aid: A New Paradigm?', *Journal of Development Studies*, 37(6): 1–16.

Herrling, S. (2006) *Enhancing Transparency and Communications of MCC Operations: An Action Agenda*, Washington, DC: Center for Global Development. Online, www.cgdev.org/doc/mca%20monitor/MCA%20Monitor%20transparencyagenda%20final.pdf (accessed 28 February 2006).

Herrling, S. and Radelet, S. (2005) *The MCC between a Rock and a Hard Place: More Countries, Less Money and the Transformational Challenge*, Washington, DC: Center for Global Development. Online, www.cgdev.org/doc/mca%20monitor/round3/rockandhardplace_MCA.pdf (accessed 11 January 2006).

Hicks, N., et al. (1982) *IDA in Retrospect: The First Two Decades of the International Development Association*, New York: Oxford University Press.

High-Level Forum on Aid Effectiveness (2005) *Paris Declaration on Aid Effectiveness: Ownership, Harmonisation, Alignment, Results and Mutual Accountability*, Paris, 28 February–2 March. Online, www1.worldbank.org/harmonization/paris/finalparisdeclaration.pdf (accessed 25 May 2005).

Hoff, K. and Stiglitz, J.E. (2001) 'Modern Economic Theory and Development', in G.M. Meier and J.E. Stiglitz (eds) *Frontiers of Development Economics: The Future in Perspective*, New York: Oxford University Press.

Hopkins, R., Powell, A., Roy, A. and Gilbert, C.L. (2000) 'The World Bank, Conditionality and the Comprehensive Development Framework', in C.L. Gilbert and D. Vines (eds) *The World Bank: Structure and Policies*, Cambridge: Cambridge University Press.

Hosmer, D.W. and Lemeshow, S. (1989) *Applied Logistic Regression*, New York: John Wiley.

Hout, W. (2002) 'Good Governance and Aid: Selectivity Criteria in Development Assistance', *Development and Change*, 33(3): 511–27.

Hout, W. (2007) 'The Netherlands and Aid Selectivity, 1998–2005: The Vicissitudes of a Policy Concept', *Netherlands Yearbook on International Cooperation*, Assen: Van Gorcum.

Hout, W. and Koch, D.-J. (2006) *Selectiviteit in het Nederlandse hulpbeleid, 1998–2004 [Selectivity in Dutch Assistance Policy, 1998–2004]*, The Hague: Policy and Operations Evaluation Department.

House of Representatives' Appropriations Subcommittee on Foreign Operations (2005) *Hearing on FY 2006 Appropriations*, 13 April. Online, www.interaction.org/files.cgi/4234_congressional_transcripts_4_14_05.doc (accessed 26 January 2006).

House of Representatives' Committee on International Relations (2003) *Hearing on the Millennium Challenge Account*, Serial No. 108–12, 6 March. Online, www.internationalrelations.house.gov/ (accessed 26 January 2006).

House of Representatives' Committee on International Relations (2005) *Hearing on the Millennium Challenge Account: Does the Program Match the Vision?* Serial No. 109–93, 27 April. Online, www.internationalrelations.house.gov/ (accessed 14 June 2006).

Hulme, D. and Chhotray, V. (2006) *Contrasting Visions for Aid and Governance in the 21st Century: White House Millennium Challenge Account versus DFID Drivers of Change*, paper presented at the Hallsworth Conference 2006, 16–17 March. Online, www.ipeg.org.uk/con_papers/d_hulme_v_chhotray.pdf (accessed 29 March 2006).

International Development Association (2001a) *Adapting IDA's Performance-Based Allocations to Post-Conflict Countries*. Online, siteresources.worldbank.org/IDA/

172   Bibliography

Resources/Seminar%20PDFs/performanceANDallocations.pdf (accessed 2 March 2005).

International Development Association (2001b) *Enhancing IDA's Performance-Based Allocation System*. Online, siteresources.worldbank.org/IDA/Resources/Seminar %20PDFs/Allocationssystem.pdf (accessed 2 March 2005).

International Development Association (2001c) *The IDA Deputies: An Historical Perspective*. Online, siteresources.worldbank.org/IDA/Resources/Seminar%20PDFs/deputS.pdf (accessed 7 December 2005).

International Development Association (2001d) *IDA Eligibility, Terms and Graduation Policies*. Online, siteresources.worldbank.org/IDA/Resources/Seminar%20PDFs/ida%20 eligibility.pdf (accessed 7 December 2005).

International Development Association (2002a) *Additions to IDA Resources: Thirteenth Replenishment. Supporting Poverty Reduction Strategies*, Report from the Executive Directors of IDA to the Board of Governors. Online, siteresources.worldbank. org/IDA/Resources/IDA13Report.pdf (accessed 2 March 2005).

International Development Association (2002b) *Linking IDA Support to Country Performance: Third Annual Report on IDA's Country Assessment and Allocation Process*. Online, siteresources.worldbank.org/ida/resources/seminarpdfs/linking2.pdf (accessed 4 July 2003).

International Development Association (2003a) *Allocating IDA Funds Based on Performance: Fourth Annual Report on IDA's Country Assessment and Allocation Process*. Online, siteresources.worldbank.org/ida/resources/pbaar4.pdf (accessed 4 June 2003).

International Development Association (2003b) *Country Policy and Institutional Assessment 2003: Assessment Questionnaire*. Online, siteresources.worldbank.org/ida/resources/ cpia2003.pdf (accessed 2 March 2005).

International Development Association (2003c) *IDA's Performance-Based Allocation System: Current and Emerging Issues*. Online, siteresources.worldbank.org/ida/resources/ mtrpba.pdf (accessed 2 March 2005).

International Development Association (2004a) *Chairman's Summary*, IDA Deputies Meeting, Paris, 18–20 February. Online, siteresources.worldbank.org/ida/resources/ chairmansummarybercy.pdf (accessed 2 March 2005).

International Development Association (2004b) *Debt Sustainability and Financing Terms in IDA14: Further Considerations on Issues and Options*, Washington, DC: mimeo.

International Development Association (2004c) *IDA Results Measurement System: Recommendations for IDA14*. Online, http://siteresources.worldbank.org/IDA/Resources/ IDA14resultsrecommendations.pdf (accessed 21 September 2005).

International Development Association (2004d) *IDA's Performance-Based Allocation System: IDA Rating Disclosure and Fine-tuning the Governance Factor*. Online, siteresources.worldbank.org/IDA/Resources/PBAFINAL.pdf (accessed 2 March 2005).

International Development Association (2004e) *Initial Draft: Part 1 of the Deputies' Report for IDA14*. Online, siteresources.worldbank.org/IDA/Resources/part1report.pdf (accessed 2 March 2005).

International Development Association (2005a) *Additions to IDA Resources: Fourteenth Replenishment. Working Together to Achieve the Millennium Development Goals*, Report from the Executive Directors of the International Development Association to the Board of Governors, Washington, DC: mimeo.

International Development Association (2005b) *Summary of IDA14 Policies for Operational Staff*. Online, siteresources.worldbank.org/INTPSIA/Resources/4900231120840449856/ SummaryofIDA14PoliciesOperationalStaff-2.pdf (accessed 7 December 2005).

International Monetary Fund (2005) *Direction of Trade Statistics Yearbook 2005*, Washington, DC: International Monetary Fund.

Jayasuriya, K. and Rosser, A. (2001) 'Economic Orthodoxy and the East Asian Crisis', *Third World Quarterly*, 22(3): 381–96.

Kanbur, R. (2002), *IFI's and IPG's: Operational Implications for the World Bank*. Paper Prepared for the G24 Technical Group Meeting, Beirut, 1-2 March. Online, ksghome.harvard.edu/~drodrik/G24Kanbur.pdf (accessed 7 December 2005).

Kanbur, R. (2005) *Reforming the Formula: A Modest Proposal for Introducing Development Outcomes in IDA Allocation Procedures*, SAGA Working Paper 181, Ithaca: Cornell University.

Kapur, D., Lewis, J.P. and Webb, R. (1997) *The World Bank: Its First Half Century*, Volume 1 *History*, Washington, DC: Brookings Institution Press.

Kapur, D. and Webb, R. (2000) *Governance-Related Conditionalities of the International Financial Institutions*, G-24 Discussion Paper 6, New York: United Nations.

Kaufmann, D. and Kraay, A. (2002) *Governance Indicators, Aid Allocation, and the Millennium Challenge Account: A Summary*. Online, siteresources.worldbank.org/ INTWBIGOVANTCOR/Resources/mca_summary.pdf (accessed 6 June 2003).

Kaufmann, D., Kraay, A. and Mastruzzi, M. (2006a) *Governance Matters V: Aggregate Governance Indicators Dataset, 1996–2005*. Online, info.worldbank.org/governance/ kkz2005/pdf/2005kkdata.xls (accessed 22 September 2006).

Kaufmann, D., Kraay, A. and Mastruzzi, M. (2006b) *Governance Matters V: Aggregate and Individual Governance Indicators for 1996–2005*. Online, siteresources.worldbank. org/INTWBIGOVANTCOR/Resources/1740479-1150402582357/2661829-115800887 1017/gov_matters_5_no_annex.pdf (accessed 9 November 2006).

Kaufmann, D., Kraay, A. and Zoido-Lobatón, P. (1999) *Governance Matters*, Policy Research Working Paper 2196, Washington, DC: World Bank. Online, siteresources. worldbank.org/INTWBIGOVANTCOR/Resources/govmatrs.pdf (accessed 1 March 2007)

Keppels, F. (2003) *Country Allocations Based on Poverty and Performance*, presentation for OECD DAC/Development Centre Experts' Seminar, Paris, 10 March 2003. Online, www.oecd.org/dac (accessed 3 December 2003).

Killick, T. (2005) 'Policy Autonomy and the History of British Aid to Africa', *Development Policy Review*, 23(6): 665–81.

Killick, T. with Gunatilaka, R. and Marr, A. (1998) *Aid and the Political Economy of Policy Change*, London: Routledge.

Klasen, S. (2004) 'In Search of the Holy Grail: How to Achieve Pro-Poor Growth?', in B. Tungodden, N. Stern and I. Kolstad (eds) *Annual World Bank Conference on Development Economics – Europe 2003: Toward Pro-Poor Policies – Aid, Institutions, and Globalization*, Washington, DC: World Bank.

Lancaster, C. (2000) *Transforming Foreign Aid: United States Assistance in the 21st Century*, Washington, DC: Institute for International Economics.

Leftwich, A. (1994) 'Governance, the State and the Politics of Development', *Development and Change*, 25(2): 363–86.

Lensink, R. and White, H. (1999) *Assessing Aid: A Manifesto for Aid in the 21st Century?*, Sida Evaluation Report 99/17:13, Stockholm: Swedish International Development Cooperation Agency.

174 Bibliography

Leys, C. (1996) 'The Crisis in "Development Theory"', *New Political Economy*, 1(1): 41–58.

Lin, J.Y. and Nugent, J.B. (1995) 'Institutions and Economic Development', in J. Behrman and T.N. Srinivasan (eds) *Handbook of Development Economics*, Volume III, Amsterdam: Elsevier Science.

Lugar, R.G. (2003a) *Opening Statement*, Hearing on Millennium Challenge Account, 4 March. Online, www.senate.gov/~foreign/testimony/2003/LugarStatement030304.pdf (accessed 26 January 2006).

Lugar, R.G. (2003b) *Opening Statement*, Business Meeting on Foreign Assistance Authorization, 21 May. Online, www.senate.gov/~foreign/testimony/2003/LugarStatement030521.pdf (accessed 26 January 2006).

Lugar, R.G. (2004) *Opening Statement*, Hearing on Millennium Challenge Corporation, 5 October. Online, lugar.senate.gov/pressapp/record.cfm?id=227135 (accessed 1 March 2006).

McClymont, M.E. (2003) *Testimony before the Committee on Foreign Relations of the United States Senate*, Hearing on Millennium Challenge Account, 4 March. Online, www.senate.gov/~foreign/testimony/2003/McClymontTestimony030304.pdf (accessed 26 January 2006).

McGillivray, M. (2003) *Aid Effectiveness and Selectivity: Integrating Multiple Objectives into Aid Allocations*, WIDER Discussion Paper 2003/71, Helsinki: UNU World Institute for Development Economics Research.

Millennium Challenge Corporation (n.d.) *Millennium Challenge Account – Indicator Descriptions*. Online, www.mcc.gov/selection/indicators/indicators_extended_descriptions.pdf (accessed 9 August 2006).

Millennium Challenge Corporation (2004a) *FY 2005 Budget Justification*. Online, www.usaid.gov/mca/Documents/FY05_Budget_Justification.pdf (accessed 26 January 2006).

Millennium Challenge Corporation (2004b) *Report on Countries that Are Candidates for Millennium Challenge Account Eligibility in FY 2004 and Countries that Are Not Candidates because of Legal Prohibitions*. Online, www.mcc.gov/selection/reports/FY04_candidate_report.pdf (accessed 26 January 2006).

Millennium Challenge Corporation (2004c) *Report on Countries that Are Candidates for Millennium Challenge Account Eligibility in FY 2005 and Countries that Would Be Candidates but for Legal Prohibitions*. Online, www.mcc.gov/selection/reports/FY05_candidate_report.pdf (accessed 26 January 2006).

Millennium Challenge Corporation (2004d) *Report on the Criteria and Methodology for Determining the Eligibility of Candidate Countries for Millennium Challenge Account Assistance in FY 2004*. Online, www.mcc.gov/countries/selection/methodology_report.pdf (accessed 26 January 2006).

Millennium Challenge Corporation (2004e) *Report on the Criteria and Methodology for Determining the Eligibility of Candidate Countries for Millennium Challenge Account Assistance in FY 2005*. Online, www.mcc.gov/selection/reports/FY05_Criteria_Methodology.pdf (accessed 26 January 2006).

Millennium Challenge Corporation (2004f) *Report on the Selection of MCA Eligible Countries for FY 2004*. Online, www.mcc.gov/selection/reports/Report_Selection_FY04.pdf (accessed 1 March 2007).

Millennium Challenge Corporation (2004g) *Report on the Selection of Eligible Countries for FY 2005*. Online, www.mcc.gov/selection/reports/FY05_eligible_report.pdf (accessed 1 March 2007).

Bibliography 175

Millennium Challenge Corporation (2005a) *Annual Report 2004*, Arlington: Millennium Challenge Corporation.

Millennium Challenge Corporation (2005b) *FY 2006 Millennium Challenge Corporation and Budget Presentation to Congress*. Online, www.mcc.gov/about/reports/congressional/budgetjustifications/budget_justification_fy06.pdf (accessed 1 March 2007).

Millennium Challenge Corporation (2005c) *Report on Countries that Are Candidates for Millennium Challenge Account Eligibility in Fiscal Year 2006 and Countries that Would Be Candidates but for Legal Prohibitions*. Online, www.mcc.gov/countries/candidate/FY06_candidate_report.pdf (accessed 26 January 2006).

Millennium Challenge Corporation (2005d) *Report on the Selection of Eligible Countries for Fiscal Year 2006*. Online, www.mcc.gov/selection/reports/FY06_eligible_report.pdf (accessed 26 January 2006).

Millennium Challenge Corporation (2005e) *Working with MCC: Overview of MCC's Steps and Processes*. Online, www.mcc.gov/countries/tools/2007/compact/english/tools-2007-09-workingwithmcc-stepsandprocesses.pdf (accessed 1 March 2007).

Millennium Challenge Corporation (2006a) *Report on the Criteria and Methodology for Determining the Eligibility of Candidate Countries for Millennium Challenge Account Assistance in Fiscal Year 2007*. Online, www.mcc.gov/about_us/congressional_reports/FY07_Criteria_Methodology.pdf (accessed 21 September 2006).

Millennium Challenge Corporation (2006b) *Report on MCC Threshold Program*. Online, www.mcc.gov/about_us/congressional_reports/032706_MCC_threshold_report.pdf (accessed 9 August 2006).

Millennium Challenge Corporation (2006c) *Threshold Countries*. Online, www.mcc.gov/countries/threshold/index.shtml (accessed 14 September 2006).

Miller-Adams, M. (1999) *The World Bank: New Agendas in a Changing World*, London: Routledge.

Minister for Development Cooperation (1995) *Hulp in uitvoering: Ontwikkelingssamenwerking en de herijking van het buitenlands beleid [Aid under Construction: Development Assistance and the Reorientation of Foreign Policy]*, The Hague: Sdu Publishers.

Minister for Development Cooperation (1998) *Brief met beleidsvoornemens inzake toepassing van criteria op het vlak van de structurele bilaterale ontwikkelingshulp [Letter to Parliament on the Application of Criteria Related to Structural Bilateral Development Assistance]*, Second Chamber, 1998–99 Session, 26200V, no. 8.

Minister for Development Cooperation (1999a) *Brief inzake het landenbeleid structurele bilaterale hulp [Letter to Parliament on Country Policy Structural Bilateral Assistance]*, Second Chamber, 1998–9 Session, 26433, no. 1.

Minister for Development Cooperation (1999b) *Brief inzake het landenbeleid structurele bilaterale hulp [Letter to Parliament on Country Policy Structural Bilateral Assistance]*, Second Chamber, 1998–9 Session, 26433, no. 2.

Minister for Development Cooperation (1999c) *Brief inzake het landenbeleid structurele bilaterale hulp [Letter to Parliament on Country Policy Structural Bilateral Assistance]*, Second Chamber, 1999–2000 Session, 26433, no. 18.

Minister for Development Cooperation (1999d) *Brief inzake het landenbeleid structurele bilaterale hulp [Letter to Parliament on Country Policy Structural Bilateral Assistance]*, Second Chamber, 1999–2000 Session, 26433, no. 22.

Minister for Development Cooperation (2000) *Brief inzake het landenbeleid structurele bilaterale hulp [Letter to Parliament on Country Policy Structural Bilateral Assistance]*, Second Chamber, 1999–2000 Session, 26433, no. 23.

Minister for Development Cooperation (2001) *Brief inzake ontwikkelingsbeleid en goed*

bestuur [Letter to Parliament on Development Policy and Good Governance], Second Chamber, 2000–1 Session, 27820, no. 1.
Minister for Development Cooperation (2003a) *Brief Ontwikkelingssamenwerking in meerjarig perspectief [Letter to Parliament on a Multi-Annual Perspective on Development Cooperation]*, Second Chamber, 2002–3 Session, 28600V, no. 65.
Minister for Development Cooperation (2003b) *Aan elkaar verplicht: Ontwikkelingssamenwerking op weg naar 2015 [Mutual Interests, Mutual Responsibilities: Dutch Development Cooperation En Route to 2015]*, Second Chamber, 2003–4 Session, 29234, no. 1.
Minister for Development Cooperation (2003c) *Brief naar aanleiding van de moties Hirsi Ali en Van der Staaij/landenlijst [Letter to Parliament regarding the Motions Hirsi Ali and Van der Staaij/Country List]*, Ref. DGIS-246/2003, 12 December.
Ministers of Foreign Affairs and Development Cooperation (2003) *Homogene Groep Internationale Samenwerking 2004 [Combined Spending on International Cooperation 2004]*, Second Chamber, 2003–4 Session, 29233, nos. 1–2.
Ministry of Foreign Affairs (2005) *HGIS-jaarverslag 2004 [Annual Report on Combined Spending on International Cooperation 2004]*. Online, www.minbuza.nl (accessed 20 February 2006).
Monterrey Consensus (2002). Online, www.un.org/esa/ffd/Monterrey-Consensus-excepts-aconf198_11.pdf (accessed 29 November 2005).
Moore, M. (2001) 'Political Underdevelopment: What Causes "Bad Governance"', *Public Management Review*, 3(3): 385–418.
Morrissey, O. (2005) 'British Aid Policy in the "Short-Blair" Years', in P. Hoebink and O. Stokke (eds) *Perspectives on European Development Co-operation: Policy and Performance of Individual Donor Countries and the EU*, London: Routledge.
Nabli, M.K. and Nugent, J.B. (1989) 'The New Institutional Economics and its Applicability to Development', *World Development*, 17(9): 1333–47.
Natsios, A.S. (2003) *Testimony before the Committee on International Relations of the House of Representatives*, Hearing on Millennium Challenge Account, Serial No. 108–12, 6 March. Online, www.house.gov/international_relations (accessed 26 January 2006).
Nederveen Pieterse, J. (2001) *Development Theory: Deconstructions/Reconstructions*, London: Sage.
Neumayer, E. (2003) *The Pattern of Aid Giving: The Impact of Good Governance on Development Assistance*, London: Routledge.
Norris, P. (2005) *STM-103 Global Indicators Shared Dataset V2.0*, updated Fall 2005. Online, ksghome.harvard.edu/~pnorris/datafiles/STM103%20Shared%20Database%20 Codebook%20Fall%202005%20-%20revised.pdf (accessed 17 May 2006).
North, D.C. (1987) 'Institutions, Transaction Costs and Economic Growth', *Economic Inquiry*, 25(3): 419–28.
North, D.C. (1990) *Institutions, Institutional Change and Economic Performance*, Cambridge: Cambridge University Press.
North, D.C. (1995) 'The New Institutional Economics and Third World Development', in J. Harriss, J. Hunter and C.M. Lewis (eds) *The New Institutional Economics and Third World Development*, London: Routledge.
Nowels, L. (2004) *The Millennium Challenge Account: Congressional Consideration of a New Foreign Aid Initiative*, CRS Report for Congress, RL31687, Washington, DC: Library of Congress, Congressional Research Service.
Olsen, G.R. (2005a) 'Danish Aid Policy in the Post-Cold War Period: Increasing

Bibliography 177

Resources and Minor Adjustments', in P. Hoebink and O. Stokke (eds) *Perspectives on European Development Co-operation: Policy and Performance of Individual Donor Countries and the EU*, London: Routledge.

Olsen, G.R. (2005b) 'The European Union's Development Policy: Shifting Priorities in a Rapidly Changing World', in P. Hoebink and O. Stokke (eds) *Perspectives on European Development Co-operation: Policy and Performance of Individual Donor Countries and the EU*, London: Routledge.

Olson, M. (1997) 'The New Institutional Economics: The Collective Choice Approach to Economic Development', in C. Clague (ed.) *Institutions and Economic Development: Growth and Governance in Less-Developed and Post-Socialist Countries*, Baltimore: Johns Hopkins University Press.

Öniş, Z. and Şenses, F. (2005) 'Rethinking the Emerging Post-Washington Consensus', *Development and Change*, 36(2): 263–90.

Organisation for Economic Co-operation and Development (2002) 'Development Co-operation Review of the United Kingdom', *The DAC Journal*. 2(4): 1–99.

Organisation for Economic Co-operation and Development (2006a) *DAC Online: Development Database on Aid from DAC Members*. Online, www.oecd.org/document/33/0,2340,en_2649_34485_36661793_1_1_1_1,00.html (accessed 6 October 2006).

Organisation for Economic Co-operation and Development (2006b) *International Development Statistics Online*. Online, www.oecd.org/dac/stats/idsonline (accessed 31 October 2006).

Palley, T.I. (2003) *The Millennium Challenge Accounts: Elevating the Significance of Democracy as a Qualifying Criterion?* Discussion Paper, Open Society Institute. Online, www.opensocietypolicycenter.org/pub/doc_26/mca_proposal.pdf (accessed 28 February 2006).

Pender, J. (2001) 'From "Structural Adjustment" to "Comprehensive Development Framework": Conditionality Transformed?' *Third World Quarterly*, 22(3): 397–411.

Picciotto, R. (2002) *Development Cooperation and Performance Evaluation: The Monterrey Challenge*, paper presented to Roundtable on 'Better Measuring, Monitoring, and Managing for Development Results', Washington, DC: World Bank.

Policy and Operations Evaluation Department (2006) *Van projecthulp naar sectorsteun: Evaluatie van de sectorale benadering, 1998–2005 [From Project Aid to Sectoral Support: Evaluation of the Sectoral Approach, 1998–2005]*, The Hague: Ministry of Foreign Affairs.

Pronk, J.P. (2001) 'Aid as a Catalyst', *Development and Change*, 32(4): 611–29.

Radelet, S. (2003) *Challenging Foreign Aid: A Policymaker's Guide to the Millennium Challenge Account*, Washington, DC: Center for Global Development.

Radelet, S. (2004) *A Note on the MCC Selection Process for 2005*. Online, www.cgdev.org/doc/commentary/Comment%20on%20MCA%20qualifying%20changes1.pdf (accessed 11 January 2006).

Ravenhill, J. (1985) *Collective Clientelism: The Lomé Conventions and North–South Relations*, New York: Columbia University Press.

Regeerakkoord 1998 [Coalition Agreement 1998], Second Chamber, 1997–8 Session, 26024, no.10.

Rice, C. (2006) *New Direction for U.S. Assistance*, Speech, 19 January. Online, www.usaid.gov/press/speeches/2006/sp060119.html (accessed 28 February 2006).

Richelle, K. (2004) *EuropeAid New Organisation*, PowerPoint presentation. Online, ec.europa.eu/comm/europeaid/general/pdf/Presentation_KR_Part_3_New_Organisation.ppt (accessed 20 October 2006).

Ritzen, J. (2005) *A Chance for the World Bank*, London: Anthem Press.

Roodman, D. (2004) *The Anarchy of Numbers: Aid, Development, and Cross-Country Empirics*, Working Paper No. 32, Washington, DC: Center for Global Development.

Santiso, C. (2001) 'Good Governance and Aid Effectiveness: The World Bank and Conditionality', *Georgetown Public Policy Review*, 7(1): 1–22.

Santiso, C. (2003) *The Paradox of Governance: Objective or Condition of Multilateral Development Finance?*, SAIS Working Paper WP/03/03, Washington, DC: Paul H. Nitze School of Advanced International Studies.

Schaefer, B.D. and Pasicolan, P. (2003) *How to Improve the Bush Administration's Millennium Challenge Account*, Heritage Backgrounder 1629. Online, www.heritage.org/Research/TradeandForeignAid/bg1629.cfm (accessed 30 June 2006).

Schuurman, F.J. (2000) 'Paradigms Lost, Paradigms Regained? Development Studies in the Twenty-first Century', *Third World Quarterly*, 21(1): 7–20.

Secretary of State for International Development (1997) *Eliminating World Poverty: A Challenge for the 21st Century*, White Paper on International Development, Cm 3789.

Secretary of State for International Development (2000) *Eliminating World Poverty: Making Globalisation Work for the Poor*, White Paper on International Development, Cm 5006.

Secretary of State for International Development (2004) *Partnerships for Poverty Reduction: Changing Aid 'Conditionality'*, Draft Policy Paper for Comment. Online, www.dfid.gov.uk/pubs/files/conditionalitychange.pdf (accessed 28 November 2005).

Secretary of State for International Development (2005) *Partnerships for Poverty Reduction: Rethinking Conditionality*, UK Policy Paper. Online, www.dfid.gov.uk/pubs/files/conditionality.pdf (accessed 28 November 2005).

Secretary of State for International Development (2006) *Eliminating World Poverty: Making Governance Work for the Poor*, White Paper on International Development, Cm 6876.

Senate Foreign Relations Committee (2003) *Mark Up on the MCA: Summary Notes*, 21 May. Online, www.mca.gov (accessed 28 February 2006).

Standing Committee on Foreign Affairs (1999) *Landenbeleid structurele bilaterale hulp: Lijst van vragen en antwoorden [Country Policy Structural Bilateral Assistance: List of Questions and Answers]*, Second Chamber, 1998–9 Session, 26433, no. 3.

Standing Committee on Foreign Affairs (2003) *Ontwikkelingssamenwerkingsbeleid voor de komende jaren: Lijst van vragen en antwoorden [Development Cooperation Policy in the Years to Come: List of Questions and Answers]*, Second Chamber, 2003–4 Session, 29234, no. 3.

Stiglitz, J.E. (1989) 'Markets, Market Failures, and Development', *American Economic Review*, 79(2): 197–203.

Stiglitz, J.E. (1998a) 'An Agenda for Development in the Twenty-First Century', in B. Pleskovic and J.E. Stiglitz (eds) *Annual World Bank Conference on Development Economics 1997*, Washington, DC: World Bank.

Stiglitz, J.E. (1998b) *More Instruments and Broader Goals: Moving toward the Post-Washington Consensus*, WIDER Annual Lectures 2, Helsinki: UNU World Institute for Development Economics Research.

Taylor, J.B. (2003) *Testimony before the Senate Committee on Foreign Relations*, Hearing on Millennium Challenge Account, 4 March. Online, www.senate.gov/~foreign/testimony/2003/TaylorTestimony030304.pdf (accessed 26 January 2006).

Bibliography 179

Tarnoff, C. and Nowels, L. (2005) *Foreign Aid: An Introductory Overview of U.S. Programs and Policy*, CRS Report for Congress, 98–916, Washington, DC: Library of Congress, Congressional Research Service.

Task Force on the Work of the World Bank Group in Low Income Countries under Stress (2002) *World Bank Group Work in Low-Income Countries under Stress: A Task Force Report*, Washington, DC: World Bank.

Thorbecke, E. (2000) 'The Evolution of the Development Doctrine and the Role of Foreign Aid, 1950–2000', in F. Tarp (ed.) *Foreign Aid and Development: Lessons Learnt and Directions for the Future*, London: Routledge.

Timmerman, M., *et al.* (2000) *Verslag van de werkgroep Allocatie structurele bilaterale ontwikkelingshulp [Report of the Task Force on the Allocation of Structural Bilateral Development Assistance]*, Internal Memorandum, 1 September.

Tørnæs, U. (2006) *Speech by the Minister for Development Cooperation for the Diplomatic Corps*, 12 September. Online, www.um.dk/en/menu/AboutUs/TheMinisterForDevelopmentCooperation/SpeechesAndArticles/Archives2006/TheMinisterForDevelopmentCooperationsMeetingWithTheDiplomaticCorps.htm (accessed 1 March 2007).

United Nations Development Programme (2000) *Overcoming Human Poverty: Poverty Report 2000*, New York: United Nations Development Programme.

United Nations Development Programme (2001) *Human Development Report 2001: Making New Technologies Work for Human Development*, New York: Oxford University Press.

United Nations Development Programme (2002) *Human Development Report 2002: Deepening Democracy in a Fragmented World*, New York: Oxford University Press.

United Nations Development Programme (2005) *Human Development Report 2005: International Cooperation at a Crossroads: Aid, Trade and Security in an Unequal World*, New York: Oxford University Press.

US Agency for International Development (2002a) *Foreign Aid in the National Interest: Promoting Freedom, Security, and Opportunity*, Washington, DC: US Agency for International Development.

US Agency for International Development (2002b) *Millennium Challenge Account Update*, Fact Sheet, 3 June. Online, www.usaid.gov/press/releases/2002/fs_mca.html (accessed 4 June 2003).

US Agency for International Development (2004) *US Foreign Aid: Meeting the Challenges of the Twenty-first Century*, PD-ABZ-322, Washington, DC: US Agency for International Development.

US Agency for International Development (2005) *At Freedom's Frontiers: A Democracy and Governance Strategic Framework*, PD-ACF-999, Washington, DC: US Agency for International Development.

US Agency for International Development (2006) *Policy Framework for Bilateral Foreign Aid: Implementing Transformational Diplomacy through Development*, PD-ACG-244, Washington, DC: US Agency for International Development.

US Congress (2004) *Consolidated Appropriations Act, 2004*, H.R. 2673 (P.L. 108–199) 23 January, Washington, DC: Government Printing Office.

US Department of State (2003) 'Millennium Challenge Account: A New Compact for Global Development', *Economic Perspectives: An Electronic Journal of the US Department of State*, 8(2). Online, usinfo.state.gov/journals/journals.htm (accessed 4 June 2003).

US Director of Foreign Assistance (2006) *Foreign Assistance Framework*. Online, www.state.gov/documents/organization/69012.pdf (accessed 26 September 2006).

Bibliography

US Government (2002) *Helping Developing Nations*. Online, www.whitehouse.gov/infocus/developingnations (accessed 4 June 2003).

US President (2002) *The National Security Strategy of the United States of America*, Washington, DC: The White House.

US President (2003) *Millennium Challenge Act of 2003 – Message from the President of the United States*, House of Representatives, H. Doc. No. 108–37, 5 February. Online, thomas.loc.gov (accessed 26 January 2006).

Van Bolhuis, F. (2005) *IDA's Performance-Based Allocation System*, PowerPoint presentation, Washington, DC: mimeo.

Van Hulten, M. (1999) '"De 19" van Herfkens' ['Herfkens' "19" '], *Internationale Spectator*, 53(7/8): 430–5.

Wade, R. (1990) *Governing the Market: Economic Theory and the Role of Government in East Asian Industrialization*, Princeton: Princeton University Press.

Warrener, D. (2004) *The Drivers of Change Approach*, Synthesis Paper 3, London: Overseas Development Institute.

Williamson, J. (1997) 'The Washington Consensus Revisited', in L. Emmerij (ed.) *Economic and Social Development into the XXI Century*, Baltimore: Johns Hopkins University Press.

Williamson, J. (2000) 'What Should the World Bank Think about the Washington Consensus?', *World Bank Research Observer*, 15(2): 251–64.

Wolfensohn, J.D. (1998) *The Other Crisis*, Address to the Board of Governors of the World Bank Group, 6 October, Washington, DC: World Bank.

Woods, N. (2000) 'The Challenges of Multilateralism and Governance', in C.L. Gilbert and D. Vines (eds) *The World Bank: Structure and Policies*, Cambridge: Cambridge University Press.

World Bank (1989) *Sub-Saharan Africa: From Crisis to Sustainable Growth. A Long-Term Perspective Study*, Washington, DC: World Bank.

World Bank (1991) *Managing Development: The Governance Dimension. A Discussion Paper*, Washington, DC: mimeo.

World Bank (1993) *The East Asian Miracle: Economic Growth and Public Policy*, New York: Oxford University Press.

World Bank (1998) *Assessing Aid: What Works, What Doesn't and Why*, New York: Oxford University Press.

World Bank (2000) *Entering the 21st Century: World Development Report 1999/2000*, New York: Oxford University Press.

World Bank (2001) *World Bank Group Strategic Framework*. Online, siteresources.worldbank.org/EXTABOUTUS/Resources/strategic.pdf (accessed 5 December 2005).

World Bank (2002) *Building Institutions for Markets: World Development Report 2002*, New York: Oxford University Press.

World Bank (2003) *Toward Country-Led Development: A Multi-Partner Evaluation of the Comprehensive Development Framework*, Synthesis Report, Washington, DC: World Bank.

World Bank (2004a) *Operational Manual OP 8.60*. Online, wbln0018.worldbank.org/institutional/manuals/opmanual.nsf (accessed 2 March 2005).

World Bank (2004b) *Country Policy and Institutional Assessment: An External Panel Review*. Online, siteresources.worldbank.org/ida/resources/cpiaexppanrepsecm2004-0304.pdf (accessed 2 March 2005).

World Bank (2004c) *Supporting Development Programs Effectively: Applying the Comprehensive Development Framework Principles. A Staff Guide*. Online,

siteresources.worldbank.org/CDFINTRANET/Resources/developmenteffectiveness.pdf (accessed 21 September 2005).
World Bank (2006) *World Development Indicators 2006 CD-ROM*, Washington, DC: World Bank.
World Bank Operations Evaluation Department (2001a) *Governance – The Critical Factor, IDA10–12*. Online, wbln0018.worldbank.org/oed/oeddoclib.nsf (accessed 2 March 2005).
World Bank Operations Evaluation Department (2001b) *IDA10–12 Replenishment Undertakings Implementation Matrix*. Online, wbln0018.worldbank.org/oed/oeddoclib.nsf (accessed 7 December 2005).
World Bank Operations Evaluation Department (2001c) *Review of the Performance-Based Allocation System, IDA10–12*, Washington, DC: World Bank. Online, wbln0018.worldbank.org/oed/oeddoclib.nsf (accessed 4 July 2003).
World Bank Operations Policy and Country Services (2004a) *Country Policy and Institutional Assessment: 2004 Assessment Questionnaire*, Washington, DC: World Bank. Online, siteresources.worldbank.org/IDA/Resources/CPIA2004questionnaire.pdf (accessed 22 December 2005).
World Bank Operations Policy and County Services (2004b) *Disclosing IDA Country Performance Ratings*, Washington, DC: World Bank.
World Bank Poverty Reduction and Economic Management Network (2000) *Reforming Public Institutions and Strengthening Governance: A World Bank Strategy*, Washington, DC: World Bank.

Index

Abonyi, G. 43
accountability 25–6, 35, 37, 42, 46–7, 49, 77, 80, 83, 90, 92, 100–1, 109, 113, 117–19, 121, 127, 131, 133
ACP group 8, 98, 106–9, *110*, 111, *112*, 113–14
Afghanistan 36, 59, *62*, 72, *99*, *105*, *111*
Africa 34–5, 45, 47, 57, 98–9, 102, 106
African Development Bank 159n1
African Development Fund 97
aid allocation 32–5, 39–40, *41*, 44–5, 47–9, 56
aid effectiveness 5–6, 12, 19, 21, *22*, 44–5, 50, 52, 64, 66–7, 98, 103, 109, 114, 134–6, 141
aid modalities 8, 21, *22*, 23, 60, 97, 101, 134
Albania *62*, *82*, 83–4, 89
Alesina, A. 140–1
Alexander, N. 46
alignment 6, 17–18, *22*, 23, 61
Angola 36, 60, *63*
Annual Report on Portfolio Performance (ARPP) 30, 33, 40, *41*, 48, 57, 59
anti-corruption *see* corruption
apartheid 55
Applegarth, P. 76, 81, 85, 164n9
appropriations (US) 78–9
Armenia *62*, 81, *82*, 84–5, *86*, *88*
Arndt, C. 93
Articles of Agreement (World Bank) 43
Asia 3, 72, 98–9, 102, 108–9, *110*, 111, *112*, 113
Asian Development Bank 159n1
Asian financial crisis 26
Assessing Aid report 4, 19–20, 45, 135
Azerbaijan 40

balance of payments support 18, 162n9

balanced budget 20
Balkans 8, 107–9, *110*, 113
Balkenende, J.P. 58, 116, 123, 161n3, 162n11, 166n2
Bangladesh 55, *62*, *99*, *105*, *111*, 165n3
Benin 56, *62*, 81, *82*, 85, *86*, *88*, *105*
Benn, H. 100
Bhutan 60, *63*, 83, 104, *105*
Biden, J.R. 76
Blair, T. 98, 103
blend countries 35, 40, *41*, 159n2, 160n13
Board of Directors (Millennium Challenge Corporation) 77, 80–1, 83, 89, 92, 94, 165n14
Board of Directors (World Bank) 38, 47, 56
Board of Governors (World Bank) 26, 47
Bøås, M. 10
Bolivia 55, *62*, 67, 81, *82*, 83, 104, 165n14
Bosnia-Herzegovina 56, *62*, 71
Brazil 60, *63*, 142
budget support 6, 18–19, *22*, 23, 60, *62–3*, 67, 97, 101, 108, 110–11, *112*, 162n9
budget surplus *see* balanced budget
Bulgaria 109
Burkina Faso 55, *62*, *82*, 83–4, 89, *105*, *111*
Burma 164n10
Burnside, C. 4, 19–21, 45, 134–5
Burundi 36, 164n10
Bush, G.W. 7, 70–1, 76, 78–9, 95
Bush Administration 70, 75–6, 93–4, 116, 163n1

Cambodia 60, *63*, *105*, 164n10
capacity building 35, 37, 107
Cape Verde 56, *62*, 81, *82*, 85, *86*, *88*, 165n13
capital formation 75

Index 183

capital market 20, 78
Central African Republic 164n10
Chad *111*
chief economist (World Bank) 27, 31
child mortality *see* health
China 60, *63*, 83, *99*, 165n3
civil liberties 14, 52, 80, 83, 92, 116, 118–19, 131–2
civil society 17, 23, 42, 53, 76, 81, 85, 89–90, 94, 101, 103, 109–10, *112*, 163n1
climate change 72
Coase, R. 12
coherence 12, 17, 100
Cold War 1
collective goods *see* public goods
Collier, P. 19–20
Colombia *62*, 73, 91, 164n4
Commonwealth 99, 102
Commonwealth of Independent States 8, 99, 109, 162n9
community participation 30
competition 15, 28
Comprehensive Development Framework 11, 26–7, 40, 48, 159n4
Conable, B. 24
conditionality 17, 19, *22*, 23, 97, 100, 113, 134
conflict prevention 105, 107–8
Congo, Democratic Republic of 36, 72, *99*, *111*
Congo, Republic of 36
Congress (US) 72, 76, 78–9, 83, 86, 89–90, 92–4, 164n4
Conservative government (UK) 102
contract enforcement 16
coordination *see* donor harmonisation
corruption 20, 26–8, 35, 53–4, 73, 75, 77, 80–1, 83, 85, 90–2, 95–6, 101, 106–7, 116, 118, 127, 129, 131, 133, 136, 140, 165n12, 165n14
Costa Rica *63*
Cote d'Ivoire 56, 164n10
Cotonou Agreement 107–8
Country Assistance Strategy (CAS) 34–5, 37, 40, *41*, 48, 160n4, 160n11, 160n12
Country Performance Rating (CPR) *see* IDA Country Performance (ICP)
Country Policy and Institutional Assessment (CPIA) 7, 20, 24, 29–31, 33, 36–40, *41*, 42, 44–5, 48–9, 57, 59, 61, 67, 136, 138–9, 144–50, 165n4
country screenings (Netherlands) *see* track records

Craig, D. 16
Croatia *111*
Cuba 137
Cyprus 109

Dalgaard, C.-J. 45
Danida 103–6, 113
debt 37, 39, 49, 67, 160n11
debt relief 12, 18–19, 162n9
decentralisation 35
democracy 53, 74, 83, 91, 104–7, 109, 113, 116–17, 133, 136–7, 141, 163n1, 164n4
democratisation *see* democracy
Denmark 8, 97, 103–6, 113–14
Department for International Development (UK) 98–103, 113–14, 139, 165n4
Department of State (US) 73, 76–7, 163n3, 165n12
Department of the Treasury (US) 74, 163n3
depoliticisation 42–3
deregulation 11
Development Assistance Committee (DAC) 3, 16–19, 50, 70, 117
development management 26
Development Partnership Arrangement (UK) 100
development theory 2
developmental state 138
Directorate-General for Development (EU) 108
Directorate-General for Enlargement (EU) *110*
Directorate-General for External Relations (EU) 108
distribution 15
division of labour 14, 16
Djibouti 83
Dollar, D. 4, 19–21, 45, 113, 116, 134–5, 140–1, 165n1
donor harmonisation 17–18, 53–4, 58, 100, 139
donor interests 8, 116–19, 121, 123, 126–7, 129, 131–2
Drivers of Change (UK) 101–2, 113, 139
Dyer, N. 98–9

East Timor *see* Timor-Leste
Easterly, W. 45, 116
Eastern Europe 99, 106, *110*, 111, *112*, 113, 162n9
economic growth *see* growth
economic management *see* macroeconomic policy

Index

Economic Partnership Agreement (EPA) 107
Ecuador 60, *63*
education 17–18, 23, 27, 59, 74–5, 78, 80, 86, 90, 105, 110, *112*, 137
Egypt 55–6, 59, *62*, 67, 71, 73, 83, 91, *111*, 164n4
El Salvador 60, *63*, *82*, 84–5
environment 104–5, 107
environmental programme (Netherlands) 7, 56, *57*, 58, *62–3*, 65–8, 162n12, 163n17
epistemic community 103
equilibrium 12, 16
Eritrea 36, 55–6, *62*
essential element clause (EU), 108–9
Ethiopia 55–6, *62*, 72, *99*, *111*, 165n3
EuropeAid Cooperation Office 108–9, *110*
European Bank for Reconstruction and Development (EBRD) 60, 159n1
European Commission 101, 107–9
European Consensus on Development 2, 107–8
European Council 107
European Development Fund (EDF) 108
European Parliament 107
European Union 2, 8, 97–8, 106–14, 166n5
Everything but Arms initiative (EU) 107
exit countries 60
ex-post conditionality 6
externality 13

Financing for Development summit *see* Monterrey Consensus
Fine, B. 42
fiscal policy 11, 67, 80
Foreign and Commonwealth Office (UK) 98
Foreign Assistance Act of 1961 (US) 91
Foreign Assistance Framework (US) 73, 94, 163n2
former Soviet republics *see* Commonwealth of Independent States
framing 6
France 47
Freedom House 42, 92–3, 118, 132
Freedom in the World 42, 118–19, 132

G-7 47
Gambia 56, *82*, 84
gap countries 35
gender 17, 104–5, 113
general budget support *see* budget support
general equilibrium model *see* equilibrium

Georgia *62*, 64, 81, *82*, 83, 85, *86*, *88*, 94, 165n14
Ghana 55, *62*, 81, *82*, 85, *86*, *88*, *99*, 104, *111*, 165n3
good governance *see* governance quality
governance discount 7, 29, 33, 48, 139
governance factor 7, 29, 32–3, 37–8, 40, *41*, 42, 45–6, 48–9, 139
governance indicators 31–2, 42, 44–5, 92, 116–33, 138–9
Governance Matters 42, 92–3, 117, 119, 131–2, 139
governance quality 1, 4–6, 8, 10–12, 19, 21, 24, 27–8, 42, 44, 50–2, 54, 58, 60–1, 64–9, 73, 75, 90, 95, 97–8, 100–2, 105–10, 113, 115, 117, 123, 129, 132–41, 162n9, 163n15
government policies 11, 14–16, 24, 53
growth 14, 19–21, *22*, 83, 85, 89–91, 95, 106, 137, 142
Guatemala *62*
Guinea Bissau 36, 60, 164n10
Guyana *82*, 83–4

Hagel, C. 76
Haiti *111*
Hansen, H. 21, 45
harmonisation *see* donor harmonisation
health 17–18, 23, 27, 59, 74–5, 78, 80, 86, 90, 105, 110, *112*, 137
Herfkens, E. 7, 50, 51–8, 61, 64–8, 162n10, 163n17
Hermes, N. 19
highly indebted poor countries (HIPC) 49, 160n4
historical cut-off (IDA) 77, 83
HIV/AIDS 59, 72, 159n2
Hoff, K. 12, 15
Honduras 60, *63*, 81, *82*, 85, *86*, *88*, 94
Hopkins, R. 46
House International Relations Committee (US) 71, 79–80, 85, 164n7, 164n8
House of Representatives (US) 71, 79, 92–3, 164n5
human development 8, 27, 105, 108, 137
human development index 66, 118–19, 121, 123, 126–7, 129, 131, 137
human rights 42–3, 49, 52–4, 75, 77, 101, 104–8, 113, 136–7
human rights, peace building and good governance programme (Netherlands) 7, 56, *57*, 58, *62–3*, 65–8, 140, 162n8, 162n12, 163n17
humanitarian assistance 72, 109

Index 185

Hyde, H.J. 80

IDA Country Performance (ICP) 29–31, 33, 37–8, 40, *41*, 44–5, 47–9, 54, 58–9, 67, 161n18
IDA deputies 30–1, 37, 39
IDA eligibility 33, 37, 39–40, 53, 59, 64, 66–9, 77, 83, 132, 151, 159n2, 161n19, 166n3
IDA Performance Rating *see* IDA Country Performance
IDA10 30
IDA11 30
IDA12 7, 30–1, 33, 35–6, 116, 121
IDA13 31–7, 116, 121, 159n2, 160n12
IDA14 31, 37–40, *41*, 142, 161n19
impasse in development theory 2–3, 5
income distribution *see* distribution
India 35, 40, 55, *63*, *99*, 160n13, 165n3
Indonesia 35, 40, 56, *62*, *82*, 84, 89, 160n13
inflation 20, 67, 80–1
information-theoretic economics 6, 12, 15–16, 43, 134
infrastructure 19, 86, 90
institutional development *see* institutions
institutions 12–14, 19–21, 26, 28, 32, 35–6, 39, 43, 53, 85, 90, 102, 107, 134, 137, 140
Inter-American Development Bank 70, 159n1
International Bank for Reconstruction and Development (IBRD) 35, 159n2
International Development Association (IDA) 6, 24–49, 59, 64, 97, 116–17, 119, 121, 123, 126–7, 132, 139, 141–2, 159n2, 160n5
international development targets *see* Millennium Development Goals
International Monetary Fund (IMF) 2, 11, 19, 48, 60, 97
Iraq 79, 95, *99*, 111
Israel 71
Ivory Coast *see* Cote d'Ivoire

Japan 97
Jordan 71, *82*, 84, 89, 91

Kanbur, R. 47, 138
Kapur, D. 46
Kaufmann, D. 61, 92
Kenya *62*, 64, *82*, 83–4, 94, *99*, 104, 165n3
Killick, T. 99

Kiribati 83
Kok, W. 51, 116, 123, 126
Kosovo 161n19
Kraay, A. 92
Kyrgyz Republic *82*, 84, 94

Labour government (UK) 98, 102
Lantos, T. 94
Latin America 8, 108–9, *110*, 111, *112*
least-developed countries 57, 66, 107
legal framework *see* rule of law
Lensink, R. 19
Lesotho 81, *82*, 165n13
Levin, V. 113, 116, 165n1
liberalisation 48; of investment 11; of trade 11, 19, 27, 72, 84
Liberia 164n10
like-minded countries 103
Lin, J.Y. 13
logistic regression 8, 117, 119, 123, 127, 131
Lomé Convention 106–7
lower-middle-income countries 77–8, 84, 91, 95, 117, 133, 157
Lowey, N.M. 79
low-income countries 78, 84, 91, 95, 102, 117, 133, 157
low-income countries under stress (LICUS) 36–7, 49
Lugar, R.G. 78, 163n1

Macedonia 35, 55, *62*, 67
McGillivray, M. 45
McNeill, D. 10
macroeconomic policy 28–30, 40
macroeconomic stability 27, 48, 52, 67
Madagascar 81, *82*, 85, *86*, *88*, *111*
Malawi *63*, *82*, 84, 89, *99*, *105*, *111*, 165n3
Mali 55, *62*, 81, *82*, 85, 104, *111*
Malta 109
market 13, 16, 24, 27–8, 32, 43, 64, 73–5, 78, 81, 103–4, 113, 163n1
market economy *see* market
market failure 12, 16, 42–3
market orientation 19, 42
maternal mortality *see* health
Mauritania 83
MCA candidate countries 77, 81, *82*, 83–4, 91
MCA Compact 8, 76, 78–9, 84–9, *86*, *88*, 90, 131
MCA eligible countries 77, 80–1, *82*, 83–6, 92–3, 95–6, 127, 129, 133, 153–6
MCA threshold countries 78, *82*, 83–90, 95, 117, 127, 129, 133, 140

Index

median 81, 83, 93, 95–6
Mediterranean Rim (EU) 8, 106–7, 109, *110*, 111, *112*, 113
methodology 20, 115–19, 135, 138–9; of Dutch development assistance 65–6, 68–9; of Millennium Challenge Account 80–1, 91–3, 94–5, 164n11, 164n12; of IDA lending 44–6, 49; of UK development assistance 101
Middle East 8, 72, 98, 106, *110*, 111, *112*
Middle East Partnership Initiative (MEPI) 94
middle-income countries 65–6, 69, 142
military assistance 72
Millennium Challenge Account (MCA) 5, 7–8, 70–96, 117, 127, 133, 142, 153–6, 164n7, 164n8, 164n10, 165n13, 165n14, 165n1
Millennium Challenge Act of 2003 76–7, 90, 94, 116, 129, 139, 164n7
Millennium Challenge Corporation (MCC) 7–8, 73, 76–80, 83–6, 90–6, 127, 131, 139, 164n7, 164n9
Millennium Declaration (United Nations) 2, 11, 37, 105
Millennium Development Goals (MDGs) 2, 4, 6, 8, 16–17, *22*, 23, 37–8, 45, 90, 97–8, 100, 102–3, 134, 141–2, 159n4, 161n17, 166n4
Moldova *62*, *82*, 84
Mongolia 56, *62*, 81, *82*
Monterrey Consensus 2, 11–12, 37, 71, 95, 105
Moore, M. 44, 138
Morocco *82*, 84, *111*, 164n9
Morrissey, O. 99
Mozambique 55, *62*, 81, *82*, 83, *99*, *105*, *111*, 165n14, 165n3
multiple regression analysis 8, 116–17, 119, 123, 127, 131
mutual accountability 8, 100
Mutual Interests, Mutual Responsibilities 58–9, 64, 123

Namibia 60, *82*, 84
National Security Council (US) 163n3
National Security Strategy (US) 70–1
Natsios, A. 164n7
natural resource management 30, 81, 83, 105, 107
neo-classical economics 11–12, 14, 16
neo-liberalism 16, 40, 42, 49, 67, 90, 95, 129, 132–3, 135–6; *see also* Washington Consensus

Nepal 60, *63*, 83, *99*, *105*, 165n3
Netherlands 5–8, 50–69, 89–90, 95, 97, 103, 113, 116–17, 123–7, 131–6, 139, 141, 166n7
Neumayer, E. 115–16
new institutional economics 6, 12–16, 43, 134
Nicaragua 55, *62*, 81, *82*, 85, *86*, *88*, 104, 135
Niger *105*, *111*
Nigeria 35, *99*, 160n13
non-decision making 47
non-governmental organisations (NGOs) *see* civil society
North, D.C. 12, 14
Norway 97
Nugent, J.B. 13

Office of Management and Budget (US) 163n3
official assistance 109
official development assistance (ODA) 52, 56, *57*, 60, *62–3*, 65, 70, 72, 110, *111*, 117
Olsen, G.R. 103
Olson, M. 13
Oman, C. 93
operational cut-off (IDA) 33, 40, 46, 64–5, 69
Operations Evaluation Department (World Bank) 29, 32, 34–5, 161n17
Organisation for Economic Co-operation and Development (OECD) 3–4, 16–17, 50, 70, 117, 134
organisational culture 44, 47, 139
Overseas Development Administration (UK) 98
ownership 6, 17, *22*, 23, 159n4

Pakistan 35, 40, 55–6, *62*, *99*, 111, 160n13, 165n3
Palestinian Authority 55–6, 59, *62*, 71, *111*, 162n8
Palestinian Territories *see* Palestinian Authority
Paraguay *82*, 84, 89
Paris Declaration on Aid Effectiveness 17, 100
participation 17, 27, 42–3, 49, 53–4, 89, 109, 131, 133, 136–7
partner countries (Netherlands) 7, 51, 58–9, *62–3*, 66–9, 123
path dependency 14
peace building 107

performance-based allocation 5–6, 24–49, 159n1, 160n12, 161n13
Peru 60, *63*
Philippines 60, *63*, *82*, 83–4, 89
Picciotto, R. 161n17
pluralism 77
policy theory 5, 7, 131, 135, 137, 140; in Dutch development assistance 61–5, 68; of Millennium Challenge Account 74–6, 89–91, 95; of IDA lending 40–4
political liberties *see* civil liberties
political rights 14, 80, 83, 92, 116, 118–19, 121, 126, 131, 133
political underdevelopment 138
Porter, D. 16
portfolio performance *see* Annual Report on Portfolio Performance (ARPP)
post-conflict countries 35–6, 40, *41*, 47, 49, 60, 72, 159n2, 161n14, 161n19, 164n4
Post-Conflict Progress Indicators (PCPI) 36
post-conflict reconstruction *see* post-conflict countries
post-Washington Consensus 15–16, 27, 40, 42–3, 137
poverty 2–3, 5, 8, 11, 16, 20–1, 33, 44, 46, 50, 54, 58–9, 61, 64–9, 104, 115–19, 121, 123, 126–7, 129, 131, 133, 141–2, 165n4
poverty alleviation *see* poverty reduction
poverty reduction 12, 21, *22*, 23, 29, 36, 57, 74, 83–5, 89–91, 95, 98, 100–2, 105–7, 113, 135, 141–2, 159n3
Poverty Reduction and Economic Management (PREM) Network 35, 140
Poverty Reduction Budget Support (UK) 99
Poverty Reduction Strategy (PRS) *22*, 23, 37, 48, 60, 97, 141, 159n4, 163n15
Poverty Reduction Strategy Paper (PRSP) *see* Poverty Reduction Strategy
Powell, C. 77
preferential ('19+3') countries (Netherlands) 7, 50, 55–6, *57*, 65–9, 123, 126, 162n12, 163n17
President's Emergency Plan for AIDS Relief (PEPFAR) 79, 94
principal-agent problem 23
private sector *see* market
private sector programme (Netherlands) 7, 56, 60, *62–3*, 65, 68
privatisation 11, 15, 26–7, 36, 48
programme assistance 12, 18

programme countries (Denmark) 103–4, 113
project assistance 12, 21, 61
Pronk, J. 51, 140
property rights 6, 11, 13, 16, 20, 27–8, 32, 42, 73, 77, 86
public enterprise 36
public expenditure analysis 35, 101
public goods 13
public sector management 7, 25, 35, 42, 44, 101, 118
Public Service Agreement (UK) 102, 142
purchasing power parity 66, 118, 163n13

Radelet, S. 91, 93–4, 163n4
Reagan, R. 1
recipient needs 8, 52, 116, 131–3
regional integration 107
regression analysis *see* multiple regression analysis
regulation 15–16
rent-seeking 26, 43–4
Rice, C. 73
Ritzen, J. 47
Romania 109
Roodman, D. 45
rule of law 6, 12, 14, 16, 19–20, 26–7, 42, 49, 52–3, 73, 75, 77, 80, 106, 108–9, 118, 136
rural development 18, 28, 74, 86, 107
Russia 47, 71, 107
Rwanda 56, *63*, 64, *99*, 165n3

Santiso, C. 46
São Tomé and Principe *82*, 83–4
Scientific Council for Government Policy (Netherlands) 52
Secretary of State (US) 73, 76–7
Secretary of State for International Development (UK) 100
Secretary of the Treasury (US) 77
sectoral approach *see* sector-wide approach
sectoral budget support *see* budget support
sector-wide approach (SWAp) 6, 8, 12, 18–19, *22*, 23, 50, 53, 61, *62–3*, 67–8, 97, 104, 113
Senate (US) 71, 77
Senate Foreign Relations Committee (US) 71, 74, 76, 163n1
Senegal 56, *63*, 81, *82*, *111*
Serbia and Montenegro *111*, 164n10
service delivery 29, 36–7, 100
Shaping the 21st Century 16
Short, C. 98, 103

Index

Sierra Leone 36, *99*
Slovenia 109
social security 27, 31
Somalia 164n10
South Africa 55, 59, *63*, 67, *99*, 109, *110*, *111*, 165n3
Soviet Union *see* Russia
Special Drawing Rights (SDRs) 33
Sri Lanka 55, *63*, 81, *82*, 165n13
state 13, 16, 138
state capture 26, 140
Stiglitz, J.E. 12, 14–16, 27
structural adjustment 21, 24, 162n9
structural reform 30, 40, 52, 60
sub-Sahara Africa *see* Africa
Sudan 60, *63*, 72, *99*, *111*, 164n10
Suriname 59, *63*
sustainable development 11, 17, 31–2, *57*, 73, 105, 107
Swaziland 83
Sweden 97

Tanzania 55, *63*, *82*, 83–4, 89, *99*, *105*, *111*, 165n3
Tarp, F. 21, 45
taxation 11, *13*
Taylor, J.B. 74–5
technical assistance 12, 21
technology 13; transfer of 15
terrorism 70–1, 106, 163n1
Thatcher, M. 1
Third World 3
tied aid 99, 103
Timmerman, M. 56–7
Timor-Leste 36, *82*, 83–4, 94, 161n19
Todd Whitman, C. 81
Tonga 83
track records (Netherlands) 58–61, 162n5
trade 12, 74, 78, 84, 107
trade liberalisation *see* liberalisation of trade
trade openness 20, 27
trade policy 67, 80
traffic-light system (World Bank) 39
transaction costs 13–14, 18, 73
transparency 7, 25–7, 46–7, 49, 52–3, 77, 92, 109
Transparency International 165n12, 165n14
Treasury Department (UK) 102
trend assessments (Netherlands) *see* track records
trickle down 91, 95, 142
Tunisia *111*
Turkey 91, 108, *111*

Uganda 55, *63*, 72, *82*, 83–4, *99*, *105*, *111*, 165n3
Ukraine 71, *82*, 84, 89, *111*
United Kingdom 2, 8, 97–103, 113–14, 142
United Nations 2, 8, 11, 71, 103, 134
United Nations Development Programme (UNDP) 118
United States 5–6, 11, 38, 47, 70–97, 113, 116, 127–31, 133–5, 141; President of the 75, 77
urban management 28
US Agency for International Development (USAID) 7, 71–8, 83, 90–1, 93–4, 96, 127, 129, 131, 133, 163n2, 163n3, 163n4, 164n7; Administrator of 77, 164n7
US Government Accountability Office (GAO) 83, 92
Uzbekistan 164n10

Van Ardenne-Van der Hoeven, A. 7, 50, 51, 58–61, 64–8, 123, 133, 161n3, 162n11
Van Hulten, M. 65
Vanuatu 81, *82*, 85, *86*, *88*
Vietnam 55, *63*, 64, 83, *99*, 104

war on terror 70
Washington Consensus 6, 11–12, 15–16, 21, 26–7, 40, 42–3, 48, 67; *see also* neo-liberalism
Webb, R. 46
weighted voting 46
Williamson, J. 11, 37
Wolfensohn, J.D. 6, 11, 26–7
Woods, N. 47
World Bank 1–8, 11, 15, 19–21, 24–49, 51, 55–7, 60, 77, 89–91, 95, 97, 113, 116, 118–22, 131–6, 138–9, 141–2, 159n1, 160n4, 161n13, 162n10, 166n1
World Bank Institute 21, 92–3, 117
World Development Report 27
World Trade Organisation 165n13

Yaoundé Convention 106
Yemen 55, 59, *63*, *82*, 83–4, 94
Yugoslavia 60, *63*

Zaire 135
Zambia 55, *63*, *82*, 84, 89, *99*, *105*, 165n3
zero-base approach 57, 163n16
Zimbabwe 35, 55–6, 60, *63*, *99*, 164n10, 165n3